A CASE OF BLACK AND WHITE

Contributions in Afro-American and African Studies
Series Adviser: Hollis R. Lynch

The World of Black Singles: Changing Patterns of Male/Female Relations
Robert Staples

Survival and Progress: The Afro-American Experience
Alex L. Swan

Blood and Flesh: Black American and African Identifications
Josephine Moraa Moikobu

From Du Bois to Van Vechten: The Early New Negro Literature, 1903–1926
Chidi Ikonné

About My Father's Business: The Life of Elder Michaux
Lillian Ashcraft Webb

War and Race: The Black Officer in the American Military, 1915–1941
Gerald W. Patton

The Politics of Literary Expression: A Study of Major Black Writers
Donald B. Gibson

Science, Myth, Reality: The Black Family in One-Half Century of
Research
Eleanor Engram

Index to *The American Slave*
Donald M. Jacobs, editor

Black Americans and the Missionary Movement in Africa
Sylvia M. Jacobs, editor

Ambivalent Friends: Afro-Americans View the Immigrant
Arnold Shankman

The Afro-Yankees:
Providence's Black Community in the Antebellum Era
Robert J. Cottrol

A CASE OF BLACK AND WHITE

Northern Volunteers and the Southern Freedom Summers, 1964-1965

Mary Aickin Rothschild

CONTRIBUTIONS IN AFRO-AMERICAN AND
AFRICAN STUDIES, NUMBER 69

GREENWOOD PRESS

WESTPORT, CONNECTICUT · LONDON, ENGLAND

Library of Congress Cataloging in Publication Data

Rothschild, Mary Aickin.
    A case of Black and white.
    (Contributions in Afro-American and African studies,
ISSN 0069-9624 ; no. 69)
    Bibliography: p.
    Includes index.
    1. Afro-Americans—Civil rights—Mississippi.
2. Civil rights movements—Mississippi. 3. Mississippi
—Race relations. I. Title. II. Series.
E185.93.M6R67   323.4′08960730762   82-6175
ISBN 0-313-23430-2   (lib. bdg.)   AACR2

Library of Congress Catalog Card Number: 82-6175
ISBN: 0-313-23430-2
ISSN: 0069-9624

First published in 1982

Greenwood Press
A division of Congressional Information Service, Inc.
88 Post Road West
Westport, Connecticut 06881

Printed in the United States of America

10 9 8 7 6 5 4 3 2 1

To the memory of my mother
Margery Myers Rothschild
with love and gratitude
for her rich spirit.

CONTENTS

PREFACE

In the fall of 1966, Otis Pease suggested to me that I could begin my graduate study in American history by writing my first seminar paper on the Southern Freedom Summers of 1964 and 1965. That gesture was as generous as it was unwise, for Pease understood even then that the summers represented an end to one phase of the civil rights movement and were already a historical entity. The suggestion was generous, because, as a Mississippi participant, Pease wanted to see the summers studied well and he also wanted to help me find a topic about which I could care deeply. I was typical of the students I came to study and, in fact, had applied and been accepted to work in the 1965 project in Mississippi, though personal reasons unrelated to the summers kept me north. The suggestion was unwise, however, because in a real sense I was studying and writing about my friends and myself: I had very little analytical perspective on the events or the participants when I began.

This book has gone through various ideological casts, many of which reflected the politics of the late 1960s and early 1970s and mirrored those phases that the volunteers themselves have gone through in claiming or recanting their southern work. I have vacillated from passionate defense of the northern students to near horror at their presumptuousness and misunderstanding of the southern movement. There has been at least some truth in all the versions, but sometimes there was precious little understanding.

Seventeen years after the first summer, I will say now that I believe the volunteers were primarily naive and had no idea what they were really committing themselves to. They had been raised in a society so infused with institutional racism that it suffused their—and everyone else's—lives. Yet, withal, they were courageous, generous, and enthusiastic foot soldiers in the southern civil rights movement. They were the cream of northern students. Children of the American Dream, they represented what is best about what some historians have called America's liberal tradition. They genuinely believed in freedom for black Americans, even if they could not visualize what freedom would entail. And they cared passionately that America get its house in order and live up to its promises. They considered themselves liberals in the classic sense: They trusted the America that had raised and nurtured them, and they believed in its promise of liberty and justice for all people. Unlike classic liberals, however, they acted on their beliefs by physically putting their bodies on the line and by that physical commitment began to change their definitions of appropriate political behavior and expose the difference between liberal and radical action and politics. When the government refused or was unable to live up to its ideals, the disillusionment the volunteers experienced profoundly influenced and inspired their northern work for years to come.

At a time when Strom Thurmond is head of the Senate Judiciary Committee and the president of the United States is uncertain he will support an extension of the Voting Rights Act of 1965, the passion, excitement, and misery of those summers seems as distant as any historical event of the nineteenth century. Students in my classes now were toddlers in 1964 and 1965 and the rest of us forget that our living past is not theirs.

I believe that the Southern Freedom Summers marked a turning point in the civil rights movement and that the people who took part in them fueled the continuing movements for social change throughout the remainder of the 1960s and to the present. This whole era in the history of American reform needs to be carefully examined, and I hope this book will make a piece of that time clearer.

ACKNOWLEDGMENTS

Sometimes I think so many people have helped me with this project in so many ways that it is in the truest sense the collaborative effort of a cast of thousands.

For their help in guiding me to manuscripts, explaining their views of the Freedom Summers, and, in several cases, giving me board and room, I would especially like to thank Jan Hillegas of the Mississippi Freedom Information Service; Bernice Morrison, Janet Smith, and Pat Watters of the Southern Regional Council; Christopher Hexter and Sarah Cooper of the State Historical Society of Wisconsin; Richard Berner of the University of Washington Archives; Carel and Charlie Horwitz for help with the Delta Ministry Collection; Richard Gillam for aid with the Stanford KZSU material; and Frayda and Justin Simon for access to the Medical Committee for Human Rights files.

To all of the people—especially the former volunteers—who were both patient with my requests for interviews and generous of their time and materials, I extend my heartfelt gratitude. In the most literal sense, I could not have done this study without their help. I want particularly to thank Emily Abel, the late Fannie Lou Hamer, Florence Howe, Shalimar, and Mimi Feingold Stein. Otis Pease, who started me on this path, has been a helpful and supportive participant-observer and has given me interviews, archival material, and advice, not all of which I've heeded.

A good many friends and colleagues have read parts or all of this manuscript, have discussed the summers, and have both encouraged and challenged me in this work. I would especially like to thank Karen Anderson, Pauline Bart, Pamela Brink, Clayborne Carson, Susan Ellmaker, Sara Evans, Shirley Harkess, Nan Hughes, Peter Iverson, Katherine Jensen, David Katzman, Beth Luey, Scott Lytle, Gerald Marwell, Rita Napier, Jack O'Connell, Anne Firor Scott, and Arvella Weir. Arizona State University gave me a Faculty Grant-in-Aid to help me return to Wisconsin for research. The secretaries in the history department cheerfully typed various stages of this manuscript, and I would especially like to thank Kathryn Brown, Kathy Hansen, and Shirley Moraga. My students and friends in women's studies and our Women's History Study Group have supported me in ways that give a new dimension to sisterhood.

Lastly, I want to thank all the members of my extended family for their love and encouragement over the years. My father and stepmother, Harvey and Ulla Rothschild, have provided both psychic and physical support with encouraging phone calls and taking care of grandchildren at critical times. Toby and Sasha Rothschild Aickin have accepted tight schedules and have kept me clear about what is really crucial in the world. But my most important debt is to my husband, Mikel Gavin Aickin, who has given me encouragement and space. He has been my most incisive critic, has unfailingly done his half of our joint work, and has treated me to the most wonderful wit I have ever encountered.

Of course, any mistakes or omissions are entirely my own, but what is useful comes from the collaboration.

ABBREVIATIONS

ADA	Americans for Democratic Action
AFT	American Federation of Teachers
ASCS	Agricultural Stabilization and Conservation Committee
CO	Conscientious objector
COFO	Council of Federated Organizations
CORE	Congress of Racial Equality
CRAG	Civil Rights Action Group
FBI	Federal Bureau of Investigation
FSM	Free Speech Movement
F-SNCC	Friends of SNCC
ICC	Interstate Commerce Commission
LCDC	Lawyers Constitutional Defense Committee
MCDG	Mississippi Child Development Group
MCHR	Medical Committee for Human Rights
MFDP (FDP)	Mississippi Freedom Democratic Party
MSU	Mississippi Student Union
NAACP	National Association for the Advancement of Colored People
NSA	National Students Association
SCEF	Southern Conference Education Fund

SCLC	Southern Christian Leadership Conference
SCOPE	Summer Community Organization and Political Education
SDS	Students for a Democratic Society
SNCC	Student Nonviolent Coordinating Committee
USDA	United States Department of Agriculture
VEP	Voter Education Project
WATS	Wide Area Telephone Service
YWCA	Young Women's Christian Association

A CASE OF BLACK
AND WHITE

1

THE BACKGROUND OF THE FREEDOM SUMMERS: AN INTRODUCTION

The Freedom Summer Projects of 1964 and 1965 were logical, almost inevitable, steps in the evolution of the southern civil rights movement. Since they entailed a massive physical invasion of the South by northerners, mostly white college students, they seemed to many Americans a sharp deviation from what had gone before.[1] But they were not; rather, they followed implicitly from previous civil rights programs, which were constantly changing and adapting to respond to the southern situation.

The movement to bring blacks equality in America has waxed and waned since it began in the nineteenth century. The turning point for the latest phase of the civil rights movement, however, was the 1954 Supreme Court decision of *Brown* v. *Board of Education*, which held that separate schools for blacks and whites were inherently unequal and therefore could not be continued. The *Brown* decision ostensibly mandated only the desegregation of public schools, but it set the stage for a series of court decisions that would strike down all forms of state-sanctioned segregation and would result in integrating most facets of American life.

The *Brown* decision increased the strength of the National Association for the Advancement of Colored People (NAACP), which had worked since its founding in 1910 for the abolition of Jim Crow laws. The NAACP was the leading civil rights group in the country, and its three main thrusts were to organize people to work for civil rights, to pass legislation, and to challenge racist laws. The NAACP

3

could take a great deal of credit for paving the way for the *Brown* decision.

In 1955, six months after the Supreme Court refined the *Brown* decision to say that desegregation must be accomplished "with all deliberate speed," Rosa Parks was arrested and briefly jailed in Montgomery, Alabama, for refusing to give up her seat near the front of a bus to a white. A local NAACP leader, Parks was also active in the church of a young black minister, Dr. Martin Luther King. King and Parks decided to organize a mass protest for the evening of Parks' trial. On the day of the trial, 90 percent of the blacks who ordinarily rode the bus in Montgomery boycotted the bus system. At the mass meeting that night, blacks decided to continue the boycott until the bus system was desegregated. Further, the Montgomery Improvement Association was formed with King as its head.

The boycott brought King, Dr. Ralph Abernathy, and other black ministers like them to the forefront of the beginning of a southern black civil rights movement. Religious leaders to the black community, these often young, black ministers preached Christian love coupled with firm nonviolent action against injustice. Blacks were to love those who were against them but to stand up to protest racist laws and actions at the same time. Drawing on the long American tradition of religious civil disobedience and the concepts of Mohandas Gandhi, this nonviolent, direct-action movement was a powerful new force for blacks in the South, and Martin Luther King became a symbol of the "new southern Negro," who was religious, educated, charismatic, and strong.

The white community in Montgomery tried to stop the boycott in numerous ways, including mass arrests and the prosecution of King. However, white resistance seemed to strengthen black resolve, and the boycott ended only after the Supreme Court late in 1956 ruled bus segregation illegal.

After desegregation, some violence against blacks occurred in Montgomery, but as before, white resistance served only to strengthen black resolve, which was growing throughout the South. Capitalizing on this developing black strength, people active in civil rights throughout the region proposed organizing a new southern based group to work for change. In 1958 the Southern Christian Leadership Conference (SCLC) was formed with Martin Luther King as its president and Ella Baker, a long-time NAACP organizer, as its executive secretary. SCLC was based in Atlanta to serve the whole region. Initially composed primarily of southern black religious leaders, SCLC stood for nonviolent change in the South. A year after its founding, King moved to Atlanta to work for a "full scale assault" against "discrimination and segregation in all forms."[2]

While the immediate response of the white South to the *Brown* decision had been cautious, within a month of the decision, important white political leaders in Virginia pledged themselves to continue segregation. By 1956 all but three of the southern senators and representatives to Congress had signed a "Southern Manifesto" pledging to find a way to reverse the decision and maintain segregation.

With white southern leaders pledging defiance and blacks challenging segregation in new ways, the stage was set for a major confrontation by whites against school desegregation. It came, somewhat unexpectedly, in Little Rock, Arkansas, with the opening of school in 1957. The integration of Central High produced a jeering, violent mob of whites determined to keep nine new black students out of school. Supported by Governor Orval Faubus, the white community successfully kept the students from regular school attendance until President Eisenhower reluctantly sent in federal troops to assure the integration of Central High. The country watched in amazement as one thousand paratroopers and ten thousand national guard ushered in integration at Central High.

The symbolic importance of Little Rock was lost on no one. For the first time since Reconstruction, federal troops were in the South to protect the rights of blacks. While the president was clearly unhappy about sending in troops, he nevertheless forcefully put himself and the executive branch on the side of upholding the Supreme Court decision. He felt he had no options. Many southern whites were horrified at what they saw as unwarranted federal intrusion into the southern way of life, while most blacks were delighted at the federal intervention.

Many southern whites began to be terrified at the thought that the federal government would use federal troops to enforce desegregation in the South. And the nascent nonviolent movement of blacks throughout the region was frightening to whites as well. By the end of the decade, the civil rights movement in the South was set for a new level of action.

On February 1, 1960, four well-dressed black freshmen from the A and T College in Greensboro, North Carolina, sat down at the segregated Woolworth's lunch counter and stayed until it closed. With that one act, the new student nonviolent, direct-action movement began and fanned across the entire South. Within two weeks, sit-ins spread to five southern states, and within the year, over fifty thousand people confronted some aspect of segregation in more than one hundred cities. Some thirty-six hundred demonstrators were jailed during the year, but hundreds of lunch counters and public accommodations were desegregated.[3]

For the student civil rights activists of the early 1960s, the Greensboro sit-in represented the beginning of their movement, and it marked the next stage of the southern civil rights movement. The moral force of the protesters absorbed the attention of the nation. The national media spotlighted the sit-ins and contributed to their spread. For the students, mostly southern blacks, there was charisma in the act of physical confrontation itself.

The new student movement was an innovation born of confrontation that significantly altered the direction of the entire civil rights movement. It garnered instant attention from the media—especially television—and greatly speeded up the course of events and the rate of change. The sit-ins broke the hegemony of the NAACP over the civil rights movement. The focus of the movement shifted to nonviolent direct action for social change in the South, resulting within the year in the birth of the Student Nonviolent Coordinating Committee (SNCC), the first student-controlled organization in the movement. With the NAACP's domination shattered, the beginning of SNCC and the student actions breathing new life into SCLC and the Congress of Racial Equality (CORE), a primarily northern direct-action civil rights group, a period of unprecedented rivalry began among civil rights groups for programs, fund raising, and attention.

In an effort to coordinate the sit-ins and projects of individual groups, Ella Baker, as the executive secretary of SCLC, organized a conference for Easter weekend in 1960 at Shaw University in Raleigh, North Carolina. Two hundred people, mostly students, assembled from fifty-eight southern communities in twelve states. Over the weekend, they hammered out a plan to form an organization to coordinate southern direct-action campaigns. The only disagreement was whether or not this new group should have an official tie with SCLC. After much debate, the delegates decided to remain unattached—friendly, but independent of all the other civil rights organizations. The conference set up a committee to continue meeting to formalize the organization.

The importance of the conference was not simply that it officially created SNCC; it was also the first gathering of the most daring and committed students that the nation had seen for years. These students had a vision for America. And as visionaries they had as a group an almost inexplicable fascination that set them apart from the other civil rights organizations. This developed into the "SNCC mystique," and it was present even in Raleigh. Jane Stembridge, a white southerner who became the first secretary of SNCC, wrote later about her feelings at that first meeting:

The most inspiring moment for me was the first time I heard the students sing "We Shall Overcome." . . . It was hot that night upstairs in the auditorium. Students had just come in from all over the South, meeting for the first time. February 1 was not long past. There was no SNCC, no *ad hoc* committees, no funds, just people who did not know what to expect but who came and released the common vision in that song. . . . It was inspiring because it was the beginning, and because, in sense, it was the purest moment. I am a romantic. But I call this moment the one.[4]

Although delegates came from all over the South, black students from Nashville, Tennessee, with Fisk University, and Atlanta, Georgia, with Spelman and Morehouse colleges, were major organizers in the beginning of the student movement. Within the year, Howard University students would play a substantial role as well as members of the new CORE chapter in New Orleans.

At a May meeting the Temporary Student Nonviolent Coordinating Committee was formally established, and a statement of purpose was drafted by the Rev. James Lawson of Vanderbilt University and SCLC. It reflected the spirit of SNCC at its foundation:

We affirm the philosophical or religious ideal of non-violence as the foundation of our purpose, the presupposition of our faith and the manner of our action. Non-violence as it grows from the Judaic-Christian traditions seeks a social order of justice permeated by love. Integration of human endeavor represents the crucial first step towards such a society.

Through non-violence, courage displaces fear; love transforms hate. Acceptance dissipates prejudice; hope ends despair. Peace dominates war; faith reconciles doubt. Mutual regard cancels enmity.

Justice for all overthrows injustice. The redemptive community supersedes systems of gross social immorality.

Love is the central motif of nonviolence. Love is the force by which God binds man to himself and man to man. Such love goes to the extreme; it remains loving and forgiving even in the midst of hostility. It matches the capacity of evil to inflict suffering with an even more enduring capacity to absorb evil, all the while persisting in love.

By appealing to conscience and standing on the moral nature of human existence, nonviolence nurtures the atmosphere in which reconciliation and justice become actual possibilities.[5]

Although the statement was an accurate reflection of the dominant church-oriented majority at the conference, there was never again such unanimity on nonviolence as a life-style. Like the civil rights movement as a whole, this total commitment to nonviolence underwent considerable change as a result of the students' experience in the South.

In June, Jane Stembridge opened the "office" in a corner of the SCLC office in Atlanta and the nucleus of the future SNCC staff began working together. They organized institutes on the subject of nonviolence, printed the first issue of the *Student Voice*, and made the office a clearinghouse for information on demonstrations throughout the South. While a few northern blacks, including Robert Parris Moses, the young man who later organized work in Mississippi, came to help, the office remained chaotic.

SCLC was not the only organization to aid the new student movement. CORE was also active in supporting the sit-ins in the South with personnel and materials. In addition, it began northern sympathy marches, boycotts, and negotiations for employment of blacks in chain stores and other public institutions. By the end of the summer, CORE opened its first major chapter in the Deep South in New Orleans, which supplied many workers for Mississippi and established CORE's primacy in nonviolent, direct-action work in Louisiana. One New Orleans member recalled, "The chapter had a deep Gandhian philosophy.... All the members were prepared to die, if necessary. In fact we spent hours talking about Gandhian philosophy and willingness to give our lives. We would not eat and talk for days as a means of acquiring discipline."[6]

In October 1960 SNCC became a permanent organization dedicated to the goals of the May statement of purpose. The committee was composed of one voting delegate from each of sixteen southern and border states, the District of Columbia, and assorted voting delegates and observers from allied groups such as CORE, SCLC, NAACP, the Young Women's Christian Association (YWCA), the National Students Association (NSA), and the Southern Conference Education Fund (SCEF).

The new year brought a tactical innovation of "jail-no-bail" with the Rock Hill sit-in. Under the course of its recently appointed director, James Farmer, CORE was helping the student sit-in at Rock Hill, South Carolina. When the first group of students were arrested, they refused bail in order to defuse the threat of jail, show their commitment, and dramatize their fearlessness. The SNCC steering committee decided to send volunteers to publicize their support and also to retain their primacy as the most militant civil rights group. The "jail-no-bail" policy, or "jail-in," made national headlines and garnered support for the students across the country.

While Rock Hill lunch counters remained segregated, the jail-in spread and indicated the students' increasing militance. It became the model for the next major tactical innovation, the Freedom Ride.

In December 1960, the Supreme Court, in the case *Boynton* v. *Commonwealth of Virginia*, desegregated all vehicle terminals regulated by the Interstate Commerce Commission (ICC). In response to this decision, CORE decided to test the desegregation of terminals with a "Freedom Ride" modelled after their 1947 "Journey of Reconciliation." James Farmer of CORE issued the call on March 13, 1961. Seven blacks, including Farmer and John Lewis, who was later to become chairman of SNCC, and six whites, including James Peck, who had been on the Journey of Reconciliation, gathered in Washington, D.C., to begin the ride in two buses to New Orleans.

From the start, the Freedom Ride was seen as a well-publicized test of the commitment of the federal government. All the riders pledged to refuse bail if they were arrested and to use nonviolent techniques if any trouble arose. Speeches and rallies were planned along the way, with a grand finale planned for New Orleans on the anniversary of the *Brown* school decision.

The riders ran into trouble in Rock Hill, but the first severe violence was in Anniston, Alabama, where one of the buses was burned and some of the riders were attacked. The situation deteriorated still more, however, when the buses arrived in Birmingham, Alabama, and they were greeted by a mob. All the riders were attacked, and Peck, a white, and Charles Person, a black, were severely beaten. The ride ended, a victim of white terrorism, when no driver could be found to continue the ride.

Civil rights organizations and influential individuals demanded protection from the Justice Department and the Federal Bureau of Investigation (FBI). They received for the first time what was to become a familiar refrain: The Justice Department and the FBI exist for investigation and prosecution only. They do not provide protection. The Kennedy administration was nervous, however, and saw itself on the horns of a dilemma. President John Kennedy had not done well in the South in the 1960 election, and he and his brother Robert, the attorney general, were already laying the groundwork for an ameliorative "Southern Strategy." On the other hand, the administration depended on the black vote, and its inability to deal with white mob violence damaged its liberal civil rights image.[7]

SNCC immediately organized another ride to complete the first one; they were determined to prove that white violence could not stop a nonviolent black revolution. Two whites and eight blacks, including John Lewis and Henry Thomas of the first ride, left Nashville for Birmingham where they were arrested and driven back to Tennessee by "Bull" Conner, the chief of police. They picked up seven more students and returned to Birmingham. Students came from Atlanta and Washington, D.C., and the press arrived in force. The Kennedys argued with Alabama officials for "safe conduct" to Montgomery for the Freedom Riders. But when the buses arrived, all police were absent, and many of the riders and observers were beaten by a mob.

Robert Kennedy ordered marshalls into Montgomery, and President Kennedy expressed his "deepest concern."[8] The riders stayed for a rally where Martin Luther King flew in and were forced by a white mob to remain in the church overnight. When they left for

Jackson, Mississippi, five CORE members, including Farmer, joined the riders, bringing the total to twenty-seven. After a well-guarded journey, all were arrested by Jackson police upon disembarking from the buses. All were tried immediately, found guilty, and refused bail, preferring instead to go to jail.[9]

Robert Kennedy sought an injunction against the Jackson police, but meanwhile asked civil rights activists to cease the rides for a "cooling-off period." To CORE's and SNCC's dismay, Martin Luther King supported Kennedy's request.[10]

This was the beginning of a steady disenchantment between SNCC and SCLC and especially with the personage of Martin Luther King. Indeed, Ella Baker later recalled, "They [SNCC students] came back from the Freedom Rides with the terrible feeling that the angel had feet of clay."[11] By joining the SNCC group in Montgomery and by going to jail in Jackson, however, James Farmer and CORE rose considerably in the students' estimation, and CORE and SNCC together issued a call to "fill Mississippi's jails" with Freedom Riders.

Riders poured into Jackson. Many were destined to become leaders of CORE, SNCC, and SCLC, including David Dennis, Lawrence Guyot, Stokely Carmichael, Julian Bond, Ruby Doris Smith, Diane Nash, and James Bevel. Two-thirds of the riders were college students. Three-quarters were men, and slightly more than one-half were blacks from the South. There was a substantial minority of rabbis and ministers and among the southern blacks many expressed strongly religious motives.[12] A total of more than 360 riders were arrested, and they did fill Mississippi's jails. However, the enormous response to the rides exhausted CORE's and SNCC's resources, especially their ability to provide legal aid. By the end of the summer, after the riders had endured horrible psychological and physical violence from Mississippi jailers, the NAACP's Legal Defense Fund, Inc. (Ink Fund) took over the Freedom Riders' cases, which resulted in a small healing of the breach among SNCC, CORE, and the NAACP. It also ultimately led to a Supreme Court decision overturning all Freedom Riders' convictions in April 1965.

The Freedom Rides breathed new life into the direct-action movement, and within the year civil rights workers had desegregated all terminals except those in Mississippi. To southern blacks, the Freedom Rides were mesmerizing, and Freedom Riders were instant folk heroes and heroines. "Freedom Rider" became a nickname of praise attached to many civil rights workers by southern blacks years after the rides. Additionally, the Freedom Rides forced the Kennedy administration to act through the ICC, even though it was reluctant to do so. The rides put the Kennedy administration on notice and garnered tremendous nationwide public support for both CORE and SNCC. They also precipitated the students' initial disillusionment with the commitment of the federal government and with the more moderate civil rights organizations, especially SCLC. Perhaps most importantly, however, the Freedom Rides initiated a truly nationwide student civil rights movement. For the first time northern students, white and black, joined with the predominantly black southern students in a direct-action campaign. The rides, then, were enormously important to the new student movement and proved again the students' improvisation skills, courage, and commitment. At exactly the time successful sit-ins began to flag, they seized the opportunity presented by the *Boynton* decision to push the movement forward. Their ability to innovate to dramatize the civil rights struggle to the world remained unparalleled.

The excitement generated by the rides brought large public donations to CORE. Membership soared and a fund-raising campaign of direct mailing, benefits, and speeches about the Freedom Rides netted over $400,000 for the organization within a few months. SNCC also received some donations as a result of the publicity, but the organization had no northern support groups, no professional fund raisers, and little money. Chronically in debt just for basic office supplies, SNCC initially received free rent and services from members of the black community and borrowed money from whomever they could to continue. A winter tour of college campuses brought in some money but not enough to erase all of SNCC's debts. Although SNCC eventually developed northern Friends of SNCC (F–SNCC) support groups, organized speaking tours, sponsored benefits, and hired a professional fund raiser, it remained the most financially precarious of the major civil rights organizations.[13]

At the same time as the Freedom Rides, Robert Moses of SNCC charted a new path for the movement by initiating a voter registration campaign in McComb, Mississippi. Moses' work touched off a fiery debate within SNCC over its priorities. Many SNCC activists believed that the only gains to be made for blacks would involve direct-action confrontations, and they saw voter registration as an "Establishment" way to cool the fervor of the student movement. They had reason to be suspicious, for the Kennedy administration, at least initially, wholeheartedly endorsed voter registration projects. Tim Jenkins of the NSA came to the August meeting of SNCC to argue for SNCC's participation in voter registration projects sponsored by the Southern Regional Council's Voter Education Project (VEP). VEP was financed by the Taconic and Field foundations and had the blessing of the Kennedy administration and all the other major civil rights organizations. Proponents of Moses' work within SNCC argued that only with voter registration would substantial fundamental change come in the South. As long as SNCC was aware of the "danger" of doing what the "Establishment" wanted, they could use the VEP money to support their projects. Ella Baker negotiated a compromise: There would be two branches of SNCC with direct-action projects headed by Diane Nash and voter registration projects headed by Charles Jones.[14]

Following this meeting and compromise, SNCC became a full-time staff operation. James Forman, a black teacher from Chicago, took over as the first salaried executive secretary. And several previous volunteers, most of them veterans of the Freedom Rides, quit school and signed on as field workers paid subsistence wages. By the fall of 1961 SNCC had a full-time staff of sixteen. Three years later it had 150.[15]

CORE also was expanding. The organization opened a southern regional office in New Orleans and hired David Dennis, a Freedom Rider, to be its first southern field secretary. By the fall of 1962 CORE hired more secretaries and organized a task force for southern projects, which consisted of white and black field workers who were paid subsistence wages. When the old guard in CORE discovered all the southern field secretaries were black, they voiced some concern over CORE's long-standing commitment to interracialism and sounded a warning bell about what was to become the burning question in the movement.

The two major voter registration projects that SNCC coordinated were Bob Moses' work in Mississippi and Cordell Reagan's and Charles Sherrod's in southwestern Georgia. Moses started in

McComb, and Sherrod and Reagan worked with him there through
the summer before going to Albany in the fall of 1961.

The McComb experience foreshadowed the projects to come.
The first step in voter registration was to overcome the local
blacks' fear of confronting the white registrar. Moses did this by
quietly working himself into the community and beginning classes
in how to register to vote. These classes included information on
the voting tests and the section requiring the registrant to interpret
the Mississippi Constitution. They also posed the questions who
has power, who governs, and why. After the classes, Moses would
accompany those blacks who wanted to attempt to register to the
courthouse. If they were allowed to fill out a form, they counted it
a victory.

Meanwhile, Marion Barry, a direct-action proponent, organized
workshops on nonviolent action in McComb. Two black teenagers
started a sit-in at a Woolworth's and were jailed. Others were
arrested and beaten. Some high school students accompanied new
registrants to the courthouse with "One Man, One Vote" signs.

White retaliation to Moses' program was swift, sure, and particularly brutal in McComb. Moses himself was jailed and beaten
immediately after escorting the first group to register. Jailings and
beatings continued and grew in ferocity. Finally, Herbert Lee, a
local black farmer, was murdered in cold blood after he had shown
interest in Moses' work. His accused assassin was completely ex-
onerated the next day at a coroner's hearing. One of three major
witnesses admitted he had committed perjury out of sheer fear; he
was murdered two years later, just before he was to move north.[16]

In late October, the entire SNCC staff in Pike County was found
guilty and jailed for contributing to the delinquency of minors as a
result of a SNCC-led march of black high school students, all 103
of whom were expelled for their part. In support of the SNCC staff
in jail, CORE tested the new ICC ruling by a series of Freedom
Rides to McComb. Many of the riders were beaten, as were assorted
journalists and observers accompanying them.[17]

When the SNCC workers were released in December, they left
McComb for Jackson, having learned several lessons. First, the
absolute police power in Mississippi could stymie any direct-action
program they could organize with their limited resources. Second,
members of the white community would go as far as murder to

stop a project. Third, voter registration was every bit as threatening to the white community as direct action. Fourth, voter registration campaigns needed a core of people who were economically independent of the white community. And last, SNCC's own division between direct action and voter registration was artificial. The experience in McComb showed that all civil rights work melded together in the field and, in the case of Mississippi, forged a bond for all of the organizations in the state. McComb was a radicalizing experience; the students were not going to be turned around. Their response was to dig in and find a new vehicle to change the position of blacks in the state.

Over the winter, Tom Gaither and David Dennis of CORE, Robert Moses of SNCC, and Aaron Henry of the NAACP formed the Council of Federated Organizations (COFO). COFO consisted of SNCC, CORE, NAACP, SCLC, and several local, independent groups. Aaron Henry was elected president; Bob Moses was director; Dave Dennis was assistant program director. At a time when the nationwide civil rights movement was splintering disastrously, COFO was conceived and born. One of the most successful coalitions in the entire movement, COFO was a direct response to the extraordinary repression in Mississippi. James Silver has called Mississippi "the Closed Society,"[18] and indeed, the severity of the oppression there provided the context for the success of COFO. As one CORE worker explained, "We can't mess around with petty organizational disagreements and with separate loyalties when the OUT THERE aspect is so pressing."[19] In addition, the people who founded COFO were movement oriented. Henry, Dennis, Moses, and Annell Ponder, who was with SCLC, were primarily concerned with their work in Mississippi and only secondarily with their national organizations. This enabled them to work extremely effectively together. They organized COFO to pool all resources and coordinate all programs—to gain what strength they could through cooperation.

Most of COFO's money came from SNCC, however, which supplied 80 percent of the budget and staffed four out of five of the state's congressional districts. CORE paid Dennis' salary and put some money into the general coffers. SCLC paid Ponder's salary and gave money to the main office in Jackson. The NAACP gave money, some legal support, and an entrée into its local groups for the students. COFO became a recipient in its own right of money from VEP, which also gave funds to the component organizations for Mississippi projects. Occasionally there were flare-ups among the group. The NAACP was often unhappy about COFO's programs and, indeed, precipitated COFO's demise in 1965. Sometimes SNCC felt that CORE and the NAACP nationally claimed credit for work that SNCC, in fact, performed and financed. Dave Dennis of CORE was continually at odds with his national office because he felt that Mississippi needed more money and legal aid, while the national office felt that Dennis submerged CORE's achievements and publicity to COFO. In an attempt to end the wrangling between Dennis and the national office, CORE officially took over and staffed all of the projects in the fourth congressional district. However, despite what the national office thought, in Mississippi Dennis and Moses continued to share decision making and take over each other's responsibilities.[20]

By the spring of 1962, Moses and Dennis planned seven new voter registration projects in Mississippi for the summer. Utilizing local students as workers, COFO financed the projects with VEP money.

For the next two years, Greenwood became the most active and repressed project in the state, though new projects continued to begin in various parts of the state under CORE and SNCC auspices. The Greenwood project experienced the expected, though dreaded, recalcitrance and violence. Local officials added new harassment, however. In retribution for the Greenwood voting campaign, Leflore County officials in October discontinued all surplus food programs, leaving 22,000 people to face a lean Delta winter. By January local people were desperate, and COFO workers asked friends for food and clothing. The response was immediate. Northern Friends of SNCC groups gathered food and clothing, which were trucked to the Delta by northern students.[21]

This food and clothing drive proved to be a turning point in the project. SNCC and COFO for the first time became identified with direct aid for the black community. And the community responded in increasing numbers to the voting campaign. The more the black community responded to the voter drive, the more the white community resorted to violence. In late February, three white men shot thirteen bullets into the SNCC car carrying Bob Moses, Jimmy

Travis, and Randolph Blackwell. Travis was critically wounded, and it was a miracle no one was killed. Dennis, Henry, and Forman all telegraphed the federal government to protest and demand protection, but they received no response. Spurred by the shooting, Wiley Branton, director of the VEP in Atlanta, requested all voter workers in Mississippi to Greenwood immediately: "The state of Mississippi has repeatedly thrown down the gauntlet at the feet of would-be Negro voters. . . . The time has come for us to pick up the gauntlet. LeFlore County has elected itself as the testing ground for democracy."[22] The Greenwood violence continued. There were more shootings, and the office was burned, destroying all the equipment.[23]

Violence also escalated all over Mississippi. Fire bombs were tossed into houses, stores, and offices connected with civil rights workers. Shots were fired into cars and houses of workers. Beatings and jailings continued, escalating with every new demonstration. And on June 12, 1963, Medgar Evers, the state leader of the NAACP, was shot by a sniper in his driveway in Jackson. His assassination touched of a series of demonstrations and jailings in Jackson. It also touched a core of statewide despair among civil rights workers: It was hard to fight murder.

The 1963 summer campaigns continued the voter registration work throughout the state. CORE opened its first separate office in Canton, and their project faced the same violence and repression that other projects had previously. Before the fall was over, partially as a response to the Birmingham bombing that killed four little black girls in their Sunday school class and to the intensified Mississippi violence, one of the local CORE workers kept a rifle in the Freedom House for self-defense.[24]

The harshness of Mississippi's racial climate dealt the movement there another blow: The Voter Education Project discontinued all grants to the state. Even after all the projects, very few blacks had been allowed to register, and the VEP regretfully decided to spend its small resources on more rewarding areas.[25]

On the national scene, the major civil rights organizations sponsored a "March on Washington" in August 1963 to lobby for civil rights legislation. Despite the students' general suspicion of the administration's commitment to civil rights, President Kennedy endorsed the march. For many SNCC workers, however, their disaffection from the administration was so great that Kennedy's very endorsement served as ironic proof that the action was pointless and against the best interests of the southern student civil rights movement. When the federal government supported the march, the already fragile coalition became severely strained. By the day of the march, it nearly split over SNCC chairman John Lewis' proposed speech. While Martin Luther King moderated the breach between SNCC and NAACP, John Lewis changed his speech, and the march was on. Over 200,000 black and white Americans came from all over the nation to participate. King's "I Have a Dream" speech immediately became famous and best expressed the feelings of the majority of the participants and the more moderate groups. However, Lewis' speech most clearly represented the southern student movement. A result of the growing disillusionment of those people working actively in the South, it illustrated the radicalizing effect of the southern experience. Lewis' speech indicated deep distress with the federal government and distrust of the government's ability to implement justice in America:

I want to know—which side is the federal government on? The revolution is at hand, and we must free ourselves of the chains of political and economic slavery. . . . For those who have said, "Be patient and wait!" We must say, "Patience is a dirty and nasty word." We cannot be patient, we do not want to be free gradually, we want our freedom, and we want it now. We cannot depend on any political party, for both the Democrats and the Republicans have betrayed the basic principles of the Declaration of Independence.

The revolution is a serious one. . . . Listen, Mr. Kennedy, listen, Mr. Congressman, listen, fellow citizens—the black masses are on the march for jobs and freedom, and we must say to the politicians that there won't be a "cooling-off period."

Already in 1963 SNCC workers were emphasizing the importance of jobs as well as civil rights. The claim of revolution was not merely rhetorical—some SNCC workers were beginning to believe that nothing short of revolution would change the position of blacks in the country.[26]

By the end of the summer, the southern civil rights projects seemed set in a pattern. Civil rights workers tried to register voters and organize the black community. In order to get publicity and support, they held demonstrations and sit-ins. They also often contacted northern support groups for aid in the form of clothes, food, and temporary volunteer workers. All the projects faced violence and repression at the hands of the white community, while blacks were only very slowly being added to the rolls. The sole variation within this framework was in the degree to which each of the three elements differed project to project, for the factors were always present and interrelated: There was always support from the black community; it depended enormously on the relative economic strength of the black community; and there was always violence from the white community in response to black organizing.

To combat the escalating violence and to reinvigorate the projects, the leaders of COFO sought a new tactic. Out of their recognition of the need for black economic as well as political independence, Moses and others in SNCC and COFO were evolving a theory of parallel institutions. Seen as an alternative to working into and becoming part of a decaying or unjust system, proponents envisioned people building their own institutions to respond to their own needs outside of established institutions.

Angered by a remark from a white Mississippi politician that "Negroes do not want to vote," Moses conceived of holding a "mock election."[27] The concept was simple: The campaign and election would duplicate a regular election, but voting would be open to anyone, white or black, who met residency requirements. People would fill out Freedom Registration forms, which would entitle them to vote when they were properly completed with name, age, and length of residency. And, in addition to the segregationist Republican and Democratic candidates, COFO would field an integrated slate of its own with Aaron Henry and the Rev. Edwin King as nominees for governor and lieutenant-governor.

This idea was presented at the October COFO meeting. A few wondered at the wisdom of risking more violence for a "mock" campaign. Anne Moody, a native CORE worker in Canton, opposed the plan: "I couldn't see us mobilizing the Negroes around a false campaign. We had enough problems getting them to register to vote, period." Another person agreed with her. He feared whites would react negatively and make it even harder to register blacks officially.[28] But most spoke in favor of the plan. The Freedom Election would bring publicity and expose the seriousness of the condition of blacks in the state. Indeed, Henry argued, "The Freedom Vote is a vote for the right to vote. . . . " It would show the strength blacks could wield in a close election.[29] Moreover, as Lawrence Guyot and Mike Thelwell explained later, the Freedom Vote was a way of politically involving the entire community and laying the groundwork for an indigenous leadership to develop. " . . . Most important, the 'Freedom Vote' was a means of taking politics to the people *where they were*."[30] By the end of the meeting, COFO decided to sponsor the Freedom Election.

All civil rights workers in Mississippi worked on the election. Balloting took place in churches, stores, and other meeting spots throughout the state. Wherever blacks gathered, workers tried to appear with Freedom Registration forms and ballots. In Canton the workers even went to the Madison County Fair during the segregated week for blacks. As usual, civil rights workers and black participants were harassed and intimidated by Mississippi officials.

In an attempt to get more blacks registered, COFO accepted the help of a white lawyer, Allard Lowenstein, who was well known in the liberal establishment. Through his contacts at Stanford University and Yale University, Lowenstein drafted about eighty college students to come to Mississippi to help "Freedom Register" voters. These students represented the first large group of previously uninvolved northerners brought into Mississippi to work in the field in civil rights. They came enthusiastically and brought with them skills, media attention, and money. So many students wanted to work and the Mississippi community resources were so limited that only a fraction of the students who were willing were chosen to go. The others organized bail money, funds for the campaign, and letter writing to congressional representatives and the Justice Department. Indeed, the Freedom Vote was "the" topic at Stanford, with every issue of the *Stanford Daily* headlining the campaign's progress. The Freedom Vote tapped a wellspring of activism on the campus.[31]

The influx of northern college students enabled COFO workers to cover the state more effectively, and after three days of balloting some 88,000 people who had completed Freedom Registrations cast their ballots for Henry and King.[32] The vote was hard work, however, for whites intimidated many blacks who wanted to vote and several cities even added temporary policemen to their force to "handle" the Freedom Ballot.[33]

Within a few days of the voting, SNCC staff and representatives from CORE and SCLC held a meeting in Greenville to discuss new directions for the Mississippi civil rights movement. At this time, field workers in Mississippi constituted about one-third of the SNCC full-time staff in the Deep South. Of these, thirty-five were black and six were white. Twenty-five of the blacks were from the Deep South as were two of the white workers. In general, all of the whites and most of the northern blacks on the Mississippi staff came from middle-class homes where the fathers were primarily ministers, teachers, or civil service workers. In contrast, the majority of the southern blacks and some of the northern blacks came from lower-class or lower-middle-class homes where the mothers worked as domestics or maids and the fathers were factory workers, truck drivers, small farmers, bricklayers, or carpenters. Twenty-nine of the staff were between the ages of fifteen and twenty-two years and twelve were between twenty-three and twenty-nine years of age. Of the group, twenty-six were college graduates or had attended college; ten had either finished or attended high school and two had attended only elementary school.[34]

The staff began the conference at Greenville with a forceful discussion on restricting the participation of whites in the movement. On Saturday Bob Moses chaired the meeting with almost thirty-five blacks and seven whites in attendance. Several black staff members formally brought up the issue of white participation and argued for severe restriction of whites in Mississippi. In direct response to the influx of students who worked on the campaign they argued that white students automatically took leadership positions, received publicity, and then left. This, they maintained, reinforced the tendency of southern blacks to believe in white superiority and also kept them from developing leadership. They suggested instead that whites should work in white communities and blacks in black communities.[35] Although the arguments against whites were certainly persuasive, another small but formidable group argued for a massive project utilizing northern students. Bob Moses, David Dennis, Fannie Lou Hamer, and Lawrence Guyot countered every argument for restricting whites. Guyot believed northern students working with blacks would truly change Mississippi society "... on a human individual to human individual relationship."[36] Hamer spoke passionately in favor of including whites. She believed the nationalist arguments were "reverse segregation." "If we're trying to break down the barrier of segregation, we can't segregate ourselves."[37] In the end, Bob Moses' calm, reflective, and idealistic statements swung the conference in favor of a massive summer project. Moses was concerned that the civil rights movement in Mississippi might become racist. And he believed, "... the only way you can break that down is to have white people working along side of you, so then it changes the whole complexion of what you're doing, so it isn't any longer Negro fighting white, it's a question of rational people against irrational people."[38]

Although the SNCC staff eventually agreed to the summer project, the meeting did not truly resolve the question of the place of whites in the movement. The first open all-staff discussion, the Greenville Conference uncovered honest doubts, resentments, and confusions. Often through the weekend, individual staff members admitted their ambivalent and unwilled emotions: "I think one way and act another way. It's not rational. But these feelings [against whites] are there."[39] The basic idealism of the SNCC staff was legendary, however, and it was the seeming "rightness" of an integrated effort, especially when Hamer and Moses espoused it, that compelled the staff to accede to the summer project.

Julius Lester, a SNCC field secretary, wrote later about the meeting that "within SNCC there had been widespread opposition to the bringing of whites into the state," and that "a small, powerful minority" got the summer project by branding those against it "racist." Countering Lester's position, Len Holt, a black SNCC lawyer, believed that those really against the project were a small, vigorous minority, while academics Emily Stoper and Howard Zinn each argue persuasively that both factions were minorities, but that the group in favor included the major figures in the Mississippi movement. Bob Moses, already a legendary figure, commanded enormous respect and support within SNCC. His arguments carried the day.[40]

The most obvious advantage of a massive project was the strength to be gained in numbers. The more workers, the more work could be done and the more difficult it would be for white Mississippians to shut the projects down. As was clearly shown by the Freedom Vote, northern students attracted both money and media. A large project could put the federal government on notice and push the question John Lewis asked at the March on Washington, "Which side is the federal government on?" Also, the project could be arranged to spotlight the challenge of the civil rights movement before the Democratic Party in an election year. Underlying all of these reasons was the conviction that Mississippi was a symbol of the worst in race relations. If the "closed society" could be significantly opened, the entire civil rights movement would make a quantum leap forward.[41]

In addition, as the staff well knew, it was true that by November 1963 the movement in Mississippi was stymied. Increasing violence seriously curtailed projects throughout the state. Despite Freedom Days, marches, sit-ins, and boycotts, Mississippi blacks were not registered to vote, and the nation seemed unaware of the situation. In one sense, the Freedom Vote was only illustrative of how bad things really were. The movement in Mississippi needed a new direction. In the established tradition of the student movement, the civil rights workers proposed the summer project as an innovation. It was a direct response to the Mississippi experience.[42]

The staff meeting ended with the participants committed to a Summer Project. Once they agreed, COFO was easily convinced to sponsor formally the Mississippi Summer Project, which from the outset was envisioned as a total community project. Inspired by the Freedom Vote, COFO workers expanded and refined their ideas on parallel structures, devising a project with three major components: voter registration, freedom schools, and community centers.

In addition to regular voter registration, the staff planned to continue Freedom Registration and begin a challenge to the regular state Democratic Party. From this idea came the Mississippi Freedom Democratic Party (MFDP or FDP), which was formally founded in Jackson on April 26, 1964.[43] In direct contrast to the state Democratic Party, the MFDP was open to all citizens of voting age, regardless of race, creed, or color and advocated a coalition of poor whites and blacks to bring substantive change to

Mississippi. The MFDP from the beginning pledged loyalty to the national Democratic Party.

COFO saw Freedom Schools as a way to free children from the confines of regular school, while still reinforcing the concept of learning. As importantly, civil rights workers believed Mississippi's future belonged to the young and that Freedom Schools would be a good organizing base for all phases of the Freedom Summer Projects.

In the established projects, COFO hoped to begin community centers to be an ongoing organizational base. Visualized as comfortable and useful centers, they would house libraries, equipment, offices, and Freedom Schools. Most black communities throughout the state had no free community space, and COFO workers hoped to remedy that lack.

Throughout the spring, plans and theories were bandied about. A series of meetings in Jackson resulted in the basic programs and project mimeos.[44] The National Council of Churches offered to finance an orientation for volunteers and also to give some money to establish the Delta Ministry. Carl Rachlin of CORE formed the Lawyers Constitutional Defense Committee (LCDC) to aid the project, and the National Lawyers Guild offered its services.[45] The Medical Committee for Human Rights (MCHR) organized to give medical support to the volunteers and the local black community. And the American Federation of Teachers (AFT) promised money and Freedom Summer volunteers. Despite all the help it received, COFO was still in debt and desperately needed money.

Northern colleges acted as recruiting centers for volunteers. Yale and Stanford were particularly involved, due at least in part to their previous association with Allard Lowenstein and the Freedom Vote.[46] Northern Friends of SNCC organized support groups, raised money, and set up screening committees to interview prospective volunteers.

Meanwhile, at the COFO offices in Jackson, staff worked eighteen hours a day to arrange housing, Freedom School sites, program outlines, and a statewide communication system based on a Wide Area Telephone Service (WATS) line.

The white community in Mississippi was terrified by the thought of an invasion of beatnik, communist race mixers. The state government added police and equipment to meet the onslaught, and the legislature passed a series of laws designed to kill the project. On the other side of town, however, the black community could hardly wait for the project to begin. Anne Moody wrote, "Among Mississippi Negroes . . . I had never witnessed such antici-pation in all my life. It seemed that for once in the history of civil rights work in Mississippi something was actually going to be accomplished."[47]

The project represented the next logical step in the continuing evolution of the civil rights movement. The students had moved from sit-ins to Freedom Rides to voter registration. A tactic of voter registration, the Freedom Vote, attracted public attention and owed part of its success to northern student volunteers. It in turn produced the plans for the Freedom Summer.

Those plans grew out of a desperate need to break out of the terrifying no-win pattern of Mississippi civil rights work and regain some momentum in Mississippi. The ramifications for COFO of bringing in hundreds of northern students were fraught with dan-ger, and the staff knew it well. Recruiting northern students entailed big risks; the question was whether the possible success was worth it. Northern students, who would almost certainly be predominantly white, had five big pluses in their favor: They would bring back the media currently bored with portraying "routine" violence against blacks; they would bring concrete skills and energy to a movement that was bruised and tired; they had contacts with money and nationwide publicity; their parents were often substantial members of their respective northern communities who would lobby for their children's cause; and their sheer numbers would render it almost impossible for Mississippi whites to stop the project with violence. Their minuses were clear, too, however: They could take over the projects, reinforcing concepts of white superiority and negating black gains and leadership; they might be patronizing or even racist with local blacks; they were almost certainly naive and unready to deal with the Mississippi experience; and they would bring danger to themselves and the black community by their presence.

When COFO went with the gamble of bringing in northern students, they bet on the side of the pluses and not the minuses. They made a public stand for continued integration, for "black and white together." Just as the experience of the southern civil rights movement brought the Summer Projects logically into existence, so the experience of the summers ushered in the next phase of the movement from self-conscious integration to conscious self-determination.

Although the southern student movement publicly indicated the shift from "black and white together" to "Black Power" only in 1966, the direction that shift would take was clearly evident in the debate over the Mississippi Summer Project as early as November 1963. And the actual experience of the large integrated Summer Projects of 1964 and 1965 provided the catalyst for that final shift. In fact, by the late fall of 1965, the southern student movement had quietly changed its emphasis from integrated programs and projects to "self-determination." That change, not brought to the attention of the national media until the Mississippi Meredith March in June 1966, was a direct result of the Freedom Summer Projects. They represented a major turning point in the civil rights movement, and they were a crucible for change for the northern volunteers as well.

NOTES

1. Louis Harris, *Newsweek*, July 13, 1964, pp. 24–27.

2. *New York Times*, December 1, 1959, p. 23.

3. Howard Zinn, *SNCC: The New Abolitionists* (Boston: 1965), p. 16; August Meier and Elliott Rudwick, *CORE: A Study in the Civil Rights Movement, 1942-1968* (New York: 1973), pp. 101–27; Clayborne Carson, *In Struggle: SNCC and the Black Awakening of the 1960's* (Cambridge, Mass.: 1981), Michael V. Namurato, *Have We Overcome? Race Relations Since Brown* (Jackson, Miss.: 1979).

4. Zinn, *SNCC*, p. 33.

5. Joanne Grant, ed., *Black Protest: History, Documents and Analyses, 1619 to the Present* (New York: 1968), pp. 289–90.

6. Meier and Rudwick, *CORE*, p. 16.

7. For a fuller discussion of the Kennedy administration and the civil rights movement, see Victor S. Navasky, *Kennedy Justice* (New York: 1971), especially chap. 3.

8. Zinn, *SNCC*, pp. 46–47, 49–50.

9. Meier and Rudwick, *CORE*, pp. 136–41; Zinn, *SNCC*, pp. 40–61; also James Peck, *Freedom Ride* (New York: 1963).

10. Zinn, *SNCC*, p. 52.

11. Meier and Rudwick, *CORE*, p. 144.

12. Ibid., p. 140.

13. Ibid., pp. 148-53. State Historical Society of Wisconsin: Stuart Ewen Papers (hereafter SHSW: Stuart Ewen Prs.); Jim Forman, "What Is the Student Nonviolent Coordinating Committee," mimeo, November 1964, esp. pp. 9-20, 29-32; Mississippi Freedom Information Services, Jan Hillegas Prs.; SNCC Staff, "Notes on Mississippi Staff Meetings," November 14-16, 1963; COFO Staff, "Summary of Minutes," January 10, 1964; Judy Richardson, "SNCC Executive Committee Meetings," April 10, 1965. I am indebted to Jan Hillegas of the Mississippi Freedom Information Service for allowing me access to her extensive private collection and for permission to use her papers at the SHSW.

14. SHSW: Stuart Ewen Prs.; Jim Forman, "What Is the Student Nonviolent Coordinating Committee." For background on the VEP, see the Southern Regional Council (SRC) Collection in Atlanta, Georgia (hereafter SRC Prs.), Box VEP Administration, Folder: Annual Report; Leslie Dunbar and Wiley Branton, "First Annual Report of the Voter Education Project of the Southern Regional Council, Inc."

15. Zinn, *SNCC*, p. 3.

16. Len Holt, *The Summer That Didn't End* (New York: 1965), p. 35.

17. Zinn, *SNCC*, pp. 62-78.

18. James W. Silver, *Mississippi: The Closed Society* (New York: 1966).

19. Meier and Rudwick, *CORE*, p. 269.

20. Holt, *The Summer That Didn't End*, pp. 31-33; Meier and Rudwick, *CORE*, pp. 269-71; Anne Moody, *Coming of Age in Mississippi* (New York: 1970), pp. 329-31; Zinn, *SNCC*, pp. 79-81.

21. Zinn, *SNCC*, pp. 86-89; SRC Prs., Box VEP Administration, Folder: Annual Report; Leslie Dunbar and Wiley Branton, "First Annual Report of the Voter Education Project of the Southern Regional Council, Inc.," March 1963, pp. 27-33.

22. SRC Prs.; Box VEP Administration, Folder VEP: Readings File Copies, January 1965-; Wiley A. Branton, "Descriptions of Problems Encountered by the Voter Education Project in the State of Mississippi Between April 1, 1962 and Nov. 1, 1963 as Prepared for the United States Commission on Civil Rights," pp. 5-7; Zinn, *SNCC*, p. 90.

23. Zinn, *SNCC*, chap. 5, pp. 79-101.

24. Moody, *Coming of Age*, p. 330.

25. SRC Prs., Box VEP Administration, Folder VEP: Reading File Copies, January 1965-; Wiley Branton, "Description of Problems Encountered by the Voter Education Project in the State of Mississippi between April 1, 1962 and November 1, 1963 As Prepared for the United States Commission on Civil Rights," pp. 9-11.

26. Grant, *Black Protest*, pp. 375–76. Cleveland Sellers and Robert Terrell, *The River of No Return, the Autobiography of a Black Militant and the Life and Death of SNCC* (New York: 1973), pp. 59–66.

27. Leslie B. McLemore, "The Mississippi Freedom Democratic Party: A Case Study of Grass-Roots Politics" (Ph.D. diss., University of Massachusetts, 1971), p. 101.

28. Moody, *Coming of Age*, pp. 330–31.

29. Reese Cleghorn, "Who Speaks for Mississippi," *The Reporter*, August 13, 1964, p. 32.

30. Lawrence Guyot and Mike Thelwell, "The Politics of Necessity and Survival in Mississippi," *Freedomways* 6 (Spring 1966):121.

31. Otis Pease Prs.; Ilene Strelitz Melish, unpublished memoir, manuscript (hereafter *Memoir*), pp. 1–18. I am indebted to Otis Pease and Ilene Strelitz Melish for their permission to use this remarkable memoir.

32. McLemore, "Mississippi Freedom Democratic Party," p. 105. Footnote 44 is a bibliographical discussion of the varied reporting of the figure. I have taken McLemore's own figure for the vote total.

33. Moody, *Coming of Age*, pp. 340–42.

34. Zinn, *SNCC*, pp. 9–10.

35. Ibid., pp. 186–87; Holt, *The Summer That Didn't End*, pp. 35–36; Julius Lester, *Look Out Whitey! Black Power's Gon' Get Your Mama!* (New York: 1969), pp. 19–20.

36. Zinn, *SNCC*, p. 187.

37. Ibid., p. 188.

38. Ibid., pp. 188–89.

39. Ibid., p. 188.

40. Lester, *Look Out*, pp. 19–20, Holt, *The Summer That Didn't End*, pp. 35–37; Emily Stoper, "SNCC: The Growth of Radicalism in a Civil Rights Organization" (Ph.D. diss., Harvard University, 1968), pp. 135–38; Zinn, *SNCC*, pp. 185–89. These are the main sources on this meeting, and they differ mainly merely in emphasis and perspective. My belief is that Lester overstates his case but that he better understood the mood of the Greenville meeting than did Len Holt. This is corroborated by interviews. See also Meier and Rudwick, *CORE*, pp. 253–54, for similar views and Moody, *Coming of Age*, pp. 329–43. Howard Zinn is the most useful, because he renders a sympathetic account of the meeting from a participant-observer view. In a classic understatement, the actual minutes of the meeting say only, "*White Students' Role*: Much discussion. Decision to choose roles on basis of qualified people . . . ," Jan Hillegas Prs.; SNCC Staff "Notes on Mississippi Staff Meeting," mimeo, Greenville, Miss., November 14–16, 1963, p. 3.

41. Holt, *The Summer That Didn't End*, Appendix II, 197–99, Melish,

Memoir, pp. 18–30. Melish and friends at Stanford wrote the "Prospectus for the Freedom Summer" on their own without benefit of attending the Greenville meeting. Perhaps that in itself exemplified the fears of the losing minority faction at Greenville. Certainly Melish throughout her *Memoir* regrets the role she played in the organizing of the project. Mary Rothschild Prs. in author's possession; "Prospectus for the Mississippi Summer," COFO undated |Winter–Spring, 1964|.

42. Emily Stoper, "SNCC," pp. 135–38.

43. Leslie McLemore, "Mississippi Freedom Democratic Party," pp. 106–11. In footnote 45, p. 106, Lawrence Guyot reports that the "seminal meeting" on the MFDP actually occurred some months before.

44. I quickly read through notes or informal minutes of some of the meetings from March to June when I was in Mount Beulah, Mississippi. Unfortunately, I was not able to copy them.

45. The guild's entry into the project brought a strong reaction from those liberals within the movement who were averse to what they felt was "Communist infiltration." Guild participation was problematic to the other legal groups as well as to the NAACP and the Ink Fund. Melish, *Memoir*, pp. 44–48, 68–74.

46. Melish, *Memoir*, details this story for Stanford students.

47. Moody, *Coming of Age*, p. 366.

2

THE VOLUNTEERS:
A TYPOLOGY

The Mississippi Summer Project began as scheduled in 1964.

The first group of volunteers arrived for orientation in Oxford, Ohio, amidst the chaos of the Jackson COFO office and the anticipation of the black community. During the summer about 650 young people went to Mississippi under the auspices of COFO, and a year later about 750 volunteers fanned throughout the entire South with several projects to work for the civil rights movement.[1]

According to a national opinion poll taken in July 1964, 65 percent of the adults of both black and white races, "opposed the trek of Northern Students to Mississippi." In the face of such majority sentiment, who were the volunteers? Why did they go south? And what did they hope to accomplish?

Knowledge of the volunteers' backgrounds, their reasons for entering the civil rights movement, and the differences in the groups is important to understanding the volunteers' experience. Any typology necessarily overlooks the individuality of the persons considered and the often highly personal motivations that compel an individual to act. Nevertheless, a typology has its uses, and this chapter examines as a group who the summer project workers were, what they believed, and why they went south.

There were two kinds of summer civil rights workers. By far the larger and more celebrated was the collection of young men and women who volunteered a summer of their time to work for the civil rights movement. For the most part, these workers stayed at least two months and became Freedom School teachers, voter registration workers, and community center organizers. The other major group comprised men and women in the professions who offered their particular skills to the movement for a specific, generally short period of time. In the movement language, members of the former group were "the volunteers," while those of the latter were "the lawyers," "the doctors," and "the ministers." In this study, only the volunteers will be examined, for they were the largest and most controversial group to answer the call to work in the South.

In 1964 most volunteers went to Mississippi for the first Freedom Summer Project under the auspices of COFO. In 1965 volunteers went to Mississippi to work for the Freedom Democratic Party, as COFO had nearly disintegrated during the winter. In addition a large number of volunteers worked throughout the Deep South under SCLC's Summer Community Organization and Political Education (SCOPE) project, which was a spinoff of the 1964 Mississippi Summer Project.

Because of changes in the political climate between the summers and because of the variety of projects, there were some differences between the individual 1964 and 1965 volunteers. The 1964 COFO project ended in August with the failure of the FDP challenge to unseat the Mississippi regulars at the Democratic convention. In September a contingent from SNCC went to Guinea as guests of the government and saw a black-run government for the first time. Later in the fall, the Free Speech Movement (FSM) shook the University of California at Berkeley and presaged widespread student unrest. During the winter, President Johnson began serious escalation of the war in Vietnam, including saturation bombing of the North. And in the spring, U.S. Marines were dispatched to Santo Domingo.

In 1965 there were differences in the style of the two main projects, and they attracted different people. SCOPE primarily registered voters pushing for the Voting Rights Act, while SNCC–FDP, in sharp contrast, focused on building parallel institutions in the community with local blacks in charge.

Despite the political change between 1964 and 1965, and the differences in style of the 1965 projects, it is possible to draw a general profile of the northern volunteers, for there was a remarkable underlying similarity among the people who went south. The group differences that evolved and the impact they had on volunteer selection will be discussed at the close of the chapter.

Because the application forms were not standardized, it is impossible to say precisely how many volunteers were white, Asian American, or black; however, the overwhelming majority were white. A random sample of 220 Mississippi summer volunteers' files showed 88 percent of the volunteers were white, 11 percent were black, and 1 percent were Asian Americans. Cleveland Sellers, a black student who first worked in Mississippi in 1964 and later became SNCC's program secretary, estimated there were "about" 135 black volunteers out of 900, which would be a total of 15 percent black and 85 percent white volunteers. A complete count of the 282 FDP applications for 1965 that mentioned race found 94 percent of the volunteers were white, 4 percent were black and 2 percent were Asian Americans. Of those 1965 applications that did not specifically mention race but gave other solid clues, fifty volunteers appeared to be white, while five appeared to be black, for a ratio of 91 percent to 9 percent. The SCOPE group reflected the national average of whites to blacks with a ratio of 88 percent white to 12 percent blacks.[2] Almost more important than the actual percentages, however, was the fact that staff and volunteers alike viewed volunteers as white. The relatively few black volunteers were usually perceived both by other white volunteers and by staff members as, at the very least, "potential" staff members and from what sketchy data are available, it seems many did become staff members. In 1964 few white volunteers were seen as "apprentice staff"; by 1965 almost none were. Because of both the relatively small number of black volunteers and a lack of material on them, and because in a fundamental sense they had a different experience from the vast majority of volunteers, who were white, in this study the volunteer experience will be discussed primarily in terms of white volunteers. This in no way means that I believe that whites were more important to the civil rights movement than blacks; rather, it means that to study the dominant volunteer experience means that I am mostly examining the roles and actions of white volunteers.

The overwhelming majority of the northern volunteers were students and teachers. These people were recruited from campuses

across the United States and from several professional teachers'
associations.[3] Those volunteers who held jobs other than teaching
often still considered themselves students.

Although volunteers went south from all types of colleges, there
was a very high proportion from the most prestigious private and
public schools, especially Harvard, Stanford, the University of
Wisconsin, and the University of California at Berkeley.[4] This may
merely reflect the sophisticated recruiting and screening centers at
these schools in both 1964 and 1965.

Even in comparison with other students, the volunteers held
high educational aspirations. In 1965, 25 percent of the FDP–SNCC
workers had more than sixteen years of schooling.[5] SCOPE volunteers indicated in a survey study conducted by sociologists Michael
Aiken, N. G. Demareth, and Gerald Marwell that 73 percent
planned postgraduate study in liberal arts fields.[6] Many volunteers
valued education for its intrinsic importance to their personal
development, in contrast to students who saw education as a
career path. The SCOPE study indicated, moreover, that while
students who remained in the North preferred careers as business
executives, lawyers, physicians, engineers, and housewives, the
volunteers preferred careers as professors, social workers, and
clergy.[7]

The civil rights movement was a national concern, and the
Freedom Summers attracted volunteers from every state in the
Union. They were overwhelmingly urbanites. More than 90 percent in 1964 and 1965 lived in towns classified urban by the United
States Census Bureau, whereas only 70 percent of the total population were considered urban dwellers. Two volunteers in five hailed
from the northeastern states, and of those states New York sent by
far the largest number. The midwestern and west coast states sent
the next largest group; if their numbers were combined, they
formed just under half of the total group. A very few volunteers
came from the mountain and southwestern states. In both 1964
and 1965, the southern states produced more white volunteers than
both the mountain and southwestern states combined.[8]

The white volunteers who came from the Deep South were a
small band. In Mississippi, white southerners worked in the small
"White People's Project" trying to interest poor white southerners
in joining blacks to form a coalition Freedom Democratic Party. In

1964, for example, there were only about twenty white volunteers from the Deep South, and all of them came from large "New South" metropolitan areas or attended Ivy League schools.[9]

In both 1964 and 1965 the volunteers were required to pay their own way, which included transportation to the South, living expenses of $150, and a guarantee for a $500 bond if necessary. Thus most student volunteers came from families with a secure economic standing. One FDP worker remarked in 1965, "My father's money has been able to buy my idealism."[10] Indeed, the SCOPE study found that two-thirds of its subjects belonged in the upper and upper middle classes, and the more sketchy data from the other projects corroborate this, although in this regard the SCOPE study found that the volunteers differed little from Wisconsin students who remained in the North.[11] For a minority of the volunteers, however, work in the South constituted a definite financial burden, and a few noted they would have to forego college temporarily, due to their loss of summer earnings. In some cases, church groups and northern civil rights affiliates sponsored individual volunteers. These groups paid the volunteers' expenses, enabling them to go south without financial aid from their parents.

In addition to their relatively high economic standing, the volunteers' parents had attained a very high educational level for their generation. Three out of four had finished at least twelve years of school, and a substantial number had more than sixteen years of schooling. Most of them held high-status jobs as doctors, lawyers, professors, teachers, business executives, and civil servants, and they were highly represented in service occupations. They were also in the political mainstream; more considered themselves Democrats than Republicans, but very few deviated from America's two major parties.

A large majority of the parents agreed with their children that attaining full civil rights for blacks in the South was an important problem that needed to be solved. One young FDP worker said of her parents, "They suggested . . . [my involvement] . . . in a sense, at about the time that the Selma crisis went on. I got a letter from them saying something to the effect that 'maybe it wouldn't be such a bad idea for you to go down to Selma and do something about what's going on since our generation failed so badly.'"[12] More frequently, however, the volunteers themselves were the first in their families to suggest their involvement. After an initial reaction of "why do you have to go?" the parents tended to support their children and share their concern. Very few parents were segregationists, according to the volunteers, but most were not active in northern civil rights work.[13] If their children had volunteered to work in the North, parental support might have been less universal: Most saw flagrant civil rights abuses in a distinctly southern context.

The volunteers' backgrounds were in the main similar to those of most students in their colleges, but certain differences are important to identify. The volunteer tended to be older than the average college student. The SCOPE group averaged two years more than the Wisconsin control group, and the median age of the 1964 COFO and the 1965 FDP–SNCC volunteers was twenty-one plus, while the median age of, for example, University of Washington students was just over nineteen.[14] This may indicate that age brings the independence and opportunity to act and also, perhaps, that it fosters activism.

In their stated political philosophy, the volunteers differed from their fellow students but not on the issue of racial equality. Most northern college students favored full equality for southern blacks.[15] The volunteers, however, veered to the left of their colleagues in their broad range of social concern. They felt that the federal government should spend a larger portion of the budget on antipoverty, medicare, and educational programs. Perhaps most important to the future of the movement, the SCOPE study found in 1965 that volunteers were more worried about the prospect of nuclear war than other college students. Fully three times as many volunteers as others wanted the United States to initiate negotiations to end the war in Vietnam.[16]

In their activities, the volunteers mirrored their spoken concern. In 1964 92 percent of the volunteers had participated in at least some civil rights activities in the North. In 1965 95 percent of the FDP volunteers and 78 percent of the SCOPE volunteers had worked in the civil rights movement before the summer. Over one-half of the volunteers participated in their communities in tutoring programs, settlement work, and voter registration. The vast majority of 1965 volunteers from California worked actively against Proposition 14, an initiative to overturn the state's existing open housing legislation. Of the 1965 Berkeley contingent of FDP–SNCC workers, over three-quarters were in the Free Speech Movement.[17] Even in 1964, 15 percent of the volunteers indicated activity in peace groups, and more than 10 percent had previously worked with the American Friends Service Committee in work camps outside their communities.[18]

The overwhelming majority of the volunteers considered themselves "Liberal Democrats," "Liberals," or nonaffiliated "Socialists." They thought the existing political institutions could accomplish their desire for a more just society and saw their wishes as consistently American in orientation. They were, in fact, not far to the left of the stated goals of the Johnson administration in its search for the Great Society.[19] For example, of those 1965 FDP volunteers who indicated membership in Students for a Democratic Society (SDS), 37 percent also indicated membership in the Democratic party.[20]

At the time, SDS was seen by both students and the press as a vanguard of the "New Left," though most members still adhered to the 1962 "Port Huron Statement," which was ameliorative in tone and sought:

... the establishment of a democracy of individual participation governed by two central aims: that the individual share in those social decisions determining the quality and direction of his life; that society be organized to encourage independence in men and provide the media for their common participation. . . . [21]

The most daring thrust of SDS in 1965 was establishing community centers in some northern cities to build parallel community institutions.

Although the majority of the volunteers believed that American political institutions could change to promote an egalitarian society, they tended to be more alienated from American society and education than their colleagues on campuses throughout the country. In the SCOPE study 42 percent of the volunteers agreed that "American culture is sick and moving along the road to destruction," while only 20 percent of Wisconsin students agreed.[22] A survey of FDP volunteers' statements indicates the majority felt alienated to some degree from contemporary society. As one FDP volunteer wrote, " . . . The corrupted and singly autonomous society which prevails in the South is evidence of the general malaise of our entire nation. I feel that in the South where freedom and human values are least in evidence, the national sickness is best attacked."[23] Another volunteer, who was very active politically, wrote in more personal terms,

I've lost faith or interest in most of the things that a lot of people get absorbed in, like academics, religion, "escapes," money, or a special hobby or "field of concentration." About the only thing I really believe in is the ability of people to sometimes get through to one another, and get close to one another, to help each other, and to make living easier for one another.[24]

This alienation provided many of the volunteers with a partial motivation for going south. Because of their profound belief in the highest American ideals of freedom and justice, the volunteers' alienation prodded them to change the society to live up to its goals. While their degree of alienation differentiates them from other students who stayed north, their desire to work to change the society in order to end their alienation differentiates them sharply from the "beatnik" drop-outs of the late 1950s and the "hippie" dropouts of the late 1960s.[25] Despite their alienation, the volunteers believed that at some level—personal, political, or societal— they could effect some change, and this conviction helped their decision to go south.

In 1965 in the Mississippi FDP–SNCC project, about 10 percent of the volunteers consciously identified themselves as "radicals." Although this was twice the number of self-described radicals in the SCOPE project, in both groups "radicals" were a small minority. Many of the radicals were members of the W.E.B. Du Bois clubs, the youth organization of the Progressive Labor Party, although a few were SDS members and some listed no political affiliation. They tended to see the civil rights struggle as intimately connected with America's involvement in Vietnam and the Dominican Republic, its anti-Castro policy and the general struggle of "third world peoples." In contrast to their fellow volunteers, radicals had almost no faith in either the ability or the desire of the United States government to effect change. As one wrote,

With SNCC the Civil Rights struggle in Mississippi or any state of the Black Belt South is not an isolated struggle, and working outside of the government-backed institutions, connections can be drawn. For example, the events of the Congo or Cuba or Vietnam or the Dominican Republic have some of the same elements as the events of Selma or Birmingham—or Harlem: an existing power wishes to maintain its foothold at the expense of people who have had quite enough of extra-popular control. Democracy is incomplete within America, and cannot, therefore, be "upheld" by America 8,000 miles away.

They wanted to work in the civil rights movement precisely because it was extra-governmental. Furthermore, they believed that viable parallel institutions could change the black community by giving it a power base to "fight the system." None advocated violent revolution.[26]

The volunteers' stated motives for going south were many and diverse. The most basic motivation, however, seemed to be their belief in the justice of their cause: Discrimination was wrong and evil and it must be ended. Time and again, the volunteers echoed the sentiments of this FDP worker:

I feel that Civil Rights is the most pressing problem of our time and that working in Civil Rights is the most useful way I can spend my summer, both in terms of duty to humanity and deep personal value.[27]

The belief that they were totally and unimpeachably right in their cause sustained all civil rights workers. This complete commitment to the justice of the movement was the single most important motivating factor for the volunteers. It underlay all the other reasons.

Working in the South was a way to demonstrate physically the depth of a volunteer's commitment to equality in American society, and many went south for that reason. They felt compelled to confront the evil of racial discrimination physically. Overwhelmingly, the volunteers stressed the importance of being able to act on a deeply held belief. One wrote, quite typically, "I *have* to go. Something inside me compels me to work for equal rights for all ....Freedom is a cause I believe in. I *have* to fight for it."[28] Indeed for a substantial number of the students, the summer projects at last offered a chance to confront a problem full time rather than study about it. For example, one graduate student wrote:

I have not spoken to the question of "personal motivation" the often unspoken question of parents and friends. . . . If little else, my work in history has shown me the complexity of this question in historical problems. Recent students have seen many levels, and "discovered" that abolitionists are neurotic, populists adolescent, and progressives maladjusted. Much of this may be; it may also be irrelevant. I know enough of myself to feel motivation operative on several levels. . . . I want to understand from the inside, the dynamic of social action; after too many years in school, I want to participate in the society I have studied for ideals which are important to me. . . . [29]

Students in every field from sociology to philosophy uttered similar statements about their disciplines. The sheer act of confronting a social problem—of laying one's body on the line—propelled many students south. Indeed, the SCOPE study found that 60 percent of those volunteers agreed at their orientation, "Almost nothing that can happen in the South this summer would make me feel my summer's work was not a success."[30]

In addition, the possibility of effecting real change in the system through one's acts proved an impetus to most volunteers. A substantial number agreed with the volunteer who wrote in 1965,

. . . I want to work for a Civil Rights organization, rather than for some other sort of organization because the racial inequality existing in this country is one of the worst of America's present problems. There are many things I would like to see changed in this country, but few are so widespread and so morally repugnant as racial discrimination. Also, I am fairly sure I could make a contribution to the Civil Rights Movement; I am much less sure that I could do anything about poverty in the North or the War in Vietnam.[31]

The SCOPE study showed that the possibility of effecting change was the major reason that the students volunteered.

To many of the volunteers the early 1960s, in sharp contrast to the 1950s, seemed to hold new and exciting directions for America. The Kennedy administration gave the illusion of being substantially more activist than the Eisenhower administration. The civil rights movement had awakened the conscience of a large proportion of the population. It seemed possible that changes could be made. A substantial number of the volunteers believed that civil rights was the historic movement of the century, and they saw in the projects a way to help form U.S. history in a positive mold. One FDP woman wrote:

I want to be a part of history, not letting history form me, but forming history itself. America is at a crossroads, not only domestically, but internationally, and what it decides about the oppressed within its own borders may well determine its attitude concerning other oppressed peoples. I have an opportunity and I do not intend to let it pass by me.[32]

This feeling of taking part in history was not always comfortable, however. One SCOPE worker wrote about joining the project,

It's kind of like a commitment to history, when I don't want to be committed to history, and I'm wary about making history at all. . . . It's like holding up your hand in front of a freight train and saying, "Stop." You just get run over. The thing to do is to . . . present your body so that you don't get annihilated. There are different ways to commit yourself, and I don't want to be destroyed in the process. I want to be effective and I didn't feel that I could be, until I became aware of the movement.[33]

Some students were motivated by more traditionally philosophical-religious reasons. Many volunteers enunciated the existentialist belief that one attains one's own freedom only when all people are free. As one SCOPE worker said, "I can't sit back and watch the world pass by; I've got to be a creator of the world. . . . I want to be free, and until all Americans are free, I can't be."[34] A much smaller number of volunteers held civil rights work as a way to further the Marxist revolution by "moving the masses and . . . spurring change."[35] The largest group of students expressing philosophical motivations held Judaeo-Christian religious beliefs, which provided them a large impetus for going south. These volunteers tended to be involved in campus ministries, where their ministers often put themselves on the front line of "social justice" activities and challenged their students to make a "personal confrontation." They saw themselves presenting an active "witness" and in that respect illustrated the evolving existentialist theology especially prevalent in campus ministries.[36] In 1965 religious motivations were more prevalent in SCOPE than FDP-SNCC volunteers, although there were some FDP volunteers who were primarily religiously motivated. A campus minister who worked for FDP wrote, "It is not only my duty, but also my desire, to commit myself to the movement which I firmly believe is the will of God. In order to be true to myself and faithful to my brothers, I must do what I can to further equality and humanity in our land."[37] A SCOPE volunteer enunciated a more common response: " . . . I am a Christian, and it is out of love that I have joined SCOPE."[38]

Many volunteers also were motivated by more personal-emotional reasons. Some volunteers suggested that they felt personally guilty for the way society had treated southern blacks; they saw work in the South as a way to atone for society's guilt and their own.[39] In 1965 SCOPE workers more often enunciated guilt feelings as a motivating factor; they also tended to be more religiously oriented than FDP–SNCC volunteers. Those FDP volunteers for whom guilt was a motivation also tended to be more religious than their other FDP colleagues. Explaining why he wanted to go south, one FDP volunteer wrote, "I feel a sense of duty and a sense of shame upon examining the Civil Rights situation today. I am anxious to act in any field of the Civil Rights struggle. . . . "[40] Another interpreted his action in terms of a way to avoid guilt, " . . . I have always blamed the German people for their apathy and silence in the face of the most brutal holocaust in world history. I do not want to blame myself today."[41] Those volunteers who enunciated guilt as a motivating factor represented a very small minority of COFO, SCOPE, and FDP–SNCC volunteers. Of the COFO and FDP group, however, there was a high correlation among guilt, religious motivation, and devotion to a nonviolent life-style. The SCOPE study does not analyze its data in this way, but one of the study's findings is that "the index of religious traditionalism" tended to be "the most potent variable" in a volunteer's expectations for the project and beliefs about the world, politics and society. The more traditionally religious SCOPE volunteers were, the more they believed in nonviolence for the movement, in the ability and desire of the government to change, and in a "hawkish" foreign policy. For these volunteers, devotion to nonviolence in their southern context did not mean they were pacifists. Indeed these volunteers were most likely to support the war in Vietnam.[42]

Suggesting another personal-emotional motivation, two psychiatrists who worked with the volunteers in 1964 believed they were also " . . . concerned with achieving, and consolidating their *own* rights and opportunities, their own dignity and self-respect, [which] made them specially sensitive to the plight of others struggling for freedom in its many senses."[43] The SCOPE study suggests the volunteers were acting out a "generational independence" in going south and sees this as a source of activism as well as a logical outgrowth of the volunteers' generally liberal upbringing. The authors believe that the SCOPE volunteers, then, were partially motivated by a desire to separate themselves from their parents in a positive way.[44] Many FDP volunteers also indicate this "independence." One wrote, "My own personal commitment to the Civil Rights Movement most probably stems from the 'White Liberal-intellectual Jewish' family background of my youth—a background of which I am proud, but, of course, not satisfied with."[45] A very few volunteers found themselves rebelling against their parents by going south. For these volunteers, the decision to work in the movement often involved a complete break with their family and also meant that they had to quit school temporarily for lack of funds.

Although the volunteers seldom concisely articulated these reasons, many discussed the benefits they would accrue from the projects in terms of understanding a new culture, expanding their education, and gaining independence. Thus, an FDP volunteer explained, "I hesitate to list any qualifications I may have, both because they seem meager and also because of my conviction that the work involved is more of a learning rather than a teaching experience for any outsider. . . . "[46] And another wrote, "Actually, I feel that the benefits of the experience for me would be greater than the service I could give. But my goal is to be useful and I would be grateful for the chance to work at it."[47] The volunteers believed that they would learn and grow from their experience in the South. For some, this represented an egotistical and opportunistic reason for joining. For the majority, however, it illustrated a genuine desire to understand another culture and another people in a real way.

Having examined the common qualities of the volunteers, we now turn to some of the differences, by groups, within the student civil rights movement.

Especially in 1965, there were some characteristic differences in the *type* of student involved in the different projects, although there were individual volunteers within each group who were atypical.

In 1964 COFO was the major project. Thus, almost all volunteers in the student civil rights movement worked in Mississippi. As a result, COFO had a wider range of people than any of the 1965 groups. As far as students were concerned, COFO was truly an umbrella organization, universal in its acceptance of volunteers. In addition, the student movement as a whole was not as politically developed and differentiated in 1964 as in 1965, and this added to the first summer project's catholicity.

In comparing a random sample of 1964 COFO applications to all of the 1965 FDP–SNCC applications, one finds several differences. The COFO volunteers had less previous political activity outside the area of civil rights than did those of FDP–SNCC volunteers. Of the 1964 volunteers, 16 percent indicated they had previously worked in the peace movement, whereas 33 percent of the 1965 volunteers indicated peace work.[48] It was in the area of previous civil rights work, however, that the most consistent differences existed. In their study of SCOPE, Aiken, Demareth, and Marwell examined the issue of the volunteers' previous civil rights activity and assigned three categories to assess that activity. They define a "very active" volunteer as having been affiliated with a group and having participated in direct-action demonstrations; a "moderately active" volunteer as having attended meetings and/or having gathered money; and a "not active" volunteer as having had no previous connection with the civil rights movement. Using this scale, the 1965 FDP–SNCC volunteers had substantially more previous civil rights activity than the 1964 COFO volunteers. The differences in the COFO and FDP volunteers show clearly:[49]

	1964 COFO	*1965 FDP–SNCC*
Very active	25%	68%
Moderately active	67	27
Not active	8	5

The categories of "very active" and "moderately active" are very nearly switched in the two years. In addition, 1964 volunteers who had previous civil rights activity tended to have only very recent activity. Many 1964 volunteers' previous activity was the organizing effort in the winter and spring of 1964 that resulted in the launching of the project.[50] Of those who had other civil rights experience, most were affiliated with CORE, NAACP, or local Human Relations Committees. Only 2 percent indicated previous affiliation with SNCC (F-SNCC) groups. Of the 1965 FDP-SNCC groups, 46 percent indicated affiliation with SNCC or F-SNCC groups, and an additional 36 percent indicated affiliation with CORE. Clearly part of the difference between the two groups in both previous political and civil rights experience is a result of the intervening year and thus the ability of 1965 volunteers to work in politics and civil rights. The difference in the civil rights affiliations, however, indicates that politics as well as time differentiated the groups.[51]

In 1965 there were two major projects, FDP-SNCC in Mississippi and SCLC's SCOPE project, which fanned throughout the rest of the South. As a result of the continuing evolution from the initial 1964 COFO project, the FDP-SNCC group identified itself as more radical than both COFO and SCOPE.

There were differences between FDP-SNCC volunteers and SCOPE volunteers on the question of religion. SCOPE volunteers set "a bimodal pattern of religiosity" which resulted in two substantial groups at nearly opposite ends of the continuum—a large group of agnostics and a large group of religious volunteers. For instance, 55 percent of the volunteers never attended church, but 25 percent attended church once a week or more. Fully 66 percent "agreed" or "strongly agreed" that "Jesus was God's only Son," and 27 percent accepted the traditional concept of God as "a person who is concerned about me and all mankind and to whom I am accountable." Organized religion didn't fare as well: Two-thirds responded, "I often find myself in agreement with religious doctrine but opposed to the policies of churches and ministers." Finally, however, 25 percent indicated that their campus clergy had positively influenced their decision to go south.[52] By contrast, in their applications to come south, only 17 percent of the FDP volunteers indicated religion played *any part at all* in their decision to work in civil rights. A large group of FDP volunteers described themselves as atheists.

There were more important differences between the FDP and SCOPE groups, however, particularly in the area of previous civil

rights activity. Utilizing the same categories as above, there is a
significant difference in all the categories, especially "very active"
and "not active."[53]

	1965 FDP-SNCC	*1965 SCOPE*
Very active	68%	18%
Moderately active	27	60
Not active	5	20

One in five of the SCOPE workers had had no previous connection
with the civil rights movement, and less than one in five had ever
participated in a civil rights demonstration of any kind. This lack
of previous civil rights experience indicates a more conservative
group of volunteers, a conclusion sustained by the relatively high
percentage of SCOPE volunteers who held traditional religious
beliefs.

There is some indication that SCOPE volunteers more closely
resembled 1964 COFO volunteers, especially in the criterion of
previous civil rights activity.[54]

	1964 COFO	*1965 SCOPE*
Very active	25%	18%
Moderately active	67	60
Not active	8	20

There are some obviously significant differences, however. On a
percentage basis, two and a half times as many students with no
previous activity went south in the SCOPE project as in the COFO
project. In the COFO project one of four students had previously
been in a demonstration, as compared with less than one in five of
the SCOPE students. In addition, of course, SCOPE students had a
crucial intervening year to act in politics and in civil rights. COFO
volunteers certainly did not have the opportunity for activism that
the SCOPE workers had.

In 1964, then, COFO was to the volunteers a truly catholic
organization. It provided an ideological home to students who
were to the left of the general student populace, but who tended
not to be radical. COFO volunteers were new to the civil rights
movement and were unlikely to be affiliated with SNCC.

In 1965 the projects differed, and they drew some different types into their groups. The 1964 volunteers who returned to the South overwhelmingly chose FDP. FDP–SNCC was much less open than COFO had been in 1964 and drew students who were at least sympathetic to the "New Left." SCOPE, on the other hand, was more open than COFO, accepting anyone who wanted to join, regardless of their previous activism. The obvious differences in the groups attracted different types within the student movement, and this in turn affected what the projects did in the summer and what success they had.

In summary, with all the group differences, there was a remarkable similarity in the volunteers over time and among groups. They were overwhelmingly white and upper middle class, supported financially and emotionally by their parents. They saw the civil rights movement as a case of simple justice, which compelled them to act, and they pledged at least a summer of their lives to the movement. From the time they began orientation, however, they were immersed in an alien culture, a new social structure, and a very different way of life. Both the volunteers and the movement changed as a result of their participation in the Southern Freedom Summers.

NOTES

1. This chapter is based mainly on the analysis and compilation of four groups of sources: Stanford University's KZSU Interviews, Commitment Sheets, and Pre-South Interview Forms; Delta Ministry's COFO Files for 1964 and FDP Files for 1965; a study of the SCOPE project; a study of CORE; and my own interviews.

Stanford University's radio station KZSU sent eight students in 1965 to interview civil rights volunteers throughout the South in all types of projects. Trained by university social scientists before they went south, they interviewed students throughout the Bay Area in the spring of 1965. Although they were not planned for this purpose, these interview reports provide a "companion-control" group for the volunteer interviews (Pre-South Interview Forms). Once in the South, the Stanford students interviewed as many volunteers as possible and wrote background reports, when they could, on standard forms (Commitment Sheets). The Quote Cards and interviews are the transcriptions of the tapes.

The Delta Ministry at Mount Beulah, Mississippi, has the files of the now defunct COFO and the barely alive FDP. I compiled a summary of all the files of the 1965 FDP–SNCC workers and a random selection of 250 1964 COFO workers' files. Each file contained the volunteer's application and whatever other material pertained to the individual. In general, all the applications gave the name, home, race, sex, school, and educational level of the volunteer. Most also contained information on previous activities that would qualify the volunteer for civil rights work and a majority included statements indicating the volunteer's reasons for joining the movement. In the major recruiting centers all applicants were screened, and these reports were also in the files. The majority of 1964 applications did not contain "statements of faith" and so were not as useful in that regard as the 1965 files.

Sociology professors Michael Aiken, N. G. Demareth, III, and Gerald Marwell of the University of Wisconsin conducted a before-and-after summer questionnaire survey of the three hundred SCOPE volunteers in 1965. To assess the volunteers better, they also ran a control survey of Wisconsin students. Their "preliminary" report analyzed the first questionnaire and was published as "Conscience and Confrontation," *New South* 21 (Spring 1966):19–28. Their final study was published as *Dynamics of Idealism, White Activists in a Black Movement* (San Francisco: Jossey-Bass, 1971).

2. COFO File Compilation, FDP File Compilation; Sellers and Terrell, *The River of No Return*, p. 82. Sellers believes that nine hundred students went south, while my figures as well as Elizabeth Sutherland's indicate only about 650. Elizabeth Sutherland, *Letters from Mississippi* (New York: 1965), p. 1; Aiken et al., *Dynamics of Idealism*, pp. 25–26. Also Interviews, Otis Pease, February 13, 1967, and March 23, 1967, Seattle, Wash.; and Miriam Feingold Stein, April 1975, San Francisco.

3. Otis Pease Prs.: "Prospectus for the Mississippi Freedom Summer," COFO mimeo, p. 5. Delta Ministry COFO Files: Staff memos from March to June 1964.

4. COFO File Compilation, FDP Compilation.

5. This is corroborated by the KZSU Commitment Sheet sample.

6. Aiken et al., "Conscience and Confrontation," p. 22.

7. Ibid., pp. 22–23. In this respect, however, there is some evidence to indicate that volunteers were simply following family patterns, as the volunteers' parents "over represented such occupations as teacher, clergyman, social worker, and at the doctoral level, those occupations requiring the Ph.D. rather than a professional degree (M.D., D.D.S.)." John L. Horn and Paul D. Knott, "Activist Youth of the 1960's: Summary and Prognosis," *Science* 171, no. 3975 (March 12, 1971):979.

8. These data are from a compilation of various address lists: COFO

Address List, FDP File Compilation, KZSU Commitment Sheets, SCOPE Address List.

9. COFO Address List; Delta Ministry COFO Files: White People's Project Folder; Staff Memos; Tracy Sugarman, *Stranger at the Gates: A Summer in Mississippi* (New York: 1966), pp. 4–5.

10. KZSU Interview 0258.

11. Aiken et al., "Conscience and Confrontation," p. 26, KZSU Commitment Sheets; KZSU Interviews; FDP File Compilation.

12. KZSU Interview 9002-4.

13. Aiken et al., *Dynamics of Idealism*, pp. 26–27; Sellers and Terrell in *The River of No Return* (pp. 78–80) indicate black student volunteers had every bit as hard a time as whites convincing their parents that they should go to Mississippi. Interviews and Quote Cards, especially group A-6; Interviews: Carol Koppel, January 30, 1967; Gary Good, January 26, 1967; Sally Shideler, February 15, 1967; Michael Rosen, February 7, 1967; Barbara Rosen, January 26, 1967; John Darrah, February 21, 1967.

14. Aiken et al., "Conscience and Confrontation," p. 22; COFO File Compilations; FDP File Compilations; Interview: Registrar, the University of Washington.

15. Aiken et al., *Dynamics of Idealism*, p. 34; KZSU Pre-South Interview Forms.

16. Aiken et al., *Dynamics of Idealism*, pp. 34–36; KZSU Interviews; Interviews: Michael Rosen; Barbara Rosen; Gary Good; Carol Koppel; Sally Shideler; Timothy Lynch, November 1966; Billy Jackson, February 14, 1967; Mary Gibson, February 9, 1967; John and Ellen Fawcett, January 25, 1967; Richard Gillam, January, 1967; Roger Dankert, January 1967; David Hood, January 24, 1967; the Rev. Roger Smith, November 1969; Charles Horwitz, November 1969, Jackson, Miss.; Jan Hillegas, November 1969, Tougaloo, Miss.

17. The criterion for FSM activity was an arrest at Sproul Hall and/or active SLATE membership.

18. COFO File Compilation; FDP File Compilation; Aiken et al., *Dynamics of Idealism*, p. 50.

19. FDP File Compilation; COFO File Compilation; KZSU Commitment Sheets; Aiken et al., *Dynamics of Idealism*, pp. 34–36.

20. FDP File Compilation.

21. Paul Jacobs and Saul Landau, *The New Radicals: A Report with Documents* (New York: 1966), p. 155; see also their discussion of SDS, pp. 27–41.

22. Aiken et al., *Dynamics of Idealism*, p. 35.

23. FDP File Compilation, #37.

24. FDP File Compilation, #231.

25. I. Solomon and J. R. Fishman, "Youth and Social Action II: Action and Identity Formation in the First Student Sit-in Demonstration," *Journal of Social Issues* 20 (1964):20, 36–45.

26. FDP File Compilation #45; FDP File Compilation; KZSU Interviews.

27. FDP File Compilation, #38.

28. FDP File Compilation, #78; Aiken et al., *Dynamics of Idealism*, pp. 38–39.

29. FDP File Compilation, #92.

30. Aiken et al., *Dynamics of Idealism*, p. 39.

31. FDP File Compilation, #2.

32. FDP File Compilation, #64a.

33. Aiken et al., *Dynamics of Idealism*, p. 21.

34. Ibid., p. 23.

35. Ibid., pp. 29–31.

36. KZSU Interviews; Interviews: John and Ellen Fawcett; the Rev. Robert Peters, March 16, 1967; see also, Philip F. Hammond and Robert E. Mitchell, "Segmentation of Radicalism—The Case of the Protestant Campus Minister," *American Journal of Sociology* 81 (1965):133–45.

37. FDP File Compilation, #54.

38. Aiken et al., *Dynamics of Idealism*, p. 24.

39. Sutherland, *Letters*, especially chaps. 1 and 11; KZSU Quote Cards, especially groups A-3 through A-6.

40. FDP File Compilation, #36.

41. FDP File Compilation, #189.

42. FDP File Compilation; Aiken et al., *Dynamics of Idealism*, pp. 59–63; KZSU Interviews; Interview: Otis Pease; SHSW: Elizabeth Sutherland Prs.

43. Otis Pease Prs.; Robert Coles, M.D., and Joseph Brenner, M.D., "American Youth in Social Struggle: The Mississippi Summer," no publication identification.

44. Aiken et al., *Dynamics of Idealism*, pp. 43–44, 27–28.

45. FDP File Compilation, #49.

46. FDP File Compilation, #41.

47. FDP File Compilation, #98.

48. COFO Compilation, FDP File Compilation.

49. COFO Compilation, FDP Compilation.

50. SHSW: Elizabeth Sutherland Prs.; "Letters From Mississippi Mss.," chaps. 1–2; R. Hunter Morey Prs.; COFO organization, Spring 1964; Melish, *Memoir*, pp. 1–80; KZSU Interviews of FDP volunteers who worked in COFO in 1964.

51. COFO Compilations; FDP Compilations.

52. Aiken et al., *Dynamics of Idealism*, pp. 29–31.
53. FDP Compilations; Aiken et al., *The Dynamics of Idealism*, p. 50.
54. COFO Compilations; Aiken et al., *The Dynamics of Idealism*, p. 50.

3

TO WORK FOR FREEDOM: THE VOLUNTEERS AND VOTER REGISTRATION

The first group of summer volunteers assigned to voter registration work arrived for orientation in mid-June at Western College for Women in Oxford, Ohio. Most were unaware of the background of the Summer Project, especially of the fiery debate that had surrounded the initial decision to invite a large number of northern students to work in Mississippi. They were, therefore, surprised at their reception. COFO staff members from Mississippi, who were mostly black, seemed cold, unfriendly, and occasionally even hostile. White volunteers, innocent and naive, held romanticized visions of Mississippi that the staff felt were dangerous. While white volunteers retreated into their own groups, black volunteers felt estranged as well. Communication among the groups was minimal.[1] For short periods the strain eased, especially during the singing of freedom songs, but it always came back. Several of the volunteers commented on this feeling when they wrote home:

. . . Us white kids are in a position we've never been in before. The direction of the whole program is under Negro leadership—almost entirely. And a large part of that leadership is young people from the South—Negroes who've had experience just because they're Negroes and because they've been active in the movement. And here "we" are, for the most part never experiencing any injustice other than, "No, I won't let you see your exam paper. . . . "[2]

As the orientation continued, the tension mounted as the sessions and lectures outlined the brutality and the dangers of Mississippi. In addition to their latent suspicion, most of the staff were convinced that the volunteers had no real conception of what Mississippi was like or what the summer's work could bring. In the staff's efforts to confront them, many volunteers felt that the staff deliberately baited them to test their courage.

In the middle of the week, a crisis occurred when the volunteers saw a "CBS Reports" documentary entitled "Mississippi and the Fifteenth Amendment." The film examined discrimination in voter registration. Some of the comments of the white southerners who were interviewed, and one obese white registrar in particular, caused the volunteers to laugh, whereupon several staff members walked out. After the film was over, the students realized what had happened, and one wrote, "We were afraid the whole movement was going to fall apart. . . . " The students and staff then "had it out" in an unscheduled and emotional meeting in the building foyer. The students claimed the staff was distant and would not accept them; the staff shouted that the students had to know what Mississippi was truly like, understand the community of the movement, and really think about why they were coming south for the summer.[3] After talking it all out, the session ended in song, and as one volunteer wrote, " . . . we all sang together, and the first time *really* together. The crisis is past, I think."[4]

The crisis for the orientation may have ended, but the tensions between the staff and volunteers at no time completely disappeared. Most black staff persons at some conscious or unconscious level resented the basic leadership and organizational skills that most of the volunteers had and the immediate media and legal attention they garnered. Behind this resentment lay the knowledge that the volunteers could always leave and return to northern, upper-middle-class America. Very few of the staff could count on an alternative to working in the civil rights movement.

The volunteers had a full week of orientation. There were classes in voter registration work, area studies, MFDP background, and nonviolent action. In some classes, the students acted "role playing" exercises. They also talked about their fears and expectations, who they were and why they were going to Mississippi. Throughout these activities, psychiatrists and staff members watched the volunteers to make a final screening.

Of special interest to the volunteers were the classes and workshops in voter registration and area studies. The staff workers gave the volunteers the history of the 1963 mock election and its subsequent blossoming into the Summer Project and the MFDP. They then explained what they wanted the volunteers to do during the summer. The first task, of course, was straight voter registration and education. With so much attention focused on the state and so many people encouraging registration, the staff hoped registration would become easier. Regardless of how the regular registration went, however, the MFDP—as a parallel institution—had a complete program compiled for the summer.

Upon the opening of the MFDP office in Jackson in the latter part of April, a campaign to elect MFDP candidates to the Congress of the United States had begun, and a full scale Freedom Registration program was initiated. As in the mock election registration of the previous November, registrants had only to be over twenty-one years of age and American citizens to register for the MFDP. On the basis of the Freedom Registration, the MFDP planned a challenge at the national Democratic convention to the seating of the regular Mississippi Democratic delegation, charging the regular delegation with discrimination in party membership and disloyalty to the national party.[5] As a part of the challenge, members of the FDP were traveling the country soliciting resolutions from state Democratic conventions and other influential party groups to support the seating of the MFDP.

During the orientation session, the precinct caucuses of the regular Democratic Party were held, and blacks throughout the state were denied access to them.[6] The MFDP leaders had anticipated this action by the regular Democrats and added it to their list of grievances.

Meanwhile, the volunteers ran workshops to educate potential black and poor white voters for Freedom Registration. Their most important task was to be door-to-door canvassing, where they would explain to each potential voter the steps of party organization, including precinct caucuses, county conventions, and the state convention, and try to persuade them of the importance of the Freedom Registration and the challenge. The staff reasoned that Freedom Registration, besides giving a legitimacy to the challenge, would organize Mississippi blacks at the grass-roots level and give them courage to try regular registration.

The volunteers soon learned that black reluctance to register came from legitimate fear of economic and physical reprisals. Fannie Lou Hamer, the MFDP candidate for Congress in the Second District, told how she was beaten by police and then evicted and fired from her job as a result of her attempts to register. The volunteers heard other stories of reprisals; convincing Mississippi blacks of the importance of Freedom Registration was an awesome task, and some volunteers wondered if it was, indeed, ethical for them to ask blacks to take such risks.

Steps in organizing and motivating whole communities were outlined, including workshops on organizing mass meetings and Freedom Days to encourage local people to register. The other major technique was to convene mock conventions where local people could learn to conduct meetings and prepare platforms. As the COFO staff had decided to abandon momentarily "tests" of public accommodations, Freedom Days and conventions provided the principal outlets for public group activity.

Bob Moses gave the volunteers some basic information on leadership development and black-white relations within the movement. He stressed that the volunteers should try merely to facilitate events and not try to do everything themselves. He warned them that whites and blacks might fear or even hate them but that they must learn to deal with those emotions. He also asked them not to perpetuate the southern past and "use" each other emotionally and sexually: " 'My summer Negro,' 'the White girl I made' are no different from the token Negro in the school—none are really known and experienced."[7]

In addition, the volunteers had classes in nonviolent action. Students learned the techniques of nonviolent protection, falling to the ground and rolling up into a ball, and they acted out nonviolent responses to harassment and violence. They also discussed the underlying philosophy of nonviolent action. At least two views emerged on the subject, both of which found proponents among staff and volunteers.

. . . We heard Jim Lawson of Nashville, who gave us the word on nonviolence as a way of life. Lawson speaks of a moral confrontation with one's enemies, catching the other guy's eye, speaking to him with love, if possible, and so on. . . .

Stokely Carmichael . . . rebutted Lawson in the afternoon session, thusly; nonviolence used to work because: 1. it was new; 2. the newspapers gave it top coverage week after week; and most important 3. the demands were minor and the resistance to change was not hard-core. . . .

. . . Stokely does not advocate violence. What he *is* saying is that love and moral confrontations have no place in front of a brute who beats you 'til you cry *nigger*.[8]

The volunteer who wrote this assessment continued, "My feelings, and I think these are common, are that nonviolence is a perverted way of life, but a necessary tactic and technique."[9] However, another volunteer wrote home:

. . . |I think I now understand| . . . the part |of nonviolence| which teaches you to love your "enemy," how to feel true compassion for the cop who is using a cattle-rod on you, how to understand him as a human being caught in a predicament not of his own making. . . . When I came I thought M. L. King and his "love your enemy" was a lot of Christian mysticism. Now I can see it as a force and support, helping those who understand it. It makes me think that maybe I can take what is coming this summer. . . . [10]

As they had almost since the beginning of the student movement, these two attitudes continued to grow more separate as the movement continued active work in the South. There was a profound difference between those workers who practiced nonviolence as a life philosophy and those who followed it for tactical reasons. Some volunteers in Mississippi were disappointed that many saw nonviolence simply as a way to exist in Mississippi and not as a philosophical base for their lives. The majority of the COFO staff and volunteers, however, seemed to accept nonviolence as a tactic only.

In conjunction with the classes at Oxford, there were many outside speakers. National civil rights leaders spoke to them about the movement. White southerners, most notably the Rev. Edwin King of the MFDP and Charles Morgan, a Birmingham attorney who was ostracized after he spoke out against the Birmingham bombings, talked about the problems of white workers in the movement. John Doar of the Justice Department explained the role of the federal government in the summer activities; he told the students that the FBI and the Justice Department would be investigative agencies only and that they could not enforce police protection unless there was a federal court order to do so. Representatives from the legal groups and the Medical Committee for Human Rights also told the volunteers about their roles in the summer project and how they hoped to help the movement.

On June 20 the orientation session ended, and the first group of volunteers left for Mississippi. They expected almost anything to happen when they entered the Magnolia State. Most of all, they wondered if they really were prepared for whatever the summer was to bring.

They were tested immediately. On June 21 Michael Schwerner and James Chaney, CORE staff members, and Andy Goodman, a volunteer, left the Meridian COFO office to examine the just-burned black church in Philadelphia, Mississippi. They wanted to reassure the black community that, regardless of harassment, COFO would help them continue their attempt at civil rights organization. Their disappearance touched off a statewide search by both federal and state organizations, which ended when they were found dead on August 3, buried in the bank of a new dam, the victims of a particularly brutal murder. Sixteen men including several Neshoba County policemen were later tried for violating the three workers' civil rights.[11]

Throughout the summer the mystery of the workers' disappearance and then the knowledge of their death caused serious tensions and anxiety in all the civil rights workers in the state. Schwerner, Chaney, and Goodman were the only workers murdered during the Summer Project, but another black volunteer died in a suspicious car crash, and there was in every community a constant backdrop of white harassment, which in many cases, especially in the towns of Greenwood and McComb, escalated to severe violence. Thirty-seven black churches and thirty more black homes and buildings were bombed or burned during the summer. More than eighty volunteers and workers were beaten and more than a thousand people were arrested for civil rights work. Stringent security regulations were detailed concerning work at night, integrated groups, and the necessity for telephone reports.[12]

Volunteers who ignored these rules were sometimes sent home for endangering the project.[13] Whether or not individual volunteers were harassed or injured, all civil rights workers in Mississippi felt the continual strain of possible violence. This tension was hard to endure and added to the difficulties of daily life in the project. Sometimes it was nearly paralyzing. A young man in the Greenwood project, who was beaten in broad daylight and who obviously had seen too much violence, wrote home:

I really cannot describe how sick I think this state is. I really cannot describe the feeling in my stomach when I hear a typical story of injustice. . . . I cannot describe the real courage it takes to stay down here. I cannot describe the fears, the tensions and the uncertainties of living here. When I walk I am always looking at cars and people: if Negro, they are my friends; if white, I am frightened and walk faster. When driving, I am always asking: black? white? It is the fear and uncertainty that is maddening. I must always be on guard. . . . When confronted with a crisis, then the action is clearly defined. But when I do not know what to expect, but always to know to expect something, then the tensions mount and I think of courage and of how deep my commitment has to be, and I think of getting the hell out of this sick state. I live day to day. I wake up in the morning sighing with relief that I was not bombed, because I know that "they" know where I live. And I think, well, I got through that night, now I have to get through this day, and it goes on and on. Even as I write this letter we are told that our office might be bombed by an anonymous voice, "to get rid of it once and for all". . . .

Cleveland Sellers wrote that the Mississippi Summer Project "was the longest nightmare I ever had: three months." Violence from southern whites was so likely that all volunteers carried fear with them constantly, even if they were not in the end themselves ever harmed. It was as one volunteer wrote later, "the psychological set of a soldier going to the front lines at a time of rather heavy and personal fighting. . . . You didn't really believe in 'beyond the Project,' just as I suppose you don't really believe in 'beyond the war.' "[14]

Once the volunteers arrived in their respective towns, they set up routines and divided jobs according to their individual communities' needs. Each project was unique, since the status and composition of the black community, the degree of previous civil rights organization, and the power structure of each community varied considerably. However, certain basic obstacles and tasks differed from project to project only in degree.

First, the volunteers found that local blacks were almost always afraid of the process of registering to vote and that this fear played a large role in limiting registrants. Economic and physical retaliation by whites was very common, since all people who attempted to register had their names printed in the local newspaper for two weeks. Many of the volunteers commented on this fear in letters home:

... Fear of the Man, fear of Mr. Charlie.... Occasionally it is the irrational fear of something new and untested. But usually it is a highly rational emotion, the economic fear of losing your job, the physical fear of being shot at. Domestic servants know that they will be fired if they register to vote; so will factory workers, so will Negroes who live on plantations. In Mississippi, registration is no private affair.... [15]

Since retaliation was so common, some volunteers seriously questioned their role in urging registration. Although most continued registration work, their doubts and uncertainty grew, especially after the Democratic convention.[16]

White harassment of the projects, staffs, and volunteers was another obstacle to vigorous voter registration campaigns. Daily incidents were always annoying and often dangerous. Every office received obscene phone calls. Among the more extreme examples were the arrest of volunteers in Drew for distributing voter registration material, the beating of workers in Hattiesburg, and the bombing of the Freedom House in McComb.[17]

In addition, the volunteers found that the overwhelming physical and economic intimidation of the black community often produced apathy within the community to the civil rights movement. Some volunteers were unable to cope with that discovery: They believed that they were risking their lives for the black community, and they felt they deserved a "better" response. Workers who felt let down generally exhibited their feelings to the community by being critical and patronizing. Although a few volunteers clearly were unable to deal effectively with their situation, most, when they found apathy, identified it, understood the reasons for it, and tried to work within its confines in a nonjudgmental way. At the end of the summer, one volunteer assessed his community:

... if I were to characterize the Negro community in one word, it would be "apathetic." This is really the most frightening thing about the whole situation, to see these masses of people, including many no older than myself, with their spirits crushed, just not seeming to care about anything. Of course, it is often difficult to tell where apathy leaves off and fear begins, and when you consider the fact that their environment has all of the characteristics associated with a northern slum . . . and when you add to that the system of total racial discrimination, which constantly tells these people they are inferior beings, with no hope of achieving a good life—it is not hard to understand how a person could grow up to be apathetic. Of course, there are many exceptions to this pattern . . . especially the kids.[18]

These obstacles of fear (both economic and physical), white harassment, and black apathy combined to make voter registration slow and difficult work. The volunteers' techniques differed, but the basic job in all communities was canvassing. One volunteer described a typical interview, in a somewhat patronizing way, in a letter home:

Hi. My name is Steve M. (shake hands, having gotten name, address, from a mailbox). I'm with COFO. There are a lot of us working in this area, going from house to house trying to encourage people to go down and register to vote. (Pause) Are you a registered voter? (This is the direct technique. Often people, being afraid, will lie and say yes, but you can usually tell because they will be very proud). Are you planning on going down soon? (This makes them declare themselves. Usually they say "yes" or "I hadn't thought about it much." The other answer is "No, I ain't going down at all"). "Well, I have a sample of the registration form." (Take it out and hand it to them). "You know, some people are a little afraid to go down, because they don't know what they're getting into. . . . "

"You know, it is so important that everyone gets the vote. As it stands now, that man downtown in charge of roads doesn't have to listen to the Negroes. They can't put him out of office. He should be working *for* you. . . . "

Then I pull out the Freedom Democratic Party application. "This is a protest party. Anyone can join to protest the laws about voter registration and the way elections are carried out."[19]

For most of the volunteers in voter registration, this was the standard approach. The work was hard and monotonous after a while. Many tried to vary the tasks in their day to avoid becoming "stale" in their presentation. As one volunteer explained:

Canvassing is dirty work. It is very tiring, and frankly boring after the first hour or so. (Three hours is about all most people, including myself, can stand). It is almost impossible to overcome the fears of people, first at seeing a white man in their house, and then of course all of the fears that the courthouse people make sure exist.[20]

Block-by-block canvassing was possible in towns, but not in certain rural areas, especially the Delta plantations of Senator Eastland's Second Congressional District. Many of the blacks in that area lived in houses on the plantations which were posted with "no trespassing" signs. As a volunteer wrote home:

Before we canvass a plantation, our preparation includes finding out whether the houses are posted, driving through or around the plantation without stopping, meanwhile making a detailed map. . . .

We're especially concerned with the number of roads in and out of the plantation. For instance, some houses could be too dangerous to canvass because of their location near the boss man's house and on a dead end road.

In addition to mapping, we attempt to talk to some of the tenants when they are off the plantation, and ask them about conditions. The kids often have contacts, and can get on the plantation unnoticed by the boss man, with the pretense of just visiting friends.

Our canvassing includes not only voter registration, but also extensive reports on conditions. . . . [21]

Once people identified themselves as willing to attempt to register, the volunteers organized voter registration classes. The classes covered everything from the particulars of how to fill out the form to an analysis of the Mississippi Constitution. They formed the basis for adult literacy programs and often acted as a major link between voter registration and Freedom School programs. A volunteer in McComb, which suffered the most violence in the state, described the voter registration program:

. . . despite its shortcomings, [it] is a beautiful thing to watch. Such a big step for these people! The voter registration classes are slightly tense, but what is more present is hope, positiveness. The people dress up carefully. They shake each other's hands, await eagerly the return of those who have gone down to the courthouse already. Two functional illiterates have come, and so many others have so much trouble filling out the form. But they're going down. . . . [22]

In conjunction with the canvassing and the classes, the workers organized mass meetings. These were generally held in the evening and consisted of speeches and singing. Both workers and local people spoke on the importance of the vote and obtaining political power. Often the speeches outlined programs to help with local concerns as well as the more cosmic challenge of the MFDP to the state's political structure.

In projects lucky enough to have community centers, the organization of mass meetings was not too difficult. Unfortunately, many projects had to rely on commandeering buildings—most often black churches—for the meeting places. In an area where the ministry was behind the movement, this was not difficult, and in fact most meetings and Freedom Schools met in black churches. But in many communities the local ministers did not want to risk damage to their churches and so refused to let their buildings be used for meetings and classes. In those communities where the workers could not find buildings for their meetings, they sometimes held them outside, although this was dangerous and avoided if possible. When the meetings were well attended, they were enormously inspirational and fostered a contagious enthusiasm:

Last night was one of those times that are so encouraging and inspiring. We had a mass meeting in Indianola. Three weeks ago, there was no movement at all in that community. A few Project workers went in and began canvassing for registration. It was decided to set up a Freedom School. Another few workers went in as staff. In that short time they had generated enough interest and enthusiasm to bring out 350 people to the meeting!

I sat and watched faces that had been transformed with hope and courage. They were so beautiful, those faces. It is hard to put into words an experience like this. That sense of hope was so strong, so pervasive, each of us there felt with complete certainty that there can, there will, be a better world and a good life if we work for it.[23]

But the meetings often attracted few people of voting age, which discouraged the civil rights workers. It was common for teenagers and older women to predominate; the least active group were young men in their twenties and thirties.[24]

The other major voter activity was the organization of a Freedom Day. After an area was canvassed and several people indi-

cated their willingness to register, the project workers would take
them to the county courthouse. In addition to the registrants, local
people of all ages would picket the courthouse with signs, and the
day would usually end with a big rally. This was an exceedingly
effective way to encourage teenagers to participate. Particularly
after the signing of the 1964 Civil Rights Act that desegregated
public accommodations, teenagers around the state wanted to
conduct direct-action demonstrations. Since COFO had decided
not to sponsor any direct-action campaigns, Freedom Day march-
ing and picketing served to enable young people to put their
energy into the movement. The Greenwood project held the largest Freedom Day of the summer with over one hundred people
demonstrating and mass arrests of participants.[25]

Registration work was slow and often discouraging. Although
blacks were able to register relatively easily in a few places like
Batesville, in most counties the white registrars turned down all
black applicants. By the middle of the summer, it was clear that in
the overwhelming majority of the counties suits against each registrar would be required to put black voters on the rolls.

In mid-July, Dona Richards[26] of the Jackson office sent out an
important memo to all projects. Emphasizing the basic facts about
Freedom Registration, Richards explained that the Democratic
convention challenge would be in large part based on the number
of signatures on the Freedom Registration books. She cautioned,
" . . . it is of the greatest importance that the entire staff, those
volunteers assigned to voter registration and the community center
people work as hard as possible from now on in order to get at
least 100,000 people on the books."[27] She outlined a statewide
organization to accomplish that goal.

Everyone who was not teaching Freedom School began working
full time on Freedom Registration. And in some projects, Freedom
School teachers also filled in "spare time" by working on the
campaign.[28] Even with the extra workers, however, only fifty
thousand Mississippians were Freedom registered by the beginning
of the MFDP precinct caucuses. One volunteer explained:

. . . One of the difficulties is that most Negroes in Mississippi are instinctively
apprehensive of the word "registration." They connect it with going to the
courthouse and answering a lengthy trickily worded form. Also, some ask

if they have to pay any money; associating it with the poll tax which is still required in state elections in Mississippi. . . . [29]

While the volunteers were working on Freedom Registration for the MFDP, the regular Democratic Party of Mississippi followed its normal course in preparation for the national convention. The party held caucuses in June, and blacks across the state attempted to attend; their treatment became part of the MFDP's documentation of discrimination against blacks by the regular party. A few blacks became delegates to the county conventions, which were held on June 23, because they were the only people to attend their precinct caucuses.[30] The state convention began on July 28, and no blacks attended. The regular Democrats adjourned almost immediately until after the national Democratic convention, so that they would not have to endorse a national candidate.[31] Before they adjourned, however, they passed several resolutions, two of which aptly indicated the feelings of the regular party. One was the state civil rights plank, which read:

We oppose, condemn, and deplore the Civil Rights Act of 1964. . . . We believe in separation of the races in all phases of our society. It is our belief that the separation of the races is necessary for the peace and tranquility of all the people of Mississippi and the continuing good relationship which has existed over the years.[32]

The other applied to the national party as a final summary, "We reject and oppose the platforms of both national parties and their candidates."[33]

In direct contrast the precinct meetings of the MFDP were called statewide for July 21. Throughout the state, local people gathered together for their first real political caucus. Local leaders chaired the meetings and COFO workers acted as parliamentarians. One volunteer reported:

The precinct meeting was the first political experience for those who attended. . . . It was tremendously interesting to watch and indicative, I think, of the innate political nature of all men. Within ten minutes they were completely at ease and had elected a chairman, secretary, and ten delegates to the district convention.

. . . The delegates were teachers, housewives, packing house workers, a toy factory worker, in short, a genuine cross-section of the community.[34]

For most of the volunteers, the precinct meetings were a superb reward for all the hours spent registering. Many agreed with the volunteer who wrote, "The precinct meeting was one of the most exciting events of my life."[35] But for some, the meetings were a disappointment. One volunteer chronicled the successes in Vicksburg and then continued:

Of course, not all our meetings were brilliantly successful. Holly and I went to |the| second precinct, and about 12 people came. Our job was to check people in the door and then find a temporary chairman who would conduct the meeting and get people elected for the county meeting. I think none of the people had ever been to a meeting using parliamentary procedure before, so we had a very difficult time. One man stood up and said flatly that he didn't understand what the purpose of the meeting was. Holly and I felt rather discouraged, but I didn't feel so bad when I remembered our minister Joe's comment about how this was democracy at its grass roots and that the issue now was exactly the same as in the Revolutionary War: taxation without representation. Most of the people in Mississippi aren't educated enough to understand government, but then I'm sure that the common man wasn't a Thomas Jefferson in 1776 either.[36]

The county conventions followed almost immediately, and the delegates at the county level chose their candidates to the district caucuses. They also discussed the issues for the state platform and passed platform resolutions. Later in the week the district caucuses across the state chose delegates to the national Democratic convention.

The state convention opened on August 6 in Jackson. Ella Baker, the woman who had set the wheels in motion to organize SNCC four years before, gave the keynote address. She stressed the hard work and study necessary to organize a new party and gain political power. She congratulated the delegates on their bravery and urged them to work even harder to spread the party to all the people in the state. Following her speech, the delegates marched around the hall singing freedom songs. One volunteer wrote, "This was probably the most soul-felt march ever to occur in a political convention. . . . You would just about have to be here to really feel and see what this means to the people who are here."[37]

Joseph Rauh, Walter Reuther's attorney and a board member of the Americans for Democratic Action (ADA), addressed the group and gave an optimistic assessment of the MFDP's chance for being seated. As a member of the Credentials Committee, he was going to present the legal case for the seating of MFDP. He felt that even if the Credentials Committee would not advocate the MFDP seating, he could bring the challenge onto the convention floor, where it would have a very good chance of approval. Bringing the matter to the floor involved only the filing of a minority report supported by at least eleven members of the 108-person committee and eight states. Nine states across the nation had already passed resolutions at their conventions supporting the challenge delegation.

Bob Moses spoke after Rauh, and he was not so sanguine. He believed that President Johnson was too afraid of losing the South to allow the seating of the MFDP.

After the addresses, the delegates ratified the district choices of national convention delegates. There were sixty-eight delegates in all, sixty-four blacks and four whites.

The white delegates were MFDP members. The Rev. Ed King was an active civil rights worker and an organizing member of the MFDP. In addition, however, over the course of the summer several more whites joined the MFDP. They were mainly recruited from the Biloxi area by Bruce Maxwell who worked in the White Folks' Project. Conceived as a small pilot program of COFO, the project consisted of southern whites organizing poor whites into the MFDP. Project workers wanted to begin to build a coalition to represent the needs of poor whites and blacks in Mississippi politics.[38]

Some volunteers in other projects also attempted to recruit whites into the MFDP, although the work was fraught with danger. In Greenwood, the 1964 summer headquarters of SNCC, one white volunteer wrote a pamphlet on the MFDP to distribute in the white community. He planned to canvas integrated neighborhoods with all white volunteers, thus enabling the MFDP to strengthen its claim of being an integrated party. This would in turn strengthen its convention challenge. The project staff and volunteers held several long, intense meetings on the issue: Some felt that the effort was "mere bravado, and that a mailing would serve as well," but others felt, "It's dangerous all over, baby, and if Negroes are going onto plantations, then whites should be able to go into the white section of town." Eventually volunteers canvassed a limited section of town. By the state convention, three whites were registered from Greenwood.[39]

Freedom Registration continued until the national convention. The MFDP goal was 100,000 Freedom Registrations to back their claim of legitimate grass-roots support.[40] As of the state convention, however, only 50,000 completed registration forms were in the Jackson COFO office. The volunteers continued to canvas during August and by the opening of the national convention, some 60,000 Freedom Registrations were filed in Jackson.[41]

In addition to their canvassing, almost all of the volunteers wrote home to their families and their communities urging support of the MFDP challenge. They wrote letters to their local papers and to their political representatives. Many volunteers' parents had formed "Mississippi Summer Project Parents" organizations, which developed into effective lobbying forces in their respective communities. They wrote letters demanding protection for their children and black Mississippians. They organized fund-raising events and gathered supplies. And they visited state conventions and delegations all over the country to plead the MFDP's case. The volunteers' parents were for the most part highly respected members of their communities, and their lobbying within the liberal ranks of the Democratic Party was highly effective. As people of community stature, they had relatively easy and consistent access to the media and high-level government officials. In 1964 one group achieved a meeting with President Johnson's top political aide. Throughout the summer the parents' meetings regularly chronicled visitations of important liberal representatives and senators. By the end of the summer, the organizations were committed to remaining as an ongoing support group for the southern civil rights groups. They continued their lobbying and support through the summer of 1965.[42]

The MFDP delegates and a large number of COFO staff and summer volunteers traveled by bus and car to the Democratic Party convention at Atlantic City for the presentation of the challenge to the Credentials Committee. The hearings opened on August 22 and were covered by national television.

The MFDP claimed that they were the only legitimate Mississippi Democratic Party. First Aaron Henry and then the Rev. Ed King spoke to the claim, but the most dramatic plea was Fannie Lou Hamer's. When the television cameras panned the committee members and the audience, many individuals were crying openly. Before Rita Schwerner, who followed Hamer, could begin her presentation, television coverage was interrupted for an unscheduled presidential press conference, which ended just after the MFDP delegates finished presenting their case.[43]

Telegrams from across the nation flooded the Credentials Committee; they suspended judgment on the challenge for three days. It was obvious that the committee would rule against the challenge, but it was equally obvious the MFDP had enough strength to bring the question to the floor. The process of finding a workable compromise began.

Essentially there were two compromises, one presented by Congresswoman Edith Green and the other by Senator Hubert Humphrey. The Green compromise held that all Mississippi delegates—from both delegations—would be seated when they took an oath of loyalty to the National Democratic Party. Upon the seating of the delegates, the votes would be distributed among the regular and Freedom delegations according to the numerical strength of each. The Humphrey compromise specified that Aaron Henry and Edwin King would be seated as at-large delegates and that the remaining sixty-six delegates would receive honorary, nonvoting seating with various northern and protectorate delegations. It also resolved that delegates to the 1968 convention would have to be selected without discrimination.

The MFDP delegation accepted the Green compromise, but refused the Humphrey compromise. The regular Mississippi delegation refused anything less than full seating and promised that a walkout, which seemed likely, would result in a four-state walkout.[44]

Meanwhile, pressure was applied to various members of the Credentials Committee to reject the Green compromise and accept the Humphrey compromise as their report. When the vote was taken on Tuesday, August 25, only four of the eighteen members who had previously pledged themselves to vote for the Green proposal voted for it in the committee. The Humphrey proposal was accepted as the committee decision on the challenge. Joseph Rauh voted for the Humphrey compromise.

Charges and countercharges flew around the convention. It was rumored that President Johnson stipulated to Hubert Humphrey that he must find a settlement that would both appease the MFDP and its supporters and avoid a southern walkout before he would receive Johnson's final approval for the vice-presidential spot.[45]

In any event, the MFDP delegation refused to accept the compromise at a closed meeting Tuesday evening. Instead, they seated themselves in the empty chairs of the contested Mississippi delegation. A sergeant-at-arms came to remove the delegates bodily but stopped very quickly; national television covered the whole scene.[46]

On Wednesday Martin Luther King, Bayard Rustin, Jack Pratt of the National Council of Churches, Joe Rauh, Walter Reuther, Senator Wayne Morse, and two congressmen urged the MFDP to accept the compromise seating. They stressed the importance of the at-large seating and the moral victory the members had won. The delegates listened and then at another closed meeting voted to reject the compromise.

For all practical purposes, the challenge was over. During the remainder of the convention, volunteers, staff, MFDP delegates, and northern friends staged a sit-in in front of the convention hall. Members of sympathetic state delegations gave MFDP delegates their badges to allow the Mississippians on the floor. The regular delegation went back to Mississippi without being seated, and only two delegates pledged loyalty to the party.[47]

The large body of people throughout the country, white and black, who supported the MFDP seating split when the MFDP refused to accept the Humphrey compromise. The bitterness arose, not over the justness of the MFDP case for seating, but over the issue of compromise itself.

In general those sympathetic to the MFDP who lived and worked outside the state felt that the Mississippians should have accepted the compromise. They argued that any recognition was a real triumph for a party four months old and that, given the context of a national convention, the gain of two seats was nothing short of miraculous. They felt the delegates missed a great chance in their refusal to participate. On the other hand, those people who worked more closely with the MFDP within the state maintained that if their cause was just, they deserved to be seated. Anything less than the Green proposal was tokenism of the most demeaning kind.

Besides, they argued, they were responsible to sixty thousand Mississippians who had risked untold economic and physical harm to register in the MFDP. As delegates pledged to represent these people fully, they were not free to accept compromise. As a final rebuttal, they maintained that the National Democratic Party lost its opportunity for a "finest hour" by not declaring itself unequivocably for a cause it had maintained was right since 1948. There was nothing to lose, because the southern delegations had indicated earlier they would not support the national candidates. COFO members, and most of the volunteers, added another complaint: They felt they had been grievously mistreated and "sold out" by the white liberals who had pledged support in the very beginning, especially Rauh. In 1973 Cleveland Sellers wrote:

The National Democratic Party's rejection of the MFDP at the 1964 convention was to the civil rights movement what the Civil War was to American history: afterward, things could never be the same. Never again were we lulled into believing that our task was exposing injustices so that the "good" people of America could eliminate them. We left Atlantic City with the knowledge that the movement had turned into something else. After Atlantic City, our struggle was not for civil rights, but for liberation.

From this point on, in the southern civil rights movement, the term "white liberal," previously used as a neutral or even praiseworthy description of a person's politics, became an epithet.[48]

The MFDP delegates and many volunteers returned to Mississippi after the convention. About two hundred volunteers remained in Mississippi to work for the statewide Freedom Elections, held from October 30 to November 2, and the Johnson-Humphrey campaign for the presidential election.[49] The volunteers continued canvassing for Freedom Registrations and by the November elections, some eighty thousand Mississippians were Freedom registered.[50]

During this time, however, the Mississippi movement was in a serious decline. COFO staff and volunteers were profoundly disillusioned by the action at the Democratic convention. Bereft of summer volunteers, many projects were floundering and would soon cease to exist. Robert Moses, COFO's project director and legendary leader, resigned from COFO but remained in SNCC, changed his name, and left the state. David Dennis, the second in command, in exhaustion, withdrew from the state and began to work solely with CORE in Louisiana. Both Moses and Dennis believed that too many people were depending on them to make decisions and run the movement and that remaining in the state would ruin all attempts to develop local leaders. The NAACP, which had never been very active, threatened to resign from the coalition because COFO continued to use the services of the National Lawyers Guild and because they believed they were not consulted over COFO decisions, which they charged were SNCC decisions made in Atlanta. SNCC itself was undergoing a crisis. Bob Moses, Jim Forman, Mendy Samstein, and other SNCC staff had worked up a proposal for an enlargement and extension of the Mississippi Summer Project for 1965 called the Black Belt Summer Project, which would build on the 1964 project but would depend primarily on black college students for volunteers. However, at a fragmented SNCC meeting in October, the organization tabled the program indefinitely and lost the momentum it had always taken as the program innovators in the southern civil rights movement. Meanwhile black and white interpersonal relations had become so volatile that the main Jackson office closed for a week in November.[51]

The fact was that COFO had always been 90 percent SNCC in Mississippi, but by the end of the 1964 summer, what illusions were left of COFO as a viable coalition of many local Mississippi groups were simply fading away. While throughout the winter and spring, memos, reports, and minutes were sent from the COFO office, it was obvious to everyone in southern civil rights work that COFO was now another name for SNCC in Mississippi or the MFDP, which was also seen basically as a SNCC-supported project.

A clear example of the ways in which COFO was simply seen as "Mississippi SNCC" was the calling of the November meeting to discuss the obvious decline in the Mississippi movement. COFO staff called the meeting for the latter part of the month to discuss where the movement was going and how to solve its "problems." The meeting was held for all current project workers, including former summer volunteers. People were asked to write position papers and reports on their projects, amid many cautions to speak to the "critical issues" and forget personality feuds: "Criticism of our present structure does not have to be criticism of the people who now hold key positions in that structure."[52] Jesse Morris, project director of the Jackson office, sent minutes of the meeting which reopened the Jackson office along with a cover letter detailing his concept of the responsibilities of the office. He included the obviously acrimonious minutes to illustrate what was happening in Jackson and admonished that:

It would be helpful if the discussion were guided along constructive lines rather than having the entire staff hurl all their brickbats at the Jackson Office.[53]

In the same mailing, workers received a broad-ranging list of questions asking, "Where is COFO headed?" While all the papers did respond to the question, most spoke as if SNCC were the only organization involved. While some workers continued to refer to COFO, many abandoned even the name. Whatever nomenclature people used, COFO was Mississippi SNCC by the fall of 1964.

The reports which were written tended to be straightforward accounts of the projects' work. It was apparent that activity had lessened, since the majority of the volunteers had returned north, but most projects seemed to be functioning on a limited basis. All the reports indicated that the Jackson office was inept, inefficient, and unable to accomplish its job of coordinating the state program.

Most also believed that black-white relations had to be examined honestly, since they clearly were a large part of the staff's inability to function. One white Jackson worker wrote of the situation in his project:

Staff and volunteer discipline has broken down so far that the state headquarters has had several race riots, white workers are often subject to severe racial abuse and even violence from Negro workers, staff and volunteers have assaulted the fellow workers, cashed checks (for their own personal use), clothes and supplies have been stolen totaling several thousands of dollars. Negro workers are frequently played-up-to and looked-down-on by white workers, juvenile delinquency sometimes appears to have taken over certain offices. . . . many workers drive cars as fast as they can, figuring COFO will pay their fines and get them a lawyer no matter what they do. Former SNCC staff going to Tougaloo steal and act rowdy in the Jackson office, etc. . . . [54]

Although those people writing reports obviously believed that the black-white situation was worst in Jackson, many indicated that they had problems in their projects, too. Some black field staff wrote anonymously about other "aspects of black-white problems." The described the difficulties of having whites on projects because of the fears of the community, the staff's own insecurities about their skills, and the near impossibility of overcoming "growing up hating white people." They "really resented" the "Missionary attitudes" of some white workers and found many whites were insensitive and " . . . came down without grappling with their own feelings about Negroes." They also believed that the racism of American society produced "sexual problems," and that these existed in integrated projects, usually to their detriment. In personal terms, they felt many "conflicts between hating whites and having to cooperate with them, knowing that much of the movement depends upon them. . . . " While they believed ideologically that they had " . . . to differentiate between good whites and bad whites," they found it very difficult to do so in practice.[55]

These position papers constituted important and controversial statements. They indicated that most people wanted some structural change within COFO and many had elaborate and varying plans for the organization. Whether written by whites or blacks, the reports spoke increasingly of community control of projects and the development of local leadership, but there was wide disagreement over the desirable methods of developing local leadership.

The most fundamental philosophical split appeared to be whether COFO's and therefore SNCC's goals were to be ameliorative reform work or thoroughgoing institutional change. People on one side of the issue asked, "Can we create a free society if we do not live, as much as we are able, the society we envision?"[56] And people on the other side attacked what

. . . they perceived as a sinister fuzzy-mindedness on the part of whole factions of the staff as to what our role in this society and the South has got to be. We think that the only useful and creative function that we can have is to mobilize and educate people so that they can use their organizational power to change the basic ills in the society. Our orientation must always be toward eliminating causes rather than trying to make their effects more bearable for a few. This is what makes us different from a goddamn social welfare agency or the Salvation Army.

Although most workers agreed with the concept of total structural change, few were as single-minded and able to ignore the welfare of individuals as the authors of "SNCC's Goals and Bourgeoise [sic] Sentimentality."[57]

Several people indicated that ironically many of the problems facing COFO were caused by its amazing success. The astounding growth of the movement, the publicity and the national attention given to it served only to make workers angry that more tangible gains were not accomplished. Outlining a classic case of rising expectations, Charles Sherrod wrote:

> . . . we are more prejudiced and bitter, frustrated and impatient than our parents, because we have had more and seen more and *think we can get more* than they did and *we think we can get it now* because we have done miracles; we have most of the time surprised ourselves.[58]

During the meeting, the staff was unable to settle the problems confronting COFO and SNCC. In fact, there were only some structural changes within the organizations and some greater agreement on goals and projects. Most of the differences set forth in the papers remained unresolved. Oddly enough, this had the effect of strengthening the staff's resolve in the one area of agreement, which was the necessity for local control and community organization around felt needs. For the time being, Silas Norman's articulate analysis of black-white relations reflected the new staff consensus. Norman, a black project director, argued that integrated projects were dangerous and counterproductive in some areas, but that in others they could work and should be encouraged. Whites attracted publicity and support for the movement and therefore were important. But, he felt " . . . that there is a sort of 'ethnic relationship' among the staff and community," which cannot "be entered into by whites."[59] This acknowledgment by consensus of the inherent ability of blacks to organize black communities, and the inherent inability of whites to do so, marked a turning point in COFO's and SNCC's public rhetoric. The majority opinion had changed since the beginning of the Summer Project, even though Sherrod closed his remarks by admonishing:

> . . . There can be no room for race hatred among us. . . . We blacks must recognize the needs of the whites are not so different from our own as regards recognition, fulfillment, status in our group and so forth.[60]

Meanwhile, civil rights workers in the state launched two new projects: the Agricultural Stabilization and Conservation Committee (ASCS) boards and a congressional challenge.

The ASCS elections renewed, at least temporarily, the enthusiasm of the COFO staff and volunteers. The campaign seemed to have a possibility of success and was a local issue which tied together positive political and economic action. Basically, COFO workers tried to get black farmers nominated and elected to the ASCS committees, which in conjunction with the United States Department of Agriculture (USDA) allot acreage for cultivation. The committees had a long history of discriminatory allotment; yet, the procedure for nominating candidates and voting in the election was simple and depended only on a person's being an active farmer in the area. Nearly all COFO workers in or near rural areas worked on canvassing and organizing farmers to participate in the December elections. As one volunteer in Holly Springs wrote to his sponsors, with an apology for not answering their letters, "For the past month I've been doing little but eating, sleeping, canvassing and attending meetings. . . . we've been out in the county most of the day and many evenings . . . working on the farmer's elections. . . . "[61]

Civil rights workers held educational meetings on voting procedures and the ASCS elections. They lobbied the USDA for protection of voters and prevention of vote fraud. And they alerted their northern supporters, including volunteers who had returned to school and parents' groups, to write to the department and to influential senators and representatives.

In some communities, the local county agent actively worked against the organization of blacks, although the main obstacles were the familiar ones from voter registration: fear, apathy, and a lack of awareness of the voting process. The workers found that organizing was substantially easier and more effective where there had been an active summer project, especially one that had an MFDP organization to serve as a communications base.

The elections were held on December 3 and were accompanied by white violence, harassment, and alleged vote fraud. In no county was a majority of black farmers elected to the committees. In most, none were elected. Black farmers across the state protested the elections, and the USDA offered to set aside some of the elections and hold new ones in selected districts of several counties. Even if blacks were elected in all of the districts whose elections had been set aside, however, no county would have had a black majority. Throughout the state, farmers refused to accept this compromise, because they believed intimidation and fraud were county-wide. Black farmers boycotted the new elections, but continued to organize for the next year's elections.

During the protracted negotiations with the USDA, COFO workers served the black farmers as "facilitators." Although they helped organize meetings and contact the USDA, they resolutely tried to keep themselves from "telling" the farmers what to do and even tried not to suggest what they thought best. This obviously confused and puzzled USDA officials, who looked to the white workers for "reasonable" decisions. In answer to a USDA official's criticism of the proposed election boycott in Madison County, a volunteer wrote:

> You said a moment ago over the phone that we [COFO workers] were wrong to bring representative farmers together to discuss the new elections. Their lives are affected by those elections, not ours. If they shouldn't have some say in them, no one should. You said we should counsel them on what's best. But we assume no right to speak for them without their knowledge. And since our primary goal is their independence and self determination, we cannot even press our counsel too far.[62]

The workers saw their actions as the best way to help develop local community leaders. This exemplified the trend in all facets of COFO to local control.[63]

The congressional challenge was the other new program for voter registration workers throughout the state. Based on the premise that the MFDP was the true Democratic Party in the state, the MFDP announced it was going to challenge the seating of the newly elected Mississippi congressional delegation. In the fall MFDP candidates had campaigned in the state for congressional positions. They were not allowed on the regular ballot, however, because the state refused to honor the nominating petitions signed by Freedom Democrats.[64]

Arthur Kinoy and William Kuntsler, two lawyers well known for their civil rights libertarian positions, agreed to handle the legal side of the project. They based the challenge on Title 2 of the

United States Code, Sections 201 through 226, which prescribe the procedure whereby a candidate who has lost an election can challenge that loss. In the specific case of challenging the election of any member of the House of Representatives, the challenger must issue a written notice to the member he or she challenges within thirty days of the election stating his or her contest and giving his or her grounds for the contest.[65]

The challenge was officially filed on December 4, and the MFDP began lobbying for congressional support immediately. The Mississippi delegation had to answer the challenge in thirty days.

Workshops were held all over the state for MFDP members and staff to explain the challenge and organize the party response. As they had since the beginning of the Summer Project, the volunteers mobilized their northern ties. They urged their families and friends to lobby their congressional delegations. Those volunteers who had returned north spoke at meetings and rallies in support of the challenge. And the parents' groups publicized the challenge, lobbied in Washington, D.C., and pressured state Democratic parties to support the MFDP claims.[66]

The challenge served to coordinate the efforts of the MFDP across the state. The local precinct and district organizations worked on their own community needs, but also supported the challenge. Partially in response to the difficulties in projects whose volunteers had left, COFO staff encouraged the local MFDP chapters to define for themselves the direction of their organization. Again, the goal of the COFO workers was to assure local control of projects led by local people.[67]

On January 4, 1965, the representatives presented themselves for the swearing-in ceremony. Congressman William Ryan of New York protested the swearing-in of the Mississippi delegation, and the Mississippi congressmen had to remain seated during the ceremony. As soon as the oath was taken, Carl Albert, the House majority leader, was recognized to resolve that the Mississippi delegation be seated. On the roll call vote, 149 representatives voted against seating the delegation, which meant that many in the House were considering the challenge seriously.

The large vote against their seating surprised the Mississippi congressional delegation, so they instructed their lawyer to file an answer to the challenge. The delegation had hoped to ignore the challenge, thereby withholding any indication of its legitimacy.[68]

Immediately after the vote, National Lawyers Guild members came to Mississippi and began the deposition hearings, which were held without hindrance throughout the state. Local MFDP members testified to their voter activity and their attempts to register through the regular state political system. A volunteer in Indianola wrote her sponsor:

> Things are going well here. Just spent 2 busy and happy days driving all over the county with 2 lawyers from San Francisco to get the stories from our people about their homes being fired into, jobs lost, etc. Got a chance to visit my old friends in Ruleville and Sunflower, though after awhile we all got saturated and sick of these stories which must be told so that the world will know how things are in Mississippi. The lawyers, as everyone who comes from outside the state, were very impressed, appalled and unbelieving about the way things are. . . . [69]

During the months of hearings, several state officials, including the governor, denounced violence and oppression of local blacks. The challenge was taken surprisingly seriously within the regular state party, for upon presentation of the evidence, the House could vote against the seating of the regular congressional delegation. If it so voted, then the House would run its own free and independent elections in the state.

Following the staff reassessments of the 1964 Summer Project and while pursuing the congressional challenge, relationships among the civil rights groups in the South grew severely strained. Without the movement-oriented men like Moses and Dennis the ever-present tensions among the civil rights organizations escalated into flashes of severe hostility by the late winter. The increasingly radical tenor of the MFDP seriously disturbed the NAACP, which formally severed all relations with COFO in April 1965, when SNCC and the MFDP were holding their first "People's Conference." CORE essentially stopped all funds to Mississippi work and concentrated its community organizing efforts in Louisiana. SCLC centered its attention on the passage and implementation of the Voting Rights Act of 1965, which was before Congress, and proposed SCOPE, a major expansion of the Mississippi Summer Project to all of the Black Belt. While the project sounded like the tabled SNCC Black Belt Project, SCLC proposed voter registration as the way toward community organization and proposed working through community leaders who were members of SCLC, mostly black ministers. The thrust of the SCOPE project was not, in fact, what SNCC members had proposed for their organization, but SCLC had in effect stolen SNCC's thunder by organizing the SCOPE project. SCLC sponsored the march from Selma to Montgomery to promote the passage of the Voting Rights Act. SNCC's relations with SCLC deteriorated profoundly after SCLC's takeover of the Selma demonstration, since SNCC had worked for over two years in Selma organizing the community, and SNCC workers bitterly resented the role of Martin Luther King and SCLC in the Selma March. Throughout the year, SNCC was also increasingly involved in internal disputes, which focused on the issues of local control, black-white relations, and internal democracy.

Although Selma was an electrifying experience, which captured the conscience of the nation and inspired many northern students to volunteer for summer civil rights projects, it exemplified the growing distances among the groups of the former COFO coalition. While Selma led SCLC to organize the SCOPE project to bring northern college students south to register blacks, southern CORE workers believed the Voting Rights Act would be of little importance to the "real" goal of building grass-roots organizations around local needs. SNCC workers went even further: They believed that new federal legislation was a "white liberal" sop, which would quickly and easily be nullified by southern officials and which deflected attention away from the real southern situation. While all of the Mississippi civil rights organizations (including the NAACP) verbally supported the challenge, only SNCC was really involved in the work. SNCC believed that only the success of projects like the congressional challenge and the growth of new political institutions would change the South. Control of institutions by local people was the only way that people would achieve real power and destiny over their lives.[70]

In April the MFDP decided to sponsor a small, decentralized summer project. To avoid the project's collapsing and to better build local leadership, the 1965 Mississippi project would be completely decentralized and controlled by the individual communities. Dave Dennis explained why the MFDP project would be different:

. . . people are going to have to begin to determine their own destiny, and the more CR [civil rights] workers you have in an area, the tendency is that they do most of the work, because there is very little for local people to do. It's a human reaction—if you're director of a project, you turn to people you can rely on, who it's easy to get—usually that's CR workers, because they're there, it's easier to get them to do the work than to explain to local people and try to train them to do certain things. As a result of that, we found last summer when the volunteers left, a lot of things collapsed because volunteers were doing all the work and the local people . . . had nothing to do with it. There was no basic attempt to get them involved as more than just . . . an audience. The volunteers were like actors in a play, and the community was like an audience, just watching and looking.[71]

Thus, the 1965 volunteers would work for SNCC–MFDP in Mississippi, CORE mainly in Louisiana, and SCLC's SCOPE project throughout the rest of the Deep South.

The emphasis of the MFDP projects focused squarely on the involvement of local people. The actual day-to-day work of the volunteers involved in voter registration was much the same as the previous summer, however, although it included more sophisticated lobbying and researching for the challenge.[72]

At the beginning of the summer, the orientation for volunteers at Mount Beulah was disorganized and haphazard. Black-white relations were tense, and the active staff members were concerned with demonstrations in Jackson, which were resulting in automatic jailing of all participants. New volunteers were encouraged to join the march, which was protesting the special session of the state legislature called to try to find a way to circumvent the new Voting Rights Act. Some eight hundred people were jailed including well over a hundred volunteers. After chronicling severe police brutality and horrible jail conditions, one volunteer wrote:

Several of us are on a hunger strike in protest against the segregated jail . . . but since the food is only bread, grits, beans and water, we're not missing much anyway. We're trying to swing vitamin pills from the doctor. (Our medical people were arrested with us), I'm not a bit hungry or ill—my voice is shot to hell from singing, and sleeping on cold concrete.[73]

The Jackson demonstrations had the effect of pulling the Mississippi civil rights organization together. An injunction against the police department secured the release of all the demonstrators and assured a peaceful march led by NAACP leaders, MFDP candidates, and COFO staff to the legislature.[74]

Another way in which the MFDP summer project differed from the 1964 project was in the breadth of programs begun in different places. Since the projects were organized around "felt needs" of the community, volunteers found themselves doing many tasks in addition to voter registration. In Natchez, for example, voter registration volunteers worked on the MFDP, regular voter registration, the integration of city parks, and the organization of a laundry workers union.[75] Throughout the state, volunteers helped organize cooperatives and unions and galvanize communities around such issues as food distribution and health care.

The varied projects hinged on local control, and for the most part, MFDP volunteers were enthusiastic supporters of the concept. One volunteer who had been in Mississippi in 1964 explained that in 1964 COFO "emphasized voter registration before the election, and community organization was almost secondary. It was a way of achieving voter registration. This year with the MFDP . . . voter registration is a way of achieving community organization. And the idea is to build up 'pockets of power,' to use John Lewis' phrase—where people have a consciousness of what power is and what they might be able to do with it."[76] In Batesville civil rights workers decided not to do any voter registration work at all or make suggestions at meetings, because " . . . this Movement is . . . more than just having people gain certain rights; it's also getting people to think and do things on their own, and make decisions on their own."[77] Although most projects did not go as far as the Batesville group to avoid having the staff influence local people, every project in the state was aware of and involved in the issue of local control. Not all groups were successful in implementing the concept, however, and some volunteers rebelled by mid-summer:

. . . One of the hang-ups that I have: I'm not so certain as is MFDP . . . |of its| . . . policy on this question of local policy and local decision. I think you can go local crazy after awhile. In other words, I think that there's got to be a medium between people who have experience and can give direction. . . . [78]

Throughout the summer the challenge and the Washington lobby continued. In August, just after the new Voting Rights Act became law, MFDP lawyers presented three volumes of sworn statements of voter discrimination to the House of Representatives. The southern-dominated Subcommittee on Elections and Privileges then examined the depositions. They reported to the full session of the House that they favored dismissal of the challenge. On September 17 the House voted in favor of the subcommittee's findings, 228 to 143. The challenge was over, and the MFDP was again defeated.[79]

Few, if any, people expected the challenge to succeed, though cause was certainly shown in page after page of depositions recounting violence, harassment, and intimidation by whites of Mississippi blacks. Unlike the convention challenge, then, this defeat was no great shock, although to many it was certainly a disappointment. Reflecting the postconvention analysis, some FDP supporters outside the state looked on the 143 votes cast in favor of the challenge as at least a "moral victory" of, in fact, surprising proportions. To confuse assessment of the challenge further, while hundreds of volunteers and supporters had lobbied for the challenge throughout the winter and spring, Cleveland Sellers maintains that within SNCC

Our objectives in pursuing the Challenge were quite different from those we had had in Atlantic City. We launched the Challenge in order to prove that the system would not work for poor black people. Our aim was to disprove the notion that black people, if they play by the rules, can acquire equal justice under the law. In that sense the Challenge was successful.[80]

It is clear that final judgment on the success or failure of the congressional challenge was itself a political issue.

The SCOPE project, which absorbed many of the volunteers rejected by COFO, most nearly approximated the 1964 Mississippi project in style. Although it did not have large Freedom Schools in its programs, it did organize some adult citizenship and literacy classes.

SCOPE began with an orientation session in Atlanta, where Hosea Williams of the SCLC staff outlined the program and project emphasis:

... first we got to get our people politically conscious. We got to get him politically aware. This is the first thing you have to do. Once we get them politically aware—and aware of everything, the development of politics, its value, its surroundings, its operation—then we got to get them organized. Once we get them organized, then we got to get them in motion. And then—and I know it's a long-term plan—once we get them in motion, then we got to get them registered. We got to get them voting. And then we got to get them all over this land, running for political office. Running if it's for nothing more than to give inspiration to our people.[81]

SCLC saw its main program as voter registration under the proposed Voting Rights Act and wanted its political action to remain within the Democratic Party. This corresponded to the 1964 program of the MFDP, which attempted to reform the party from within, but it contrasted dramatically with the MFDP stand in 1965 in which the MFDP declared itself to be the only legitimate Democratic Party in the state.

One volunteer perceptively compared the differences between the approaches of SCOPE and SNCC when she was working on an SCLC project:

SCOPE has wanted to work through the leadership down to the people, if you ever get a chance to get to the people. I think I prefer SNCC's method of working from the people and letting them ... bring up the leadership. It's like working from the top down or from the bottom up and I think I prefer SNCC's idea of a people's movement whereas SCOPE has chosen to work through the ministers and the local Negro leadership who may not even speak for the majority of the Negro people.

But then she seemed to admit the inherent difficulty in the SNCC style by adding, "... I don't think that I'm ready [to work] for SNCC."[82] In contrast, she fit well into the SCOPE program with its straightforward voter registration program of canvassing, mass meetings, and voter classes.

Most SCOPE volunteers seemed glad that they had chosen to work in their project rather than in the MFDP project. They were much less interested in the issues of local control and community organization than MFDP workers, but their most common complaints were against the leaders with whom they had to work. Some also felt that SCLC was too concerned with the numbers of blacks registered and not enough with what blacks would do with the vote. Most SCOPE volunteers, however, liked the SCLC leaders and appreciated Martin Luther King's position in the movement. One volunteer, who had been "bothered" by "charisma," explained:

I don't mind the image they're making out of King any more; it has its place and I've begun to see it. Because I can go into a Negro community which is terribly scared, and say, "Martin Luther King sent me," and all of a sudden, I'm listened to. Now I don't know whether that's right or wrong, but I make a break there that I could never have made before.[83]

As far as the daily work was concerned, the volunteers working on voter registration in 1965 did virtually the same jobs as the 1964 workers. However, the broad goals and strategy of the movement were shifting toward local control and self-determination, especially in CORE and SNCC. In the student wing of the movement, the major emphasis was on grass-roots community organization utilizing workers to help facilitate flexible programs determined for each community by the people of that community. The movement also wanted to build really viable political bases in predominantly black areas. This kind of organization was long-term work; summer programs were no longer relevant. At summer's end, Lawrence Guyot, head of the MFDP, assessed the shift, which was quite profound in SNCC, CORE, and the MFDP, but which was barely beginning in SCLC:

Mississippi is not only changing, but the people involved in the Movement, by the very scope and analysis of what's going on are going to have to revamp the way that they approach certain problems . . . the issues are becoming very clear. The need for self-determination is becoming more pronounced and more exaggerated.[84]

The time for northern student volunteers to work registering potential black voters was nearly past.

NOTES

1. Sellers and Terrell, *The River of No Return*, pp. 82–83.
2. Sutherland, *Letters*, pp. 3–4.
3. Sutherland, *Letters*, p. 5; SHSW: Jane Hodes Prs.: Bill Hodes, "Dear Folks," June 16, 1964, Oxford, Ohio, pp. 1–2; Sugarman, *Stranger at the Gates*, pp. 8–23.

4. SHSW: Jane Hodes Prs.: Bill Hodes, "Dear Folks," June 16, 1964, p. 1.

5. Otis Pease Prs.: Aaron Henry to COFO Members, "undated letter," COFO ditto [early April 1964], Jackson, Miss.; Mississippi Summer Project Staff (MSPS), "Memorandum re Freedom Registration," COFO, mid-July, Jackson, Miss.; McLemore, "Mississippi Freedom Democratic Party," pp. 77–122.

6. Holt, *The Summer That Didn't End*, p. 162; William McCord, *Mississippi: The Long Hot Summer* (New York: 1965), p. 114.

7. SHSW: Lise Vogel Prs.: Lise Vogel, "Notes at 1964 Orientation for Mississippi Summer Project," p. 4.

8. SHSW: Jane Hodes Prs., Bill Hodes, "Dear Folks," June 26, 1964, Oxford, Ohio.

9. Ibid.

10. Sutherland, *Letters*, p. 29.

11. The best book on the conspiracy and the murders is William Bradford Huie, *Three Lives for Mississippi* (New York: 1965).

12. "Mississippi Summer Project: Running Summary of Incidents," in possession of author; Sellers and Terrell, *The River of No Return*, p. 94.

13. SHSW: Lise Vogel Prs.: Lise Vogel, "Notes at 1964 Orientation for MSP"; Delta Ministry Collection: Volunteer files, Note from Liz Fusco on woman volunteer; Interview: Florence Howe, June 1972, Seattle, Wash.

14. SHSW: Jane Hodes Prs.: Phil Moore, "Letter," July 11, 1964, Greenwood, Miss., pp. 2–3; Sellers and Terrell, *The River of No Return*, p. 94; Melish, *Memoir*, p. 87.

15. Sutherland, *Letters*, p. 71.

16. Otis Pease Prs., Otis Pease, "Notes," "Reflections on Voter Registration Problems."

17. Holt, *The Summer That Didn't End*, pp. 207–52; for Drew, see Sutherland, *Letters*, pp. 81–85; Leon Friedman, ed., *Southern Justice*, (Cleveland, Ohio: 1967), pp. 25–42; Interview: James B. Wilson, 1967, Seattle, Wash.; James B. Wilson Prs.: Tapes diary; for McComb see: Hodding Carter, *So the Heffners Left McComb* (New York: 1965); Otis Pease Prs.: Ilene Strelitz, "Dear Friends," MFDP, Washington, D.C., "Sporadically, July, 1964," p. 7; for Hattiesburg see: Sutherland, *Letters*, pp. 116–20, Otis Pease Prs.: Otis Pease, "Notes," July 10, July 11, July 14, 1964; Larry Spears, "Dear Friends," August 12, 1964.

18. SHSW: Charles Stewart Prs.: Charles Stewart, "Report on Mississippi Summer Project—1964," September 1964.

19. Sutherland, *Letters*, p. 70.

20. SHSW: Jane Hodes Prs.: Bill Hodes, "Dear Folks," July 2, 1964, p. 1.

21. Sutherland, *Letters*, p. 73.

22. Ibid., p. 78.

23. Ibid., p. 77–78.

24. Otis Pease Prs.: Otis Pease, "Notes," July 13, 1964, July 14, 1964, for his reflections. There were many reasons for the underrepresentation of young adult men, not the least of them being the high rate of emigration from the state by young people with talent and ambition.

25. For the Greenwood story see Sutherland, *Letters*, pp. 173–76; Sally Belfrage, *Freedom Summer* (New York: 1965); William McCord, *Mississippi: The Long Hot Summer*, pp. 89–93; Stanford University Archives: Lorna Smith Collection, entire; SHSW: Janes Hodes Prs.: Bill Hodes, "Dear Folks," Letter Series, Phil Moore, "Letter Series," July–August, Greenwood, Miss.

26. Dona Richards was a key staff member in Jackson. She was married to Robert Moses but retained her family name.

27. Otis Pease Prs.: Dona Richards and MSPS, "Memorandum: Re: Freedom Registration," |undated, mid-July|, p. 1.

28. SHWS: Elizabeth Sutherland Prs., Unused and uncat. Letters: Judy—"Dear People," July 28, 1964, Shaw, Miss.

29. Sutherland, *Letters*, p. 189.

30. "Negroes Come Too Late at Leflore Convention, Greenwood," *The Jackson, Mississippi Clarion-Ledger*, June 24, 1964, Greenwood, Miss.; Otis Pease Prs.: MSPS, "Mississippi: How Negro Democrats Fared; Part II," COFO. For a detailed analysis of the FDP and the state party, see McLemore, "Mississippi Freedom Democratic Party," pp. 106–76.

31. "Mississippians Put Off Endorsing Goldwater," *Atlanta Constitution*, July 29, 1964, p. 2.

32. Stokely Carmichael and Charles V. Hamilton, *Black Power: The Politics of Liberation in America* (New York: 1962), p. 93.

33. Holt, *The Summer That Didn't End*, p. 163.

34. Sutherland, *Letters*, p. 192.

35. Ibid., p. 191.

36. SHSW: Jan Louise Handke Prs.; Jan Louise Handke, "COFO Reporting," August 5, 1964, Vicksburg, Miss., p. 3.

37. Sutherland, *Letters*, p. 194.

38. SHSW: Bruce Maxwell Prs.: entire collection; Jan Hillegas Prs.: Bruce Maxwell, "Memo: COFO Staff," 9/7/64 on White Folks Projects; also Bruce Maxwell, "Position Paper: Organizing Poor Whites"; undated (Fall 1964); Holt, *The Summer That Didn't End*, pp. 128–48; Sutherland, *Letters*, pp. 195–98; Interview: Sally Shideler, 1967, Seattle, Wash.; Grace Maxwell, 1977, Tempe, Ariz.

39. SHSW: Jane Hodes Prs.: Phil Moore, "Letter," August 1964,

Greenwood, Miss., p. 2; Bill Hodes, "Dear Folks," July 9, 1964, p. 2, and July 10, 1964, p. 1, Greenwood, Miss.

40. Otis Pease Prs.: Dona Richards and MSPS, "COFO Memorandum: Re: Freedom Registration," COFO, p. 1.

41. Sutherland, *Letters*, p. 198.

42. SHSW: Jean Kates Prs., Minutes of Meeting of Mississippi Project Parent's Group, New York; from June 18, 1964–September 2, 1964; Harold B. Light, "To All Parents of Volunteer Workers in the Deep South," California Parents Assoc., June 23, 1965; SHWS: Matthew Zwerling Prs., Series of lobbying letters, June 18, 1964, July 1, 1964, July 17, 1964, August 20, 1964: These letters had very specific instructions of whom to contact and what to say to people in the government about Mississippi. They also asked for money, supplies, and services and advertised fund-raising events. SHWS: Christopher Wilson Prs., Parents Mississippi Emergency Committee, Los Angeles Area Newsletter, Series, Summer 1964; Mississippi Freedom Committee of Southern California, Newsletter, Series, Fall–Winter 1964–1965; Christopher Wilson, "Dearest Parents and Paula," July 31, 1964, Hattiesburg, Miss.; Stanford University Archives: Lorna Smith Collection; Bob Laurence, ed., "The Wesley Foundation Reports on the Miss., Summer Project," June 30–August 10, 1964.

43. Holt, *The Summer That Didn't End*, pp. 168–69; McLemore, "Mississippi Freedom Democratic Party," pp. 128–52.

44. "Convention May Refuse Seats for Alabamans, Spark 4-State Walkout," *Atlanta Constitution*, August 22, 1964, p. 1; "Alabama Delegates Must Pledge or Go," *Atlanta Constitution*, August 22, 1964, p. 1; "Alabama Democrats Refuse to Vow Loyalty; Delegation to Fight for Seats," *Atlanta Constitution*, August 24, 1964, p. 1; McLemore, "Mississippi Freedom Democratic Party," pp. 152–68.

45. As McLemore points out, if this charge was true, the MFDP was "high stakes," indeed, Ibid., p. 146, footnote 42.

46. "Police Slam the Doors on Freedom Delegates," *Atlanta Constitution*, August 26, 1964, p. 8.

47. "Mississippi Sides Turn Down Accord as Regulars Pack to Leave," *Atlanta Constitution*, August 26, 1964, p. 1; "Governor Johnson Threatens to Pull Mississippi Out of Party," *Atlanta Constitution*, August 26, 1964, p. 9.

48. Sellers and Terrell, *The River of No Return*, p. 111; McLemore, "Mississippi Freedom Democratic Party," pp. 152–68.

49. Sutherland, *Letters*, p. 211; SHSW: Mary Short Prs.; Mary Sue Gellatly, "Dear Mrs. Franz," Letter Series, Shaw, Miss., p. 2.

50. "It Takes Guts to Work for LBJ in Mississippi," *The New Republic*, October, 10, 1964, pp. 6–7.

51. Sellers and Terrell, *The River of No Return*, pp. 113-15; James Forman, *The Making of Black Revolutionaries: A Personal Account* (New York: 1972), pp. 411-47; Meier and Rudwick, *CORE*, pp. 337-44. Interviews: Jan Hillegas; Sally Shideler; Timothy Lynch.

52. Jan Hillegas Prs.: COFO mimeo, untitled, explaining meeting at Gammon which led to call for staff retreat.

53. Jan Hillegas Prs.: Jesse Morris, "Dear Staff," mimeo, undated |October 31, 1964|.

54. SHSW: R. Hunter Morey Prs.; Box 5; R. Hunter Morey, "Crossroads in COFO," December 3, 1964.

55. Jan Hillegas Prs.: Field Staff, "Some Aspects of Black-White Problems," mimeo, undated |December 1, 1964|, pp. 1-2.

56. Jan Hillegas Prs.: Jane Adams, "Federal Programs: Fourth Attempt," mimeo, undated |December 1, 1964|, p. 5.

57. SHSW: Stuart Ewen Prs.: Anonymous |white, more than one author|, "SNCC's Goals and Bourgeoise |sic| Sentimentality," mimeo, undated |December 1, 1964|, p. 1.

58. SHSW: Stuart Ewen Prs.: Charles Sherrod, "From Sherrod," undated |December 1, 1964|, p. 1. Underlining in original memo.

59. Ibid., p. 3.

60. Ibid.

61. SHSW: Nick Fischer Prs.: |Joe Maurer?|, "Dear Nick, John, Dave, Dale and all my other sponsors," December 10, 1964, Holly Springs, Miss., p. 1.

62. Otis Pease Prs.: George Raymond, "Latest Development in ASC Elections in Madison Co., Miss.," COFO letter which reprinted a letter from Joann Ooiman, "To Mr. Seabron, USDA," undated |April 1965|.

63. SHSW: Nick Fischer Prs.: |Joe Maurer?|, "Letter Series," Holly Springs and Aberdeen, Miss.; Winter-Spring 1964-1965; Otis Pease Prs.: George Raymond, "Latest Developments in ASC Elections," COFO; Meier and Rudwick, *CORE*, pp. 342-43; Interviews: Sally Shideler, February 1967; Gary Good, January-February 1967, Seattle, Wash.; Miriam Feingold Stein, 1975, San Francisco, and 1976, Los Angeles.

64. Jack Minnis, "The Mississippi Freedom Democratic Party," *Freedomways* 5, no. 2 (Spring 1965):273.

65. Holt, *The Summer That Didn't End*, p. 182. By far the most complete account is in McLemore, "Mississippi Freedom Democratic Party," pp. 169-249. However, Sellers and Terrell in *The River of No Return* (pp. 113-16) disagree totally with McLemore's analysis.

66. SHSW: Christopher Wilson Prs.: "Parents Mississippi Freedom Association of California Newsletter," series; Jean Kates Prs.: "Minutes of Parents Meeting," September 2, 1964; SHWS: Linda Seese Prs.: Linda

Seese, "Dear Mrs. Franz," December 12, 1964, Shaw, Miss.; Linda Seese, "Dear Mrs. Wm. Rice," January 23, 1965, Indianola, Miss.; Linda Seese, "Dear Friends," February 11, 1965, Indianola, Miss.; Linda Seese, "Dear Ladies," undated [April 1965]; Linda Seese, "Dear Mrs. Rice," March 30, 1965, Indianola, Miss.; Harry J. Bowie Prs., Box 2, Folder MFDP, 1964-1966; Lewis E. Campbell, "The MFDP Challenge," undated [January 1965]; SNCC Staff, "The New Voting Bill: Rhetoric or Reality?" March 23, 1965.

67. McLemore, "Mississippi Freedom Democratic Party," pp. 213-14.

68. Ibid., pp. 185-91.

69. SHSW: Linda Seese Prs.: Linda Seese, "Dear Mrs. Rice," January 23, 1965, Indianola, Miss.

70. Clayborne Carson, "Toward Freedom and Community: The Evolution of Ideas in the Student Nonviolent Coordinating Committee, 1960-1966" (Ph.D. diss., University of California at Los Angeles, 1975), pp. 260-316; Meier and Rudwick, *CORE*, pp. 338-44; McLemore, "Mississippi Freedom Democratic Party," pp. 213-14; Pat Watters, *Encounter With the Future* (Atlanta, Ga.: 1965), pp. 5-8; August Meier, "The Dilemma of Negro Protest Strategy," *New South*, 21 (Spring 1966):7-8; Jack Minnis, "MFDP," *Freedomways* 5, no. 2 (Spring 1965):277; David H. Lewis, *King: A Critical Biography* (New York: 1970), pp. 264-305; Aiken et al., *Dynamics of Idealism*, pp. 4-18; Emily Stoper, "SNCC," pp. 134-200; SHSW: Harry J. Bowie Prs., Box 2, Folder MFDP, 1964-1966, SNCC Staff, "The New Voting Bill: Rhetoric or Reality?" March 3, 1965.

71. KZSU Interview 0442, pp. 3-4.

72. Otis Pease Prs.: Larry Spears, "Dear Friends," August 6, 1965; Interview: Donna Goodman, 1972, Seattle, Wash.

73. SHSW: Jean Kates Prs.: Jim Kates, "Dear People," June 26, 1965, Jackson City Jail, p. 1; See also KZSU Interview 9007, pp. 8-14, and 0132, pp. 3-7, FDP Orientation for Joyce Brown's speech.

74. SHSW: Jean Kates Prs.: Jim Kates, "Dear People," June 26, 1965, Jackson, Miss.; Jim Kates, "Dear People," July 6, 1965, Natchez, Miss.

75. SHSW: Jean Kates Prs.: Jim Kates, "Dear People," July 17, 1965, Natchez, Miss.; KZSU Interviews 0219 and 1218.

76. KZSU Interview 0218, p. 2.

77. KZSU Interview 0326, p. 7.

78. KZSU Interview 0291.

79. Carmichael and Hamilton, *Black Power*, pp. 94-95. Lawrence Guyot and Mike Thelwell, "Toward Independent Political Power," *Freedomways* 6, no. 3 (Summer 1966):pp. 247-49; McLemore, "Mississippi Freedom Democratic Party," pp. 226-29.

80. Sellers and Terrell, *The River of No Return*, pp. 115-17.

81. KZSU Interview; Hosea Williams, Orientation, 0089, p. 4.

82. KZSU Interview 0220, p. 8.
83. KZSU Interview 0056, p. 12.
84. KZSU Interview 0305, p. 10.

4

TO SEE THE LINKS:
THE VOLUNTEERS AND THE
FREEDOM SCHOOLS

Shortly after the Greenville meeting that established the 1964 Summer Project, Charlie Cobb, a black member of SNCC, wrote a memo entitled "Prospectus for a Summer Freedom School Program." His premise was that Mississippi schools were inadequate, that black students in them received an education that was in every way inferior to that available elsewhere, and that in consequence they were victims of a pervasive "social paralysis." He argued that COFO needed to organize students around the state to work in educational programs and that students needed " . . . to articulate their own desires, demands, and . . . to stand up in classrooms around the state, and ask their teachers a real question."[1] He proposed that those needs could be met with Freedom Schools, which would benefit both COFO and Mississippi students and which could be staffed by the student volunteers and professionals from colleges in the North.

Cobb's initial proposal envisaged a two-month session for tenth and eleventh grade high school students to achieve three things:

1. Supplement what they aren't learning around the state;
2. Give them a broad intellectual and academic experience during the summer to bring back to fellow students in the state, and

93

3. Form the basis for statewide student action, such as school boycotts, based on their increased awareness.

Since these students were still in high school, they would remain in the state to put their knowledge to work.

Compensatory education in basic areas, in addition to skills like typing, would be combined with cultural programs. Social studies and political education would be a "prominent" part of the curriculum. Special projects combining curricular areas, such as writing a newspaper or planning a conference, would stimulate learning and build practical skills.

As part of the rationale for his proposal, Cobb stressed his belief that Freedom Schools would have a "special appeal" to the volunteers. Primarily students themselves, they would be able to try out their educational philosophy and experiment pedagogically with new ways of teaching. Under Cobb's plan, the ratio of students to Freedom School teachers would be small to ensure dialogue, with perhaps four or five students per teacher.

Summarizing the purpose of the program, Cobb wrote, "The overall theme of the school would be the student as a force for social change in Mississippi." Freedom Schools were to be a training ground for the next generation of local civil rights workers. The background that the schools would supply to students would clarify issues, nurture new skills, and strengthen them for their future movement work. As Cobb argued:

If we are concerned with breaking the power structure, then we have to be concerned with building up our own institutions to replace the old, unjust, decadent ones which make up the existing power structure. Education in Mississippi is an institution which can be validly replaced. . . . [2]

From the first proposal, then, Freedom Schools were seen as a political organizing tool for COFO, which could ably use the skills of northern volunteers. The schools would become a "parallel institution" and would produce students able to work for social change.

The National Council of Churches held a meeting in late March to organize a curriculum for the schools. Four main areas of concern were identified: (1) leadership development, (2) remedial academics, (3) contemporary issues, and (4) nonacademic curriculum, which would emphasize fieldwork and projects designed to encourage student organization. Dr. Staughton Lynd, a northern white professor and civil rights activist then teaching at Spelman College, was chosen to be director of Freedom Schools. During the ensuing months, various individuals worked on curriculum and teaching aids. Since COFO was always strapped for money, materials were generally mimeographed or dittoed, often by the departments of interested individual faculty or student groups in northern colleges. The "core citizenship curriculum," especially, benefited from the work of several notable American historians, including Howard Zinn, Staughton Lynd, Martin Duberman, Norman Pollack, C. Vann Woodward, and Otis Pease.[3]

Starting from Cobb's first premise that education is political, the "core citizenship curriculum" was designed to give students a sense of dignity and a link with their past. Curriculum planners made special efforts to present black history and American government and economics to students at all levels. Planners believed that students should know their black heritage for knowledge's sake and for the sake of their self-esteem. Additionally, they believed that if students found their past, of which they were deprived by Mississippi schools, they could work actively for a better future. Learning about American government and economics would help students understand the roots of their oppression. This understanding, in turn, would provide the key to change blacks' position in society.

As information was disseminated in the North, however, a subtle change in the Freedom School rationale occurred. Increasingly, memos and mimeographed announcements discussed the schools as primarily a purely academic endeavor, a kind of educational challenge to the "closed society." The COFO staff's initial emphasis on schools as a tool for organization and social action faded into the background and became secondary to a more traditional academic emphasis for the schools.[4]

This happened because those people who took over the planning for the schools, particularly the northern volunteers, acted out of their experience, which was for the most part traditionally academic and light-years away from the Mississippi movement. To the volunteers, mainly college students and professors, schools were not automatically connected with political action and social change. Conversely, Cobb and the other black and white SNCC staff who initially envisioned the schools worked out of their world, which was dedicated to political action for social change. Given the enormity of the problems facing Mississippi blacks, from their point of view, allocation of money and staff to Freedom Schools could only be countenanced if it would lead to substantial political action. When the summer program began, the two strains of thought about Freedom Schools formed the context for tension within the schools and for differing assessments about their usefulness to the movement.

Throughout May Freedom School teachers received information on the project to prepare them for orientation and the summer. The proposed daily schedule and curriculum were outlined, along with the case studies that would illustrate each topic. The volunteers were informed that some teachers might be holding classes without classrooms and that they almost certainly would not have ideal materials and facilities for teaching. The Jackson staff clearly indicated their belief that:

> ... academic experiences should relate directly to ... [the students'] ... real life in Mississippi, and since learning that involves real life experiences is, we think, most meaningful, we hope that the students will be involved in the political life of their communities.... The way students can participate in local voter registration should be worked out by the teachers and local COFO voter registration staff at a meeting before the opening of school.... It is important that voter registration staff and teachers stay in close touch with each other so these things can be worked out.... [5]

Volunteers were encouraged to begin thinking about special areas they would like to teach and to collect visual aids, books, and teaching aids for both the "citizenship curriculum" and their special subjects. Above all, they were urged "to think creatively about what could be done in the schools and with *small groups*."[6]

The 1964 volunteers who were to become Freedom School teachers began their summer at an orientation program in Oxford, Ohio, sponsored by the National Council of Churches. Like the voter registration workers who had preceded them by one week, the volunteer teachers were introduced to one another, to the staff, and to the problems awaiting them in Mississippi. The volunteers had a crash course in Mississippi politics, race relations, and black history. Speakers presented varied views on the purpose of the summer projects and movement philosophy, including the issue of nonviolence as a tactic or life commitment. The volunteers learned intensely practical safety rules, such as how and when to report to headquarters and how to travel safely after dark. Additionally, they acted out sociodramas of possible situations and actively practiced nonviolent techniques to protect themselves against the eventuality of violent retaliation to the projects from the white community. The only major planned difference between the two orientation sessions was the substitution of training in Freedom School techniques and curriculum for training in voter registration.

On the second day of the Freedom School orientation, however, a shock occurred that materially affected the atmosphere of the meeting and the remainder of the summer. Rita Schwerner, a CORE staff member, announced to the group of volunteers that her husband Michael and James Chaney, who were both CORE staff workers, as well as Andy Goodman, a summer volunteer, were missing from Philadelphia, Mississippi. She urged the volunteers to telegraph their representatives and senators for federal protection and assistance in the search and to write their relatives and friends to do the same.

One volunteer wrote her parents:

I cannot begin to tell you how it feels to be here . . . knowing about them [the three missing workers]. You feel like it couldn't be real. no—uh—huh. They were in Oxford only a few days before—they couldn't already be in such danger. But then all of a sudden—the disbelief is countered by a vivid picture of reality—that it could be you. And then there's this weird feeling of guilt because it wasn't you—and there you are on a beautiful campus trying so hard to understand just what danger is anyway. . . . A lot of kids are trying to be real casual and cool and funny about everything so they don't worry their folks. This seems silly to me—especially with you— you're in this with us . . . you realize the significance of this summer as much as I do. . . . [7]

The training session continued with the planned program, but the Freedom School volunteers experienced more extreme psychological reactions than the previous group of volunteers, especially as the search continued with no sign of the missing men except their empty, charred station wagon. Two psychiatrists who were at the orientation to screen the volunteers for their final field assignments, Robert Coles and Joseph Brenner, noted:

There was a noticeable increase in the consultations we made. In point of fact we worked almost round the clock because the conference almost did. Minor medical complaints, bruises, cuts, aches and pains came in high numbers, we thought because many students were quite doubtful of their strength—of body and mind both—to face a continuation of what had happened in Philadelphia. There was an increase in those openly anxious, fearful or unable to sleep soundly. Yet the general drift of those tense hours and days after Philadelphia was toward a final consolidation of the entire group. . . . [8]

Despite this psychological and physical shock, the vast majority of the 280 Freedom School volunteers stayed through the orientation and went to Mississippi. But the disappearance, and later the discovery of the three mutilated bodies, framed the summer project in violence. No one ever forgot the tension; rarely did anyone ever feel safe.

For the volunteer teachers, area studies were practical and immediately useful. Sections of the state were analyzed and discussed, so that the volunteers would know the economic and political background of their geographic areas. They reviewed more specific information when they were assigned to their schools. Thus, volunteers bound for Canton learned about cotton chopping and were warned in advance of the possible necessity of double-shift sessions to accommodate their working students. Those designated for Hattiesburg found that they could count on a well-established and active black community with reasonably urban resources and attitudes. Each small group of volunteers, then, was introduced to "their" new community: its power structure, economic situation, and physical circumstances.

The intrinsic appeal of Freedom Schools became even greater as the volunteers learned more about the existing educational structure in the state. The staff gave a blistering précis of Mississippi Negro education. The underlying premise, according to them, was repression of all kinds—physical, emotional, psychological, and intellectual—to the end of keeping the Mississippi black in his place. Charlie Cobb wrote:

... |in Mississippi| ... an idea of your own is a subversion that must be squelched; for each bit of intellectual initiative represents the threat of a probe into the why of denial. Learning means only to stay in your place.[9]

As the volunteers read of the discrepancies in black and white schooling from the 1962 report of the state superintendent for education and SNCC reports, they began to comprehend the bitterness of Charlie Cobb. On the state level, Mississippi paid $81.86 for each white student and $21.77 for each black.[10] In 1960 for those twenty-five years or older, blacks had completed a median of six years of schooling, compared with eleven years for whites. Only 4.2 percent of the blacks twenty-five years or older had graduated from high school, but 24.6 percent of the whites in that age group had graduated.[11] Even more shocking appeared to be the difference in monetary expenditures in the rural areas, which were heavily black in population. For instance, Holly Bluff spent $191.17 per white student per year as opposed to $1.26 per black student per year.[12] The volunteers also found to their dismay that the rural areas were the hardest to reach although they often needed the workers most. Few were scheduled to have Freedom Schools.

After introducing the volunteers to the background of the educational situation, the staff discussed what the Freedom School teachers should do in their new jobs. They pressed the point that the volunteer's most important task was to encourage the students to discuss problems and ask questions, so that students would begin to appreciate their intrinsic importance as people.

Noel Day, a SNCC staff member, gave the volunteers several suggestions about teaching Mississippi black children. He advised the teachers to encourage their students in all possible ways:

The leader should not be critical—particularly at the start. For many of the students, *just being able to verbalize in this situation is progress* that can easily be inhibited by a disapproving remark or facial expression.

He suggested that volunteers simplify their language and learn the student's slang: Their job was to communicate and to encourage expression.[13]

Another full-time COFO staff member, Mendy Samstein, told the volunteers about the physical conditions of Freedom School teaching. They were warned that COFO had few funds, that supplies would be limited, and that few of the communities could give financial help. Indeed, he wrote, "particularly in rural towns there are really no suitable facilities available either in the white or in the Negro communities. As a result, most Freedom Schools will have to be held in church basements, homes, backyards, etc."[14]

Exemplifying the somewhat simplistic COFO staff feeling about their new educational structure, Jane Stembridge cautioned the volunteers "to be trustworthy. It's that simple." She also wrote from the Jackson office: "We can say that the key to your teaching will be honesty and creativity. We can prepare materials for you and suggest teaching methods. Beyond that, it is your classroom. . . . "[15]

Along with the staff cautions and explanations, the volunteers were given intensive classes in the core curriculum, expecially black history, federal and state government, and the history of the movement. They needed to know facts as well as interpretations. And they struggled to absorb enough information to help students understand their personal experiences in the light of the history of black and poor white people in the world. This forging together of personal experience and academic data was the rationale of the Freedom School method. Only with both emphases could the students realize the goal of the organizers that they see " . . . the link between a rotting shack and a rotting America."[16]

At the end of the one-week orientation, most of the volunteers were scarcely prepared for their tasks, but they did have some ideas about what they should do and how they might attempt teaching. They had practical information and teaching ideas for projects and role playing. Furthermore, they could count on support from the resource people based in Jackson who had special skills and who often brought mimeographed teaching aids and book lists.[17]

On the last night of orientation, Bob Moses talked to the group about the prospects, the dangers, and the rewards that the summer might bring. He concluded with a plea to the Freedom School teachers " . . . to be patient with their students. There's a difference between being slow and being stupid, he said. The people . . . [the teachers would] . . . be working with aren't stupid. But they're slow, so slow."[18]

The volunteers left for their respective schools and began working within the week. The staff had estimated that one thousand black students would attend the twenty-five Freedom Schools located throughout the state.[19] After the second week, however, over two thousand students had registered, and by the end of the summer an estimated twenty-five hundred to twenty-seven hundred black Mississippians had attended at least some classes.[20] The Freedom School sites expanded from twenty-five to forty-one.[21]

A typical Freedom School day began with the core curriculum of black history and philosophy of the movement. This was usually a history lesson or reading followed by a discussion. For example, many teachers gave lectures on W.E.B. Du Bois of whom most of the students had never heard. They compared him to Booker T. Washington, whom they had all studied in school. The discussion period would examine questions like:

Who do you think the Movement is proving right—Booker T. Washington or W.E.B. DuBois? And what comment on your own upbringing is made by the fact that you knew all about Booker T. Washington but most of you had never heard of W.E.B. DuBois?[22]

Following the core curriculum, there was generally some project or discussion aimed at helping students examine themselves and their environment. The teachers used various methods for this class, which ranged from question sessions to impromptu role playing. Often the teachers introduced a poem and had their students respond with their own creative writing, and some beautiful and expressive pieces came out of those classes.

After a break for the hottest part of the day, the Freedom School held afternoon sessions, which were generally "special interest" classes requested by the students. The most popular ones were foreign languages, higher mathematics, art, drama, typing, and journalism. None of these were taught on a regular basis to black students in Mississippi schools. As in the other classes, the teachers tried to relate these subjects to the students. One teacher who taught a French class discovered the students requested it because foreign language classes, taught only in white Mississippi schools, were a symbol of equality to them. She found, however, that "...teaching French turned out to be a good way to develop grammar and phonetic skills that would bore them in English...."[23] Thus, the class was related to the regular program in an academic way. Art and drama sessions gave the students a way of exploring and expressing their emotions. It also made them aware of the art media as an important avenue for protest. In Holly Springs, for instance, students wrote and produced a play, "Seeds of Freedom," based on the life of Medgar Evers. Typing was also a favorite class, and students begged to learn, both to obtain better employment and to help in the movement.

Journalism was the most eclectic class of all; the students produced special "freedom" newspapers and in so doing practiced creative writing, typing, news writing, and editing. They also spurred on an indigenous black press. A volunteer wrote about his freedom paper:

Most of that week was spent working on the "Clarksdale Freedom Press." Getting all the interested kids in the basement of Haven Methodist Church, examining possible articles, editing them, typing them, etc., was great! The place looked like a newspaper office with people running in and out, with typewriters going, and newsprint everywhere. It was excellent experience for the kids too. . . . They did most of the work and made most of the decisions.[24]

In the evening, classes continued, usually with adults. Informal discussions were held about the movement and what could be done to change Mississippi. Additionally, there were literacy classes, which used Dr. Frank Laubach's "Each one-teach one" method. Freedom School students helped the teacher on this one-to-one project, thereby learning to teach others and helping the adult students learn to read. The literacy project aided local people in registering to vote and often used the registration form as a reading text.

The teachers themselves had classes. In informal discussions, the volunteers often taught each other in areas with which they were familiar and in methods that were successful in their classes. Additionally, several professors who had joined the project were assigned to work with the Freedom School volunteers and to discuss subjects relevant to their teaching. Otis Pease, then at Stanford University, volunteered to work with COFO in Mississippi in July. Before he went, he prepared a paper on "The Development of the Negro in American Politics Since 1900," which was distributed to Freedom School teachers around the state and which constituted Pease's first research in black history. When Pease arrived in Mississippi, he was assigned to work in Hattiesburg, where among other things, he led a seminar with local Freedom School teachers and used his paper as a basic text. Addressing the controversial issue of working inside or outside the system, Pease held in the paper that blacks exercised power at the national level as a direct result of having the vote in northern states. Essentially, the paper was a historically accurate brief reflecting Pease's belief that working within the system was the most practical way to obtain real political power. The seminar "sparked a lively discussion" on what the goals of the movement should be. While several teachers agreed with Pease's position on working within the system, even with the risks that entailed, a CORE worker from New York adamantly disagreed, because "the System is córrupt." He believed, instead, that the movement should build a new system and revolutionize America. Before Pease could comment, a second volunteer disagreed: Building a new system was impracticable, and it was the movement's duty to get what it could within the system and help blacks now. Waiting for a utopian situation was paralyzing and futile.[25]

While most of the volunteers agreed with the expediency of working within the system for what could be gained quickly, the Hattiesburg Freedom School seminar was a microcosmic form of the major debate within the civil rights movement throughout the country, and staff workers, as well as volunteers, remained divided on the issue for several years. The issue was not, after all, small or "academic," for everyone knew it was a fact that people had lost their lives in Mississippi for movement work and that it was a possibility that people would continue to lose their lives "simply" trying to get into the southern political system. Seminars such as this, with heated debates on topics clearly relevant to real people's lives, helped the volunteers examine major issues in the movement and bring back to their students a new awareness of the facts of the black experience and the various interpretations that could be ascribed to these facts. Additionally, the volunteers often came to question their "ivory tower" academic beliefs of "value-free scholarship" and "objectivity" and to formulate alternative visions of what constituted "real" education for their students and themselves.

For the most part, the volunteers were enthusiastic about their new vocation and found it exciting to be in an unstructured "learning situation." Some realized fond dreams when they were able to test their theories of education, and many others began for the first time to consider alternatives to the traditional academic classroom seriously. The most consistently appealing and rewarding aspect of Freedom School teaching, however, was that the volunteers' efforts clearly helped children overcome their previous experiences in school and respond positively to their teachers. One volunteer wrote home:

I can see the change. The 16-year-old's discovery of poetry, of Whitman and Cummings above all, the struggle to express thoughts in words, to translate ideas into concrete written words. After two weeks a child finally looks me in the eye, unafraid, acknowledging a bond of trust which 300 years of Mississippians said should never, could never exist. I can feel the growth of self-confidence.[26]

And another exclaimed:

Every class is beautiful. The girls respond, respond, respond. And they disagree among themselves. I have no doubt soon they will be disagreeing with me. At least this is one thing that I am working towards. They are a sharp group but they are under-educated and starved for knowledge. They know that they have been cheated and they want anything and everything that we can give them.[27]

Although the majority of the teachers adapted ably to their tasks, there were a few who should not have been in Mississippi at all. Some of them, unable to resolve their frustrations, vented their aggressions on their students. Less often, they were just incapable of conversing with young black students on anything approaching an equal basis; still others were not able to arrive at a psychological balance between the clear short-run futility of teaching in a Freedom School and the potential long-run progress, when faced with the enormity of the racial problem in Mississippi.[28] Unfortunately, incapable teachers in several cases materially affected their Freedom School, especially if the school was small or in a rural area.[29]

All of the schools varied in their offerings and their composition.

Some case studies illustrate the scope of the schools and the different kinds of experience that the volunteers had.

Hattiesburg, which was the home of a strong COFO community center, became, in the words of Director Staughton Lynd, the "Mecca of the Freedom School world." What happened there the first week illustrates the predicament in which teachers throughout the state found themselves. One volunteer from Hattiesburg wrote home:

... All this week we have been working on curriculum, schedules, registration of students and assembling materials for the Freedom Schools at Hattiesburg. It became evident quite early that we are going to have more than the expected 75 students. We called Jackson and got a promise of more teachers—at full strength we will have 23. This was when we expected 150 students. On registration day, however, we had a totally unexpected deluge: 600 students! They were expecting only 700 for the whole state.[30]

Although it was rewarding to the volunteers to find so many students interested in the schools, it was also frustrating. They had hoped to have a teacher-student ratio of about one to five in order to give necessary personal attention to the students. Instead, they found themselves in some cases with twenty or more. They also discovered that, although the Freedom Schools were originally planned for fourteen- to eighteen-year-olds, Mississippians of all ages registered, and they had to adjust their programs for the wide age spread.

By the end of the second week, there were some five schools in and around Hattiesburg. The "deluge" of students was the result of strong civil rights activity in Hattiesburg prior to the summer. The success of the schools was due in large part to the excellent organization of Arthur and Carolyn Reese, a black couple from Detroit who supervised the project. Professional teachers themselves, they adapted their knowledge and experience of structured teaching to the ideals inherent in Freedom School education.[31]

The Reeses were exceptions, however. Often professional teachers seemed to have a more difficult time adapting to the Freedom School concept than student volunteers. A professional teacher who taught as a volunteer in a school just outside of Hattiesburg exemplified this problem:

... It has been rough. Much of what we know about teaching must be unlearned or relearned here. The standard academic approach has not worked at all well, even when material has been simplified. . . . The kids we are dealing with are not trained to listen and absorb information presented in an organized, "logical" manner. . . . The students do not seem to be able to follow a point-by-point presentation at all, whether simple or complex. They learn by talking, by conversation, by rambling around and beating the nearby bushes, and they learn by acting things out. . . . [32]

While this was frustrating to her, it was exciting to many volunteers, one of whom wrote:

... the students are on a much higher level than I had been led to expect. . . . If reading levels are not always the highest, the "philosophical" understanding is almost alarming: some of the things our 11 and 12 year olds will come out with would never be expected from someone of that age in the North. . . . [33]

Because of their innovation and organization, the Freedom Schools in Hattiesburg remained "bright lights" in the state. The Hattiesburg group was particularly successful in instituting the "Each one-teach one" method of teaching literacy to older people, generally in community centers.[34] And the students from the Hattiesburg School at Palmer's Crossing wrote a "Declaration of Independence," which was widely quoted and accepted as "policy" at the Freedom School convention in Meridian in early August.

The declaration paraphrased the American Declaration of Independence and included a list of grievances, which indicated students' awareness of their position in society and how government might change that position:

The Negro does not have the right to petition the government for a redress of these grievances:
    For Equal Opportunity
    For better schools and equipment
    For better recreation facilities
    For more public libraries
    For more schools for the mentally ill
    For more and better senior colleges
    For better roads in Negro communities
    For training schools in the state of Mississippi

For more Negro policemen
For more guarantee of a fair circuit clerk
For integration in colleges and schools.[35]

This list of demands was a clear example of Hattiesburg students "seeing the link between a rotting shack and a rotting America."

A Freedom School–Community Center project continued throughout the year at Hattiesburg. Seven volunteers remained in the face of increased white harassment. And the project instituted a proposal made by the Reeses that older students teach younger students, thus expanding teaching capabilities.[36]

In contrast to the Hattiesburg schools, volunteers who went to Shaw, Mississippi, faced many problems. Shaw is a poor rural Delta town. Aside from a teenage group, the movement had scarcely touched Shaw prior to the summer, so the volunteers had to make their own introduction. Most arrived originally in Ruleville, local movement activist Fannie Lou Hamer's hometown, and were transferred to neighboring Shaw. As one volunteer wrote home, exemplifying her upper-middle-class background and exhibiting the ethnocentrism that COFO staff members had worried about before the project began:

Ruleville is a comparatively wealthy community, if Shaw is to be considered typical. I don't really mind the lack of indoor toilet facilities, the crowded conditions of our sleeping quarters or even the horrible poverty of these people. But the people here in Shaw don't seem to have the same educational background — their homes are infested with roaches and they leave perishable food out in the heat. . . .

And then she demonstrated the ambivalence and guilt volunteers often felt about their experiences by continuing:

I hope I don't sound as if I were complaining. I don't mean to. The people here couldn't be any more wonderful if they were a club of potential saints.[37]

The Shaw volunteers were all housed in the community, and they rented a house for a community center. After installing electricity, building shelves and tables and scrubbing it all down, they were ready to set up their equipment, arrange the books for a library, and begin the Freedom School.[38]

Since Shaw is a cotton town, schools run during the summer to allow students to work in the fields at chopping and harvest time. As the children had to go to school from seven to one o'clock, a volunteer wrote, " . . . they want to sleep, not to have to study in the blazing heat of the Mississippi sun and dust." And he continued, "So would I in their place. Furthermore, they don't see how we can help them be free. At this point, neither do we. Slow change is unthinkable when so much change is needed. . . . "[39] Another volunteer, who was the center librarian, wrote home:

> The project here is in a strange situation now; no one is really sure just what his job is now, except maybe me. As a result, there are a lot of people who are really discouraged about their presence here and feel that their time could be much better spent than it is now. I won't agree with them, but I sometimes feel the same because the local reaction here has not been the kind that I would really like. . . . [40]

The Shaw volunteers grew more anxious, uncomfortable, and jealous as they read reports of Freedom School successes in other areas.

Well into what should have been the second week of classes, the Shaw Freedom School director, Wally Roberts, wrote on July 11, 1964, to Staughton Lynd, the statewide director, expressing his discouragement, which was compounded by family problems:

> I think I am rapidly losing whatever effectiveness I may have had as a coordinator, or even as a rights worker. Part of it is family trouble. Virtually all letters and calls from my wife are depressing. . . . I could probably straighten this problem [with my little boy] out, if it were not for something else even more important. I realize things are bad with us here because all we have been able to do is fix up the school and community center and attend a few mass meetings. But during this time the depressing reality that surrounds me has been gnawing at my emotions until now I am completely frustrated. Living conditions are so terrible, the Negroes are so completely oppressed, so completely without hope, that I want to change it all NOW. I mean this as sincerely as I can. Running a Freedom School is an absurd waste of time. I don't want to sit around in a classroom; I want to go out . . . shake [the white people] up, destroy their stolen property, convince them we mean business. . . . I really can't stand it here. . . . [41]

Although local people were beginning to use the library and the center, there were still virtually no students in the school.[42]

Roberts' letter brought Staughton Lynd to Shaw on July 14, three days after it had been written. He and Roberts had a long talk that evening, and the next day Lynd and all the volunteers discussed the situation. One wrote home:

There was a good meeting this morning of the volunteers. We ironed out most of the problems that faced us within our group and gained a new desire and purpose for continuing to work. It was really great. The thing lasted four hours, but every single one of us really needed the chance to air our grievances and doubts. And a lot of personality conflicts that have been eating away below the surface have come up and have become much more nearly manageable than they were before. . . . [43]

The volunteers decided to try a new tack and turned to full-time voter registration. They immediately organized a Freedom Day and took forty blacks to Cleveland, the Bolivar County seat, to register. To support the registrants, the volunteers organized teenagers to picket the courthouse and sing freedom songs. As one wrote:

Not only was this the first time *any* picketline has occurred in this county, but the Sheriff ignored a newly passed state law forbidding picketing. He hired 35–40 auxiliary police for the day, and posted them around the block with their helmets and rifles in case of incidents. . . . [44]

In giving the young people workshops in nonviolence and picketing, the volunteer teachers found, "They had enjoyed them because they understood and valued the end to which we were directing them. . . . It suddenly became clear to us that what we should do was to have special tutoring in anything the students desired."[45]

Through this Freedom Day activity, the Shaw Freedom School began. Over a third of the high school students came, some thirty-five students, and the volunteers gave classes in anything the students wanted:

Not only are they having special workshops in leadership and non-violence, but we are sneaking in all kinds of citizenship education, and they are enjoying it. We even have several who are interested in straight

Negro history, and not too few who want academics, the normal type. So in this more limited, but under the circumstances healthier extent, we are underway as a Freedom School, the last in the state to do so.[46]

The Shaw school began finally by linking its academic program to political activity and reflected Cobb's original plan and rationale for Freedom Schools.

The school so successfully joined its studies with political activity that it became the focal point of local organizing in Shaw. Students organized a chapter of the Mississippi Student Union and committed themselves to working with adults to begin the Bolivar (County) Improvement Association. Conceived in a political science class, the association hoped to apply for federal funds to form cooperatives to combat local black unemployment. Furthermore, at a meeting in Shaw's black high school, white volunteers, who had been invited by the community, were asked by the black principal to leave the school if they did not have permission from the white superintendent. As a result of this incident, black students began a school boycott on August 4. Supported by more than 75 percent of the students, the Student Union called the boycott "because of the inadequate education we're getting" and demanded new texts, libraries, Negro history materials, new laboratories, foreign languages, and more college preparatory classes. The white superintendent closed the school, and armed deputies patrolled the grounds. Boycotting students attended the Shaw Freedom School. Despite its difficult start, the Shaw Freedom School represented Cobb's initial ideal much more clearly than most.[47]

The culmination of the Freedom Schools was the statewide convention held in Meridian in early August. Planned mainly by Freedom School students, elected delegates from each school were to analyze the problems in the state and propose demands they would make on the government if they were a voting majority. Delegates from almost every school attended, although in some instances parents were reluctant to risk their children's safety by letting them be publicly involved in civil rights.

Florence Howe, who was coordinator of the Blair Street Freedom School in Jackson, recounted her surprise when no one from her school wanted to attend the convention:

I asked for volunteers and got no response again. Then I asked a thirteen year old girl, who had been particularly articulate the day before in a discussion, whether she would like to go. She said, first, only an abrupt "no," but when questioned in disbelieving tones, she admitted to, "Yes, but I can't." "But why not, then? All your expenses would be paid, and you know you'd enjoy it." She finally said that her father would not allow her to go, in general, and that he did not even approve of her attending Freedom School. . . .

The Blair Street parents did not relent, and no students attended the convention from the school. Through the fall, however, many parents slowly became involved in the movement through the impetus of their children's positive Freedom School experiences.[48]

When the Freedom School students assembled in Meridian, they immediately began working on a program. One volunteer wrote:

The purpose of the convention was to formulate a youth platform for the Freedom Democratic Party, and the kids did a fantastic job of it. . . . There were eight different committees, each concerning a different area of legislation: jobs, schools, federal aid, foreign affairs, voting, housing, public accommodations, health. Sometimes the committee discussions were long and even bitter, particularly on foreign aid where a demand to boycott Cuba and all countries that trade with Cuba was adopted but then finally voted out in the general session. Resolutions in favor of land reform were voted down because they were considered too socialistic, but there is a history of Negroes' land being taken away from them here that was the basis of these vetoes. The kids really learned something from the convention, for the first time, Negro students from all over the state came together to discuss their common aims.[49]

The students accepted the Palmer's Crossing Declaration of Independence as an ideological statement. They made guidelines for housing projects and health programs, and they advocated swift equalization of public schools and job opportunities. Resolving active support of SNCC's Mississippi Student Union (MSU), they called for a political challenge to the all-white Mississippi Young Democrats and for school boycotts in particularly repressive districts.[50]

As the summer drew to a close, most Freedom School teachers left for the North and home. The schools were initially analyzed a success and Director Staughton Lynd issued a final report, which

made confident plans to continue the project. The report proposed that a school be kept in every area and that some of the
summer Freedom School volunteers remain in Mississippi to staff
them. Additional volunteers were to be recruited by SNCC and
CORE to complete the staffing. The report also proposed that
community center and Freedom School staffs unify to consolidate
their strength and acknowledged that the schools would mainly be
held in the evening after public school. Liz Fusco, formerly coordinator of the Indianola and Ruleville schools, was appointed the
new director of Freedom Schools, since Lynd was going to Yale
University to begin an assistant professorship. Lynd's final suggestion was that the schools should allow time for restructuring and
not go back into session until October.[51]

Continuing and expanding on Lynd's ideas, in September 1964 a
staff member drew up a "Proposal for a Freedom Education Program," which advocated building a "new community institution, a
community center" to act as the meeting place for educational
programs, serve as a social service center, and be the home base
for political education. The plan called for an integrated model
preschool and Freedom School program, which would supplement
public schools, and it outlined a strong, new adult education
program. The physical plans for the building were detailed in the
proposal. Since buildings of that sort were not readily available in
most black communities, " . . . we must build our centers, symbolic
of building a New South when the old South does not meet our
needs."[52]

Although each center would initially be staffed by a "trained
outsider" and long-term northern and local volunteers, completely
local leadership would be the goal of a successful center. The
proposal concluded:

As a final argument, we can, in this project, discover for ourselves and
show the world what kind of society we envision. The center can be an
example of our goal in microcosm. The concept of an integrated group of
workers applying their brains and bodies to the solution of social problems
is needed in America now, to show the average American an alternative to
racism, materialism and cynicism.[53]

The new, smaller Freedom School program began again in the
fall. As it was less formal than the summer project, Freedom

School teachers made more of their own curriculum and continued to exchange useful units among themselves.[54] Many more clearly realized and emphasized the importance of experiential knowledge: Mississippi blacks knew how to survive politically whether or not they could read or write. Although the summer experience brought this belief, the stress on the educational validity, and in some cases superiority, of experiential knowledge marked a profound change from the summer program. Indeed, Jimmy Garrett of Los Angeles SNCC wrote exemplifying that feeling, "People are called 'ignorant' if they know nothing but their own lives. Are people 'educated' if they know about everything except their own lives?"[55]

This refocusing, which emphasized a more immediate political awareness, was an evolutionary process, and it did not automatically happen in all of the schools, although it was accelerated statewide by the dissolution of most of the pretense of a viable COFO by the winter of 1965. With the ascendance of the more politically radical civil rights groups, SNCC and CORE, over the more ameliorative groups, the NAACP and SCLC, it was obvious that programs would become more critical of local institutions and more oriented toward developing the political awareness necessary to "see the links between a rotting shack and a rotting America." While volunteers continued to teach subjects not taught in the public schools, as the year drew to a close, the subjects taught and the emphasis of the classes became more oriented to the individual local people attending them. The students helped each other learn and make their own standards for the classes.

The evolution had its difficult moments. The Freedom School staff meeting in November 1964 was an example. In a discussion about what the new Freedom School program should be, a white volunteer suggested that the staff work mainly with the "educated" people, because there were fewer communication problems with them and because they were the ones who would ultimately make important political decisions in the state. In response Liz Fusco wrote: "An irate Negro girl from Greenwood screamed, 'Yes I'm ignorant, cause they taken me and putten me in a cotton field. ' " "And so," Fusco continued, "we began discussing who we should talk to—which was our way of beginning to discuss who should make the decisions, and what education is. . . . In fact, it became

'local people' year!" The new Freedom School goal was "an education based on people," which would acknowledge the importance
of the black community's survival and experience which was
the crux of Jimmy Garrett's question, "What constitutes education?"[56]

It became clear to the staff and the remaining volunteers that an
evaluation of the Freedom School program had to come to grips
with the previous thrust of the program. Supplementary education,
while it might well boost the ego and self-image of the students,
probably did not in a practical sense help students survive in
Mississippi and might even fail to illuminate the reasons why the
material was not taught in Mississippi schools. Summer Freedom
Schools taught remedial reading: Did they confront why people
could not read? Also, the staff and remaining volunteers watched
students drift away in the fall, when specialty subjects like foreign
languages, which had drawn large numbers of people in the summer,
no longer were taught because the volunteer teacher with those
skills had returned to the North.

Just as the reassessment of the program was accelerated by the
staff changes in COFO and the disavowal by the more conservative
civil rights groups of SNCC's programs, the change in the volunteers who staffed the Freedom Schools hastened the process. Those
volunteers who remained in Mississippi after the summer made a
long-term commitment to the movement and tended to be more
consistently left-wing in their views and radical in their politics.
Dedicated to thoroughgoing social change, they tended to join the
criticism of the intent and content of the previous program and to
advocate augmenting experiential knowledge to facilitate blacks'
changing their society.

Of course, this reevaluation of the Freedom Schools—judging
"success" by actions taken by the community as a result of the
school, rather than by the numbers of school students involved—did
not contradict the original intent of the Freedom Schools as they
were proposed by Charlie Cobb in early 1964. Rather, the assessment brought the program back to the original idea of Freedom
Schools as an organizing tool for action within the movement. No
one denied that good experiences had come from the schools, for
both white volunteers and black local students, but the staff found
the schools had not been as organizationally effective as they had

first planned. And their lack of effectiveness seemed in direct proportion to the supplementary, nonexperiential nature of their programs. Those schools which were the most "northern academic" in content had the least continuity in the fall and winter.[57]

One action legacy from the summer program was the idea and statewide endorsement of public school boycotts. Several communities proposed or held boycotts.[58] Moreover, in Issaquena and Sharkey counties, students organized a long-term Freedom School when they began a boycott of their public school after the school principal forbade students to wear SNCC buttons. For the remaining staff, this became the new ideal for Freedom Schools.[59]

By any traditional academic standards, the Issaquena-Sharkey Freedom School "classes" were chaos, but they represented the free expression of students that the staff had only theorized could be possible in November. And they showed that Freedom Schools could indeed be what Cobb had initially envisioned: foci for community organizing to bring community change.[60] Although some Freedom School teachers came to help and bring supplies, they stayed in the background. The students themselves discussed what they wanted to discuss: The subjects ranged from major league baseball players, to why the earthworm needs the earth, to math, to "how would you like to see Issaquena County run?"[61] They put ideas together on their own. After examining pictures in *Look* and *Ebony* magazines, and comparing them with what they saw around them everyday, one eleven-year-old boy reported,

By looking at the magazines it let me *know* that they [rich blacks and whites] didn't care nothing about them [poor blacks and whites].

I learned that rich white people gettin' all the water, and them rich Negroes get all the water from the poor Negroes; the poor whites, they ain't gettin' no water either.[62]

The longest boycott in the state, the Issaquena action, continued until September 1965, when the majority of the children went back to the Issaquena-Sharkey school, still without the right to wear buttons. The main leaders did not go back; the boys took paying jobs with the Delta Ministry, while one girl went north and the other became the first black in the white Issaquena-Sharkey school. The Freedom School experiment lasted eight months.[63]

A more orthodox work-study program was held by SNCC at the Waveland Institute in Waveland, Mississippi, and many of the finest movement teachers came to teach at least one class. While Jane Stembridge was there, she wrote up a speech class by Stokely Carmichael, who was then on the Mississippi staff. One day he wrote eight sentences on the board with four on each side. On the left side were sentences in the local black dialect like "The peoples wants freedom," and "I wants to reddish to vote." Corresponding to those sentences, he wrote on the right side, "The people want freedom," and "I want to register to vote." He turned and asked the class of teenage Mississippi blacks what they thought about the sentences. While they thought that the ones on the right were "correct," they believed the most commonly used ones were those on the left:

STOKELY: If most people speak on the left, why are they [teachers] trying to change these people?

GLADYS: If you don't talk right, society rejects you. It embarrasses other people if you don't talk right.

HANK: But Mississippi society, ours, isn't embarrassed by it.

SHIRLEY: But the middle class wouldn't class us with them.

STOKELY: Will society reject you if you don't speak like on the right side of the board? Gladys said society would reject you.

GLADYS: You might as well face it man! What we gotta do is go out and become middle class. If you can't speak good English, you don't have a car, a job, or anything.

STOKELY: If society rejects you because you don't speak good English, should you learn to speak good English?

CLASS: No!

ALMA: I'm tired of doing what society say. Let society say "reddish" for awhile. People ought just to accept each other.

ZELMA: I think we should be speaking just like we always have.

ALMA: If I change for society, I wouldn't be free anyway.

ALMA: If society speaks on the left, then a minority must rule society? Why do we have to change to be accepted by the minority group?

STOKELY: Let's think about two questions for next time: What is society? Who makes the rules for society?

In what could have been a commonplace class in language, Carmichael, through directed questions, urged his students to think about language, power, control, and politics. With a brilliantly executed pedagogical method, he helped his students make some vital connections about their language and their lives.[64]

In these sometimes subtle but real ways, the Freedom Schools became more freewheeling and politically radical. The best of them—like Stokely Carmichael's class—integrated the personal experiences of the students with the political ideology of the movement.[65] This integration of experience and ideology was concretely action-oriented. Students at the Waveland Institute, for instance, pledged themselves to work in the movement for at least as long a time as they took classes. And students in Issaquena-Sharkey actively tried to change their school system.

The change in the Freedom School program was accentuated and aggravated when the federal government appropriated money in the spring of 1965 for the development of Head Start, an enrichment program for preschool children. The National Council of Churches project, the Delta Ministry, organized the Mississippi Child Development Group (MCDG) which was an integrated, but mainly black, parent group for the Head Start program. The policy of the MCDG was to employ mostly local black women, many of whom were active in the movement, while the federal government paid the salaries. The classrooms had to meet a certain government standard, and the children had to be properly registered. Freedom School staff workers, almost completely SNCC and CORE staff by now, were angry at the new program, because they believed the local women would probably be "coopted into the morally bankrupt middle class." They also feared that the schools would quickly become bureaucracies, and they were sure that the most needy children would not come, because they would not meet the cleanliness standards or have the right clothes. They felt that the Head Start program would take away their students and their local adult leaders and turn the Freedom School concept into a way of training students to become a part of middle-class American society. Whereas earlier in the movement's Mississippi work COFO might have strongly supported the MCDG as a local parents' group, SNCC and CORE were too politicized and too committed to alternative institutions to support the MCDG by the spring of 1965.[66]

After all the program reevaluations by the Mississippi civil rights staff, the Freedom Democratic Party formally decided to sponsor a small, decentralized project as the political branch of the state's civil rights movement. The summer project would be based solely on community needs and requests. Some communities decided to have Freedom Schools; many did not. The COFO enthusiasm of the summer before toward the schools had diminished by 1965, since the criterion for a "successful" school had changed and the movement emphasized the FDP and concrete political action.[67] Indeed, as late as the middle of April, movement staff were still debating whether Freedom Schools taught by whites were any longer appropriate for the movement. Many staff members at the April meeting did not believe that there was a place for white teachers in the state, but SNCC leader Jim Forman argued the case for assigning "aware people—white or black" to Freedom Schools, and his view seemed to prevail, although each project would determine its own needs and staff.[68]

The group of volunteers that came to the 1965 FDP Project numbered about 280, and Freedom School teachers were a much smaller percentage of the group than they had been in the 1964 Mississippi Summer Project. Volunteers who taught were requested by the community and were expected to have useful skills. Furthermore, they were seen primarily as "facilitators" for the expression of practical political awareness. Although Liz Fusco continued to hold the title director of Freedom Schools, the summer classes were much less formal than the previous year's. Compared to 1964, the orientation program was less organized, and the teaching emphasis was on the movement and the student's place in it. In 1965 Lawrence Guyot, head of the FDP and a SNCC veteran, commented:

Last summer you didn't really have the politicalness, the political thrust of people involved in the movement. You had a lot of nonpolitical ideology and a lot of very creative abstract thinking that couldn't be implemented.[69]

The focus had indeed shifted. To many in the movement, the

Freedom Schools of 1964 would have seemed anachronistic and irrelevant in 1965. Although some Freedom School classes were quite like the previous summer's, most had become more political. Karel Weisenberg's literacy class in 1965 was an example:

> Could I have everyone's attention please? . . . Mrs. Ervy's written something and I thought if she read it we could talk about it some. . . .
> Mrs. Ervy: Here's one thing: I want to know how come we pay taxes so much and don't get our roads fixed into our house.
> And here's another thing—how come they put the rocky floors in our houses? I just don't understand that.
> Cow barns is better than some of these houses. I work hard for what I get. I work from 6 to 6 for three dollars a day. That ain't no money. . . . I want more. . . . I labor a whole week and don't earn but fifteen dollars. We wants better; We wants food to eat. . . .
> We cook for a white, we washes, we irons, we bathes the children and when it comes to the real part of it, we are used as a dog. . . . something got to be done about it. We got to stick together more.[70]

Thus the classes changed from adult literacy for its own sake to literacy as a means of political expression.

Light-years away from the simple "good citizenship" basis of the previous summer, the McComb Freedom School blazed a controversial path. McComb was widely known as the most violently anti–civil rights town in the state. More black churches were bombed in McComb than in any other area, and two blacks associated with the movement had been murdered since Bob Moses had begun working there in 1961. Every civil rights worker in McComb had been beaten and jailed on more than one occasion. In fact, in June 1964 Moses initially refused to assign any white volunteers to McComb because it was so dangerous, although he later relented and allowed three special white male volunteers to integrate the project, which hung on in the black community in the face of terrible, violent white harassment. In the 1965 McComb Freedom School political education classes, students examined racism in American society, studied theories of third party politics, and worked for the FDP. Encouraged by their northern volunteer teachers, McComb students began questioning the role of the United States' involvement in Vietnam and the links between the civil rights movement and the peace movement. When a local black, who had supported Bob Moses in 1961, was killed in Vietnam, the teachers and students composed the "McComb Project Position Paper on the War in Vietnam." In a clear and concise statement, the students argued that blacks should not fight in Vietnam for "the White Man's freedom, until all the Negro People are free in Mississippi." Furthermore, they urged black men to avoid the draft and called on mothers to encourage their sons to stay home. Finally, while alleging economic aggrandizement as the reason for American participation in the war, they began to see themselves as allies with what soon became generally called the Third World:

We will be looked upon as traitors by all the Colored People of the world if the Negro people continue to fight and die without cause.[71]

With their "Statement on the War in Vietnam," McComb students made the first connection between the direct-action civil rights movement and the burgeoning peace movement. Their statement was the first of any civil rights groups to condemn American fighting in Vietnam.

The leaflet was printed in the *MFDP Newsletter* and created an enormous controversy.[72] State politicians and the local press charged that the students advocated treason. They predicted that the FDP challenge of Mississippi's congressional delegation, at that moment under consideration by the House of Representatives, would fail because of the statement, and, of course, they argued it should fail because of the "irresponsibility" of such a stand. FDP leaders Lawrence Guyot and Edwin King felt compelled to assert that the statement represented only the views of the McComb branch of the FDP and was not the policy of the statewide party, but they agreed that " . . . it is very easy to understand why Negro citizens of McComb, themselves the victims of bombings, klan-inspired terrorism, and harassment arrests, should resent the death of a citizen of McComb while fighting in Vietnam for freedom not enjoyed by the Negro community of McComb."[73] When questioned by the local press, one of the volunteers who helped author the statement explained, "It came from the people, this is how they felt. We just put their feelings into words after talking with them, singing with them and living with them."[74]

The more radical political nature of the majority of the Freedom

School classes represented a substantial change from the previous summer. Those volunteers who taught in 1965 drew connections between the peace and civil rights movements and organized their classes around viable local issues. They came much closer to enacting the original "Prospectus on Freedom Schools" than most of the 1964 schools, and they cast aside most notions of integrating Mississippi blacks into a basically "benign" American system.

An important educational and organizational experiment, the schools demonstrated the possibility of integrated education based on the premise that everyone has much to offer the community. The schools at their best showed both black and white Mississippi society that integrated students and teachers could laugh and talk and see together "the link between a rotting shack and a rotting America" and that they could then act on their vision. At their worst, the schools deflected energy from movement work and became a diversion that helped fill up time for students and kept volunteers occupied.

By the end of the 1965 summer, the staff in Mississippi did not believe that Freedom Schools taught by northern whites were relevant to the problems of Mississippi blacks, and the program turned solely to direct political action. The life cycle of the organized Mississippi Freedom School project was complete, but the legacy of the schools endured in the Mississippi black community.[75]

NOTES

1. Otis Pease Prs.: Cobb, "Prospectus," p. 1.
2. Ibid., p. 2.
3. SHSW: Howard Zinn Prs.; Staughton Lynd Prs.; Interviews: Otis Pease, Seattle, Wash. 1967-1968, Howard Zinn, Boston, Mass., 1969.
4. Otis Pease Prs.: "Prospectus for a Mississippi Freedom School Program," COFO, no date [probably April 1964], includes original Cobb proposal; Melish, *Memoir*, especially pp. 29-30; "Prospectus for the Mississippi Freedom Summer," COFO, no date [probably late April], includes only edited version of Cobb's proposal, in possession of the author; Liz Fusco, "To Blur the Focus of What You Came Here to Know: A Letter Containing Notes on Education, Freedom Schools and Mississippi," undated [Spring 1966]; Liz Fusco, "Issaquena Freedom: "A Play Written in Jail in

Mississippi," April 1965; SHSW: Howard Zinn Prs.: Dr. Robert L. Zangrando to Zinn, Rutgers University, August 20, 1964, p. 3; Elizabeth Sutherland Prs.: "Unused and Uncatalogued Letters," Letter Series "Judy" to parents and sponsor church in Denver, June 30, 1964–August 11, 1964, Ruleville and Shaw, Miss.; Staughton Lynd Prs.: Kristy Powell, "A Report, Mainly on Ruleville Freedom School Summer Project, 1964"; Florence Howe, "Mississippi's Freedom Schools: The Politics of Education," *Harvard Educational Review* 35 (Spring 1964): 144–60: Sutherland, *Letters*, pp. 100–2; Interviews: Otis Pease, Seattle, Wash., 1967; Paul Lauter and Florence Howe, Seattle, Wash., June 1972.

    5. Otis Pease Prs.: Mississippi Summer Project Staff (MSPS), "Memorandum: Overview of the Freedom Schools," COFO, May 5, 1964, Jackson, Miss., p. 1.

    6. Ibid., pp. 1–3; Staughton Lynd and Harold Bardanelli, "Dear Freedom School Teacher," COFO, May 30, 1964, Jackson, Miss.; MSPS, "Dear Summer Project Worker," COFO, undated [late May], Jackson, Miss.; Note the subtle differences in tone and purpose between the MSPS memos and the Lynd and Bardinelli memo.

    7. Sutherland, *Letters*, pp. 26–27.

    8. Otis Pease Mss.: Robert Coles, M.D., and Joseph Brenner, M.D., "American Youth in a Social Struggle: The Mississippi Summer Project," p. 12.

    9. Mary Rothschild Prs.: Charles Cobb, "This is the Situation," in "Notes on Teaching in Mississippi," COFO, undated [about June 1964], p. 2.

    10. William McCord, *Mississippi: The Long, Hot Summer*, p. 35.

    11. Gary Good Prs.: "The General Condition of the Mississippi Negro," SNCC, undated, p. 15.

    12. McCord, *Mississippi: The Long, Hot Summer*, p. 35; report of state superintendent of education as cited in the *Memphis Commercial Appeal*, January 15, 1962.

    13. Noel Day, "Remarks to the Freedom School Teachers about Methods," "Notes on Teaching," p. 5, in possession of the author.

    14. Mendy Samstein, "Problems of Freedom School Teaching," "Notes on Teaching," p. 2, in possession of the author.

    15. Jane Stembridge, "Introduction to the Summer," "Notes on Teaching," p. 1, in possession of the author.

    16. Cobb, "This is the Situation," "Notes on Teaching," p. 2, in possession of the author.

    17. Francis Hoague Prs.: MSPS, "Some Statistical Facts," COFO mimeo, undated; John and Ellen Fawcett Prs.: Delta Ministry mimeos on teaching; Otis Pease Prs.: Teaching mimeos, series; Gary Good Prs.: "The

General Condition of the Mississippi Negro," SNCC, undated; SHSW: Lise Vogel Prs.; Howard Zinn Prs.; Staughton Lynd Prs.

18. Sutherland, *Letters*, p. 39; SHSW: Lise Vogel Prs.: "Orientation Notes," handwritten.

19. Otis Pease Prs.: "Background Information—Mississippi Summer Project," Tuesday, June 30, 1964, Press Release, Jackson, Miss., p. 2.

20. Otis Pease Prs.: Untitled clipping, *The Daily Journal*, Tupelo, Miss., Xerox.

21. Otis Pease Prs.: "Freedom School Data," COFO, undated, p. 1.

22. Liz Fusco, "Deeper Than Politics," *Liberation* 95 no. 8 (1964): 18; SHSW: Howard Zinn Prs.: "Negro History Study Questions: 20th Century," COFO, undated [Spring/Summer 1964], p. 1.

23. Sutherland, *Letters*, p. 95.

24. Ibid., p. 97.

25. Otis Pease, "The Development of the Negro in American Politics Since 1900," COFO, undated [June 1964], in possession of the author; Otis Pease Prs.: Handwritten notes on July 16, 1964; Interviews: Otis Pease, February 13, 1967; March 23, 1967. Since that summer experience, Pease has always included a substantial component of black history in his courses. Previously he did not.

26. Sutherland, *Letters*, pp. 94–95.

27. Ibid., p. 94.

28. Otis Pease Prs.: Coles and Brenner, "American Youth in a Social Struggle," p. 16; Kenneth Keniston, *The Committed* (New York: 1968), pp. 140–45.

29. Interviews: Otis Pease, February 13, 1967; March 23, 1967; Sally Shideler, February 15, 1967.

30. Sutherland, *Letters*, p. 92.

31. SHSW: Elizabeth Sutherland Prs.: "Unused and Uncatalogued Letters"; Interview: Otis Pease, 1967.

32. Sutherland, *Letters*, p. 98.

33. Ibid., p. 96.

34. Otis Pease Prs.: Barbara and the COFO Office, "Hello from Hattiesburg," August 31, 1964, ditto; "Report from Hattiesburg, July 1–14, 1964," Hattiesburg Minister's Project; Sutherland, *Letters*, p. 103.

35. "Freedom School Data," including "The Declaration of Independence by the Freedom School Students of St. John's Methodist Church, Palmer's Crossing, Hattiesburg, Mississippi," COFO, p. 6, in possession of the author.

36. Otis Pease Prs.: Barbara and the COFO staff, "Hello from Hattiesburg," August 31, 1964.

37. SWHS: Elizabeth Sutherland Prs.: "Unused and Uncatalogued

Letters," Letter series from Judy to parents and home church in Denver, Colo.; July 3, 1964, Shaw, Miss., p. 2.

38. SWHS: Lise Vogel Prs.: Letter from Bonnie Guy to "Friends," July 18, 1964, Shaw, Miss., p. 1.

39. Sutherland, *Letters*, p. 100.

40. SHSW: Elizabeth Sutherland Prs.: "Unused and Uncatalogued Letters," Judy to parents and Denver church, July 8, 1964, Shaw, Miss., p. 3.

41. Sutherland, *Letters*, p. 101.

42. SHSW: Elizabeth Sutherland Prs.: "Unused and Uncatalogued Letters," Judy to parents and Denver church, July 15, 1964, Shaw, Miss., p. 1.

43. Ibid., p. 3; Sutherland, *Letters*, p. 101.

44. SHSW: Lise Vogel Prs.: Bonnie Guy, "Letter to Friends," July 18, 1964, Shaw, Miss., p. 3.

45. Sutherland, *Letters*, p. 102.

46. Ibid.

47. Mississippi Summer Project: Running Summary of Incidents, in possession of the author.

48. Florence Howe, "Mississippi's Freedom Schools: The Politics of Education," *Harvard Educational Review* 30 (Spring 1965): 148. Interviews: Florence Howe and Paul Lauter, June 1972, Seattle, Wash.; Florence Howe, Summer 1974, Seattle, Wash.

49. Sutherland, *Letters*, pp. 104-5.

50. Fusco, "Deeper Than Politics," p. 19; SHSW: Howard Zinn Prs.: "Freedom Schools—Final Report, 1964," undated [about August 20, 1964].

51. Ibid.; Staughton Lynd, "Mississippi Freedom Schools: Retrospect and Prospect," July 26, 1964; Staughton Lynd Prs.: Howard Zinn, "Educational Frontiers in Mississippi."

52. "Proposal for a Freedom Education Program," p. 3. I am indebted to Jan Hillegas of the Mississippi Freedom Information Service of Tougaloo, Miss., for allowing me access to these private files.

53. Ibid., p. 4.

54. "Outlook for Fall, 1964—Community Centers," p. 1, in possession of the author.

55. Fusco, "To Blur the Focus," p. 9.

56. Fusco, "To Blur the Focus," pp. 1-4.

57. Fusco, "To Blur the Focus," "Outlook for the Mississippi Community Center Program," a position paper, March 1965; Position Papers for COFO reevaluation, November–December 1964, ditto. Again I am indebted to Jan Hillegas of the Freedom Information Service for giving me a complete packet of these papers just as they were given to all the staff

members before the meeting. Interviews: Nancy Davis, October 1973, San Francisco; Linda Davis, October 1973, Washington, D.C.; Fannie Lou Hamer, November 1969, Ruleville, Miss., Charles Horwitz, November 1969, Jackson, Miss., Barbara Rosen, January 1967, Seattle, Wash.

58. SHSW: Staughton Lynd Prs.: Kristy Powell, "A Report, Mainly on Ruleville Freedom School, Summer Project, 1964," pp. 10–11; Florence Howe, "The Politics of Education," *Harvard Educational Review* 35 (1965): 155–57; Pat Watters, *Down to Now: Reflections on the Southern Civil Rights Movement* (New York: 1971), p. 302.

59. Otis Pease Prs.: "Freedom School Data," COFO, undated.

60. This boycott-Freedom School tradition continues in the Amite, Mississippi, school boycott over sex segregation in the Amite schools, which integrated under federal mandate in 1969, but kept the sexes separate so that white girls would not be in the same classrooms as black boys. The boycott began in September 1977 and is not yet completely resolved. *Newsweek*, September 19, 1977, p. 97.

61. Fusco, "Issaquena Freedom," pp. 5–9; Fusco, "To Blur the Focus," p. 14.

62. Liz Fusco, "Tommy Jr., A SNCC Poster (For Food, For Freedom) and some questions," mss., p. 3. Underlining in original mss. In possession of the author.

63. Fusco, "To Blur the Focus," p. 14.

64. Paul Jacobs and Saul Landau, *The New Radicals, A Report with Documents* (New York: 1966), pp. 131–35.

65. This became an important legacy of the civil rights movement. It has perhaps most strongly influenced the women's liberation movement, for which the statement "The personal is political" is an important ideological premise.

66. Fusco, "To Blur the Focus," p. 14; KZSU Quote Cards; Interview: Barbara Rosen, January 26, 1967; John and Ellen Fawcett, January 24, 1967; Polly Greenberg, *The Devil Has Slippery Shoes, A Biased Story of the Mississippi Child Development Group* (New York: 1969).

67. Fusco, "To Blur the Focus," pp. 11–14; KZSU Cards.

68. SHSW: R. Hunter Morey Prs.: Box 5, COFO Staff, "Fifth District's COFO Staff Meeting," April 14–17, 1965, Waveland, Miss., "Freedom School Joint Meeting with 3rd Dist.," pp. 12–15.

69. KZSU Quote Card 0305-1, mark 10; G-5, Lawrence Guyot.

70. KZSU Interview 0356, pp. 15–16.

71. Grant, *Black Protest*, pp. 415–16; "The War on Vietnam," A McComb, Miss., Project; Interview: Dorothy Smith, January 24, 1979, Lawrence, Kans.

72. McLemore, "Mississippi Freedom Democratic Party," pp. 234–42.

73. Grant, *Black Protest*, p. 415, footnote explanation of the background of the statement.

74. McLemore, "Mississippi Freedom Democratic Party," p. 237. Quoted from James Bonney "Letter's Author Recalls Praise of FDP Leaders," *Greenwood Commonwealth* (Miss.), August, 4, 1965.

75. See the discussion of the Amite boycott, footnote 60. Interviews: Fannie Lou Hamer, November 2, 1969, Ruleville, Miss.; Henry Kirksey, November 11, 1969, Jackson, Miss.; Dorothy Smith, January 24, 1979, Lawrence, Kans.

5

TO LEARN TO BE STRONG:
WOMEN VOLUNTEERS IN THE SOUTH

In 1964 approximately 300 white women went to Mississippi as volunteers, and in 1965 around 350 white women fanned throughout the entire South. Unlike the vanguard of strong southern black and white women who joined the movement early (often at great personal cost) and were by 1964 seasoned staff workers, these northern women represent a relatively anonymous group who lived the dailyness of women's work in a social movement. Many of the dynamics of their participation are similar to the early abolition and temperance movements, but there are some obvious twentieth-century differences, particularly the one of living together in racially integrated groups.[1]

While sometimes women volunteers seemed to have the same experiences as their male colleagues, more often their life in the South was different in both quality and texture, and they had to contend with many problems not shared by their male colleagues. In fact, there were differences between men and women volunteers from the beginning of their involvement in the movement.

Even before the volunteers went to orientation, recruiting material implied that men were more desirable than women, ostensibly because of the danger and the need to act in the community. In 1965 when CORE staff recruited volunteers, they made formal priorities and sought, in order, black men, black women, white men, and lastly, white women. Dave Dennis, the director of CORE's Southern Office, explained their policy:

... we had low on the list the white females, because they cause problems usually, you know. That's one thing that infuriates a white male in the South especially, but just about anywhere, any place, you know.... it's that whole interracial ... sex problem, you see.... white people can usually, in the South especially, can usually stomach to see a white male and a Negro female, you know, it's accepted, to some extent. But it infuriates people, it causes tremendous reactions, when there's a white female and a Negro male involved, walking down the street.... so to somewhat get out of that we decided that maybe the best thing to do would be to use that priority system.... [2]

Also, it was more common for men than women to receive financial support from northern organizations to reduce the financial hardships of volunteering.

Most volunteers' parents were at least initially somewhat reluctant for their children to participate in the Summer Projects. Parents feared for their children's safety and often wondered why they had to go south. Most recovered quickly, however, and supported their children emotionally and financially. Referring to her daughter's participation and reflecting the majority of parents, Katherine Schwarz told a reporter in 1964, "We were reluctant to let her go—not because we don't believe in it, but because it's a dangerous business. On the other hand we are very proud that she wanted to go. We tried to discourage it until she was older and more mature, but I don't think we ever would have stopped her."[3]

Despite this general pattern, however, many more women than men spoke of difficulties in obtaining parental approval to go south, and unlike men volunteers, women were not allowed to work on any COFO or FDP project without parental approval if they were under twenty-one years old.[4] This also held true for the more conservative, and therefore perhaps less threatening, SCLC-sponsored SCOPE projects. Indeed, many men and women volunteers echoed the views of one self-described "conservative" SCOPE woman: " ... most of ... [my girl friends] ... believe in what I'm doing! A lot of them would be here with me, but their parents won't let them."[5] When another woman explained her troubles in obtaining permission from her parents, she articulated what many more women implied, "My parents rather looked askance. It was not a woman's place really."[6]

Two examples of absolute parental disapproval of their daugh-

ters' involvement in the Mississippi Summer Project illustrate the
degree to which a few parents, black and white, were willing to
fight their daughters' decisions to go south. Cleveland Sellers, a
young black SNCC worker, recalls in his autobiography how very
determined two black mothers were that their daughters, Carol
Martin and Doris Wilkerson, not go to work in the Mississippi
Summer Project. The "well-dressed" mothers hit Sellers and
demanded their daughters get their belongings and leave with
them. Their daughters refused:

The girls and their mothers argued back and forth while the rest of us
listened. When Stokely tried to act as a mediator, one of the women told
him to "shut up" and mind his own business. After a few moments, the
girls' mothers asked them to walk down the street where they could talk in
privacy. They walked about a half-block before resuming the argument.
The women did most of the talking.

When the mothers realized that their daughters were not going to abide by
their wishes, they hailed a passing police car and told the officer that the
girls were runaways. The officer informed the mothers that there was
nothing he could do after he found out that the girls were . . . too old to be
considered juveniles.

The girls returned to the porch while their mothers were talking to the
policeman. Their mothers followed and issued the ultimate parental threat:
"If you don't come home with us tonight, don't come home at all. If you go
to Mississippi with *these* people, you can consider yourselves homeless!"
The girls stood fast. . . . [7]

A white mother similarly determined to keep her daughter from
going to Mississippi kept up a reign of harassment even while her
daughter was in Oxford at orientation. Many years later her daughter wrote:

Every night in complete fear and anguish I waited to see my mother on the
|TV| screen. She had sent me a telegram signed with my brother's name
saying that she had had a heart attack and I must come home immediately
(none of this was true). Telephone calls, with her screaming, threatening,
crying until I hung up, came every day. Long vituperative letters came
from her for me. After the phone calls I would disappear into the ladies'
room, and cry out the engulfing rage and accumulated frustration. When I
recovered, I desperately threw cold water on my face as it was rather well
advertised that there were psychiatrists around looking for people show-

ing signs of breaking down in the face of the project and who thus should be weeded out before they got to Mississippi. Mississippi had nothing over a Jewish mother, and I had conscious fear of some unseen psychiatrist spotting me red-eyed and misinterpreting the source of my difficulty.[8]

Black or white, Jewish or Protestant, parents seemed to resist their daughters' involvement more than their sons', although most parents ended by supporting all their children.[9]

As a result of these obstacles, women volunteers often had to be more motivated than men and felt they especially had to prove their political worth. In the main, they were more qualified in terms of previous social-action work and tended to have more direct political expertise than their male counterparts. When divided according to sex, 1965 FDP volunteers show a significantly different pattern of previous political activity. Four out of five FDP women had been "very active" in the movement, which is defined as having affiliation with a civil rights group and participating in direct-action demonstrations. By contrast only three out of five men fit that category. It was almost twice as likely, however, for an FDP man to have been only "moderately active," defined as having attended some meetings or gathered money, than an FDP woman, and it was more than three times as likely that an FDP man had had no previous civil rights activity than it was for an FDP woman. Women volunteers, then, consistently had substantially more civil rights experience, and it was also generally of a more radical nature than their male colleagues' experience.[10]

This prior activity manifested itself in women's southern work. Interviewed in 1965, Alvin Poussaint, a black psychiatrist who worked with the civil rights movement, had a "general impression" that " . . . white girls are more militant. . . . they seem to be right in there."[11] Their prior activity and possibly greater militance are indicators of the strong motivation that women had to have to overcome the barriers to their participation in the Freedom Summers.[12]

Additionally, some women indicated that their motivation to go south for these projects lay partially in their realization that, as women, they had only a short time to act on their political beliefs physically. In America in 1964 it was assumed that middle-class women would be "settled" before their early twenties were past.

Women of this class could certainly go to college and they could even work for a while, but there was a clear expectation that these were but phases in a woman's life, filling in the blanks before her true vocation of marriage and raising a family began. With an uneasy bow to that tradition, a substantial number of women volunteers discussed the necessity for them to go south at that time, since they had "no obligations," were not married, and had no family.[13] By contrast, few men mentioned freedom from family ties as a reason for being in the South. Women volunteers saw their lack of family ties as something unique about them, which enabled them to act on their beliefs and which differentiated them from other women their age. Thus a woman volunteer said, after the usual reasons, " . . . you see, I went because it was very easy for me to go: I have money of my own, so I don't have to work; I have no husband to consult; I have no degree to finish. . . . "[14] The more radical women volunteers, particularly FDP women, articulated this lack of ties and sense of urgency more than the moderates. It may be that their very involvement in direct political action and their commitment to far-ranging social change posed conflicts with the major role they saw for themselves and so led to this perception of their situation.

Women volunteers often saw themselves as very different from their old friends who were locked into a traditional female role. At the time, however, none voiced a radical challenge to, or seemed to discard, the ultimate inevitability of the traditional wife-mother role. Instead, many of the women appeared confused and ambivalent about what they would ultimately do, expressing with great pain their alienation from what they considered the norm. In a long 1965 interview an FDP woman, who throughout the rest of the interview was poised, committed, and articulate, verbally fell apart when she discussed how she differed from her friends:

The whole, my whole life, I mean, I guess I'm exaggerating a little, but I mean our lives are that different and they do, I think they would think I was absolutely crazy. . . . they didn't think I was, I was even that wise in finishing college, you know. They thought it would have been smarter to go out and find a husband instead. . . . they're all married.[15]

Although men volunteers, especially the radicals, expressed alienation from nine-to-five "establishment" or businessman's occupations, they rarely were ambivalent about what they would do instead. Since men in American society are socialized to view their occupation, rather than their role in a family-unit, as their life work, male volunteers escaped the pain many women experienced precisely because they could discard, and in some cases radically challenge their proposed life work. They saw many occupational avenues for social action open after they rejected "establishment nine-to-fivism." Most of the women were not so lucky. Without easily visible alternative avenues, it was much more difficult to avoid the prescribed role of wife and mother. And so, one woman volunteer, who in 1971 was trying to remember, said, "it seemed back then that life was so short for me, I had to act then, before everything was over and closed in on me. I didn't question it at the time."[16]

When the volunteers, both male and female, arrived in the South, they found themselves in projects in which the social structure of American society was turned on its head. In general, young black men and then black women held the power and status in the project and, in most cases, considerably below them were white men and then white women. In a few projects, due to the individuals involved, the women shared some of the men's status, though they rarely shared their power, unless they ran their own project without male staff members.[17] The racial dynamics changed only very infrequently when, in response to some particular tension, the men would bond, black and white together, in a controlling position over the women, who remained divided.

The black-white divisions in the projects became more pronounced as southern civil rights work continued. Particularly in 1965 the concepts of local control and self-determination assured the extension of the racial divisions within the project and depended on the expansion of black-controlled organizing in the community. Working in projects with the usual structure of black men and black women in control was an education in itself, particularly for the men volunteers. While most volunteers at the time saw the black and white positions in the structure, few identified the male and female dynamics.

During both summers, women volunteers did all kinds of work, but in 1964 in Mississippi, when the projects tended to be more structured, women were generally cast in traditional women's jobs.

They were most often Freedom School teachers or project office workers, and they were dedicated to their work. A Freedom School teacher wrote home, not untypically, telling about her hopes and beliefs:

> . . . I have set as my goals for the summer to be the best teacher possible and the best follower possible. Never having been a follower, this of course has been hard! . . .
>
> . . . There is so much in my head and heart that I want to say but cannot, It has been a big week filled with so much enthusiasm and love that I feel overwhelmed. The girls I work with who range from 15–25 years of age have accepted me completely. They have told me this in the way they have responded in class, and some have told me this directly in their essays they have written me or in actual conversations. . . . this abundance of love and gratitude and acceptance makes me feel so humble and so happy. I wish you could meet and see the ways some of my girl's faces shine when we talk. And I wish you could see how hard they work and how much they want to be part of the movement. . . . I wish you could see their smiles and you could hear the excitement in their voices because they have now met white people who not only see them as equals but care enough to risk their lives to share their knowledge with them. . . .
>
> There is no doubt in my mind this is worth dying for. . . . this love is growing every day and will continue to expand and expand until it defeats all hate all over the world.[18]

Unlike Freedom School teaching, which most women enjoyed, office assignments often disappointed women volunteers, since fieldwork was where the action was and held a higher status. Nevertheless, unromantic office work was crucial to the running of the projects, and many women performed tirelessly in those jobs. A volunteer assigned to communications in the main COFO office chronicled her situation:

> This office is almost beyond description. Hot . . . very full of people doing very important things apparently without any order. The office is one long room partitioned by plaster board. No windows! Perspiration runs down the back of my legs at 4:00 AM! Plywood desks are nailed to the walls around the room. Dogs, paper, pop bottles, glasses, newspapers and people are strewn everywhere. A visitor would see no order in the madness, but it is there. . . .
>
> I am very happy tonight, though I have had no sleep in 2 days, hardly, and

only one meal today. We in communications have the responsibility of running the telephone system and handling the press, knowing where everyone in the state is. We are the security system. The FBI, local police, Justice Dept., press from around the nation are our constant 'phone companions'. . . . I am now chief WATS [Wide Area Telephone Service] operator. . . .
This evening I happened to be the one who answered the phone to hear "emergency" from Moss Point. One more incident you will see in the morning paper about the "battle for civil rights in Mississippi." The strange thing is that even here in the heart of the organization and of the state, I have a hard time believing what really goes on. . . . [19]

Office workers in projects in the field often echoed the feeling of distance the communications worker expressed; however, they continued to handle the phone, type, and mimeograph for others in the field.

In a kind of middle ground between teaching and full-time office work, community center positions, especially librarian-cum-social workers, tended to be solely a woman's prerogative. In sharp distinction, relatively few women in 1964 were assigned full-time to voter registration, though many occasionally canvassed part time after their other jobs were finished for the day. During the 1964 summer, no women were assigned to canvas sharecroppers who lived on plantations, for instance, because plantation canvassing was viewed as an almost paramilitary venture, and each episode was seen as an assault on a prominent and powerful white citizen's "land and people." White women volunteers were also not sent to especially dangerous towns, like McComb, Mississippi, which took the 1964 summer record for local bombings. When integrated teams were needed in particularly dangerous areas to show the movement's dedication to "black and white together," those teams were always male.[20]

Although the prohibition on white women in particularly dangerous areas or jobs was primarily to protect the women volunteers, it also served to protect the projects themselves. As Dave Dennis noted in 1965, white southerners often became enraged at seeing white women with black men. Thus, projects integrated both racially and sexually sometimes were attacked or harassed at least partially because white women and black men and, to a lesser extent, black women and white men were working together, not solely because they were doing civil rights work. Conversely and paradoxically, sometimes having women, white or black, on a picket line or on a voter registration team inhibited violence against the men, because of the more general social inhibitions against public violence against women. Women in general were less likely than men in general to experience violence for their civil rights work, and white women were less likely than black women to be attacked or arrested by southern whites.[21]

While no women were killed in Mississippi in 1964 and considerably fewer women were beaten or arrested than men, Cleveland Sellers recounted an incident that was typical of the type of verbal and psychological abuse that white women volunteers endured and inspired from white southern men. On the way home from a Freedom rally, three cars of civil rights workers were followed and then stopped by a Marshall County sheriff in Oxford, Mississippi's university town. A crowd of about 250 whites gathered while the sheriff questioned the three black male drivers. After he finished, he called out of one of the cars a young white woman, Kathy Kuntsler, daughter of civil rights lawyer William Kuntsler. The sheriff questioned her about her background in a loud voice so the crowd could hear. Then he started baiting her:

"Which one of them coons is you fuckin'?" The crowd roared its approval of the question. "Slut, I know you fuckin' them niggers. Why else would you be down heah? Which one is it? If you tell me the truth, I'll let you go. Which one is it?"

Throughout this interrogation, Kuntsler seemed calm, though frightened. Finally the sheriff let them all go yelling:

"Take your white whores and get the hell out of Oxford!" . . . "If'n I ketch anyone of you heah again, um gonna see to it that you git a quick trip to hell."

The incident was not finished, however, because the group was followed and chased. Dangerously breaking through a road block, all three cars eventually made it back to Holly Springs project without injury. In this case it seems that the presence of white women made the sheriff more abusive. On the other hand, it is possible to speculate that more physical violence might have happened without the presence of women.[22]

Women volunteers, then, were typically assigned to teaching, office, and community center work for several reasons. First, of course, those were women's "traditional" jobs, and the COFO staff seemed not to question sexual stereotypes in job assignments.[23] Additionally, however, especially in 1964, COFO wanted to keep women out of the more dangerous jobs, to protect both the individual women and their male colleagues from white southern violence. By 1965 in the FDP project there were many more women canvassers and even some women union organizers of women laundry workers. This seeming enlargment of roles for women was due mainly to the concept of local control coupled with the logistics of running smaller projects, which meant that most volunteers did several tasks. It did not represent a conscious expansion of women's work in the movement.

The SCOPE projects were different because they were more often focused primarily on voter registration. SCOPE workers rarely tried community organizing or freedom schools; therefore, both men and women canvassed, since that was essentially the sole job of a SCOPE worker. There is some evidence to suggest, however, that as in Mississippi, women routinely covered less dangerous areas than men, for the same reasons.[24]

In those projects located in Freedom Houses, women volunteers usually did the housework, too. Women particularly resented their role in the Freedom House, as one volunteer explained, "working with fifteen people, it takes one person almost all day just to cook and clean up, and do laundry, which is difficult. Especially the girls, we wound up doing much more work than the fellows did. We didn't come down here to work as a maid this summer. We came down to work in the field of civil rights."[25]

While women performed the menial work of the offices and Freedom Houses, they rarely made policy decisions, although decision making differed greatly from project to project. When time permitted, policy decisions seemed, in general, to be made by higher-level staff, who were mainly men. The more structured the project, the more this was true. In SCOPE projects decisions often were made almost unilaterally by the project leader or by SCLC staff itself, few of whom were women.[26] In contrast, some FDP groups in 1965 were so egalitarian in policy decisions that they were called the "freedom highs," though this again reflected the trend to local control, not the position of the volunteers.

All the northern volunteers arrived in the South besieged by many strange and difficult new experiences. The extreme poverty, established community racism, black staff suspicion, and power construct of the offices combined to make the volunteers' first days and weeks a continual test. But women volunteers had an additional problem that many simply did not know how to handle. They faced what two professional volunteers described as a "sexual test," which became a sort of "rite of passage" before women could be considered serious workers.[27] This test was whether or not women volunteers could deal with sexual advances from black men in the movement. While men and women volunteers generally accepted premarital sex, reflecting the attitude of their college colleagues, out of a desire to please the black community and to lessen the chances that projects would be attacked by southern racists, in every orientation session project leaders counseled volunteers to be discreet in their sex lives, if not to forego sexual activity for the duration.[28]

There were obviously several ways for women volunteers to deal with sexual advances. Some women simply accepted, and there was sometimes joy and freedom in that interracial sex, an exhilaration born of breaking the last major social barrier between the races. Interracial sex for some women took on a kind of totality of integration in their lives, which represented a unity of belief, work, and life. For others, sleeping with black men was a way to "prove" their "commitment" to black and white equality. And some women tried to demonstrate their liberalism in that way. It has also been suggested that white women expiated their "guilt" about racism by sleeping with black men. Indeed, black psychiatrist Alvin Poussaint found this a component in what he ironically (and cruelly) called "the White African Queen Complex."[29]

Whether women volunteers accepted or rejected the advances of black men, sex became the metaphor for racial tension, hostility, and aggression. Nearly every project had real problems with interracial sex, and many white women volunteers were in a painful double bind from the moment they arrived. One FDP woman advised:

I think that the white female should be very well prepared before she comes down here to be bombarded. And she also has to be well prepared to tell . . . [black men] to go to hell, and prepared to have them not give up. . . . I don't know from an intellectual point of view what the role of sex is. . . . I mean if you go into a community, they're going to be talking how you're going to bed with a Negro fellow . . . and the Negro fellows are going to be hitting on you too. . . . I think it's because, just because, you're white. . . . [30]

Another woman FDPer, who was very bitter, described her situation, "I've seen the Negro fellows run after white women. It's quite obvious that they're after a white woman, not this particular woman. And I'm quite disillusioned about that. . . . "[31] But it was not only a problem of the more radical projects, for a black staff member at the SCOPE orientation warned:

The only way or place a Negro man has been able to express his manhood is sexually and so you find a tremendous sexual aggressiveness. And I say, quite frankly, don't get carried away by it and don't get afraid of it either. I mean don't think it's because you're so beautiful and so ravishing that this man is enamored of you. It's not that at all. He's just trying to find his manhood. . . . so, in a sense, what passed itself off as desire quite often . . . is probably a combination of hostility and resentment, because he resents what the society has done to him, and he wants to take it out on somebody who symbolizes the establishment in that society. And at the same time it's a search for his own personhood, for his own freedom.[32]

It was this scarcely veiled hostility which troubled most of the women.

The woman who simply accepted the advances and "slept around" faced grave consequences, for ultimately she failed the "sexual test." In most cases she was written off as an ineffective worker, and she often became the focal point for a great deal of bitterness for the black women on the project. Additionally, her behavior was seen as scandalous by many within the black community, and this profoundly inhibited community organizing, one of the main goals of the projects. Finally, in some instances such open flouting of the prevailing mores physically endangered the project.[33] When that happened, the woman was usually chastised and in some cases sent home, while the man was rarely reprimanded. In one incident in 1964 a black man and a white woman had sexual relations in the man's car under a street light in a white section of Jackson, obviously jeopardizing themselves, the project, and the black community. The woman was sent home, and the man remained on the staff. When a woman professional volunteer complained, Staughton Lynd, the director of Freedom Schools, told her, "We just couldn't get along without Flukey, could we?"[34]

While many women volunteers had sexual relationships with black men, there were obvious pressures against such affairs. They were seen as disruptive to the projects and the community. Reflecting the consensus of civil rights workers, one white FDP woman earthily explained:

I think that people like that, if they come down just to screw around, they ought to stay up north. They can screw around in their own communities. It's going to hurt the Movement. I don't care if they screw around themselves, but it's going to hurt the Movement, and that's what I care about.[35]

It was not easy, however, to escape problems. Women who did not wish to become sexually involved—at least not with several men—faced a classic dilemma. Black men "in search of their manhood" were persistent and aggressive. If a woman refused them, they called her a racist, and she generally became a focus for the hostility of the black men on the project. Furthermore, "racist" was an exceedingly effective epithet: It was, quite simply, the worst thing a volunteer could be.

Accusations and verbal abuse were not the only pressure that women volunteers faced. Some white women were raped by black men in the movement.[36] In 1965 before the Jackson demonstrations, one black man, whose father had been shot by a white man and who was a long-time SNCC worker, violently attacked at least three women in one evening, though he was not successful in his attempt to rape them. As one of his victims explained,

. . . he had a real deep-seated emotional hatred . . . and bitterness against white people. So that he hated most of the girls who were white, and most of the guys who were white, but he took out his hatred on the girls. . . .

While she and her friends managed to avoid him in Jackson, a few weeks later they met him in Hattiesburg with another white woman volunteer.

... The three of us just looked at each other, and we just said to each other, "Somebody should warn her." So, when she came over ... to the cafe where we were ... we just said "really be careful. You know, like if you're going to go out with him, be sure that he doesn't get you alone, because he doesn't really like white girls, and he's got a real racism problem, and be careful around him, 'cause he might try to take it out on you the way he tried to take it out on us. ... if you don't want to get yourself involved in the same kind of fight that we had to, you know, protect yourself, like we had to do, stay with us rather than with him."

The young white woman volunteer ignored their advice and told the man what the women had said. He came back "absolutely furious" and began arguing with a male volunteer in their group but left just as it seemed a fight would begin. Unfortunately the next day, one of the young women met the SNCC worker, and he attacked her again.

... I was in a car with two white boys and we were going to the church after orientation session. The car broke down on a lonely road. The two boys walked down the road to a gas station, and phoned in to the church and said "can somebody come out and tow us in? And they said, we'll send somebody as soon as possible." Well, who came out, but my dear friend, who was very angry at me at that point. And I was sitting alone in that car. He came over, and he started cursing at me, and ... he said "Why did you do that?" And I said "You know very well why I did it. I did it because you attacked me and you attacked the other girls, and we feel that we don't like you for it, we don't like your ideas, we felt that it was only right to warn this girl of the danger." And I said "I don't like you, and I have every intention of doing it again if I see you with another girl who doesn't know what she's going out with. Until you learn to treat a woman as a woman, until you learn how to behave yourself ..." "and he got very angry at that. ... And he was holding a hatchet, and he said, "I'm going to whup you good." And I said, "Go right ahead." So he started hitting me over the head with the hatchet, and I put my hand up. And the hatchet had a case around it, but the case didn't cover the blade part, and the blade hit my hand, and my hand got cut open. That's really what happened. And by that time he was really furious, because he said "next time. . . . " The boys, the two boys, then started coming back to the car, and he put the chains on, and he said he wasn't going to tow me in town because I was a white bitch, you know, and then they finally talked him into towing us into town. And when we got back to the church, he walked up to me again, and he said, "When I get you alone again, I'm really going to beat you up good."

And at that point, I was really angry cause my hand was bleeding, and 'cause I was badly frightened. He is a lot bigger than I am, and I do feel that he is mentally imbalanced. . . . He's been so frustrated, that he can't take any kind of action in a constructive way any longer. He's just got to hit. And, as I say, this is not a general case. I really think he is emotionally disturbed, but his emotional disturbance is a result of what the white people have done to him. And you know . . . so what can I do?

The terrible irony of this case is that this woman volunteer was a fair-haired, fair-skinned woman whose father is black and whose mother is white. Because her parents did not want her and her sister, who looks black, to grow up with racism, they had lived in Europe until she was through high school.[37]

Women who did not wish to have casual sexual encounters evolved tactics of their own to deal with their situations. Married women had the least trouble avoiding casual encounters, if that was their choice. Nearly everyone seemed to see extramarital sex negatively (although it certainly went on), and married women could refuse sexual encounters without fear of being branded racist. One married volunteer explained:

. . . I'd seen a great deal of conflict between white girls and Negro guys. . . . I found once I was down here that being married, a lot of those problems were solved. But there is a tremendous amount of conflict between Negro boys who think that white girls owe it to them to sleep with them or to go out with them, and there's a good deal of competition among them. I found if I said I was married, there was this big thing about being married, and they'd say, "Okay, is that your husband? I'll go away."

She also believed that if white girls would just be "very firm and not get completely intimidated," they would then find working in the South easier.[38]

Obviously unmarried summer volunteers did not get married to avoid problems, but many found that attaching themselves "steadily" to one man served nearly the same function. One woman, who found, " . . . it took a little while . . . sort of building a reputation," said,

I find it's almost a necessity to associate yourself with one person, so the other people will not bother you as much if you have a boyfriend. . . . if you don't . . . then you're much more likely to be continually bothered. But if you have a boyfriend, particularly one that's nice and strong, he doesn't want . . . anyone bothering with his girlfriend, see. In a sense, you're in a better position.[39]

Certain projects were more troubled than others and, especially in 1965, some women switched to other projects to avoid problems. One woman volunteer moved to rural Sunflower County, because, "one had to put up with a lot of social difficulties in Jackson, and I didn't like that. And I felt that my rights were being encroached upon by other people. . . . I thought that I'd do better to work out of it."[40]

Sometimes, women simply put up with their situations and wrote out all their problems to special confidants in the North. This was not a viable alternative for most, however, because they needed immediate help and also, paradoxically, because their problems were too emotionally painful to verbalize. Most women volunteers were too involved in and dedicated to their projects to allow themselves to criticize the movement even to sympathetic outsiders. It was particularly rare for a white woman to complain in the case of real violence, like a rape or a beating, from a black man. Women in the movement who were in some way brutalized usually held a clear vision of what would happen to a black man accused of raping a white woman, even if she were a civil rights worker. The horror of the southern lynching tradition kept them silent.[41]

A more ordinary response than writing to outsiders was to find one other woman on the project in whom to confide. The two would help each other and talk over their mutual problems. Very rarely, a group of women would join together, but this seemed to happen only in extreme cases, like the one above, when there was a real possibility of physical violence toward one of the women. And the reasons for this were obvious: attaining civil rights for brutally oppressed southern blacks was the goal of the summer projects and was held firmly by most volunteers. Even when women believed they were not being treated fairly, their personal situations were never as bad in any dimension as the local blacks', and thus their own had to be a clearly secondary concern, in their view. For both men and women, the volunteers' life in the South *was* the movement, and nothing else was of comparable importance. In fact, it usually took an extreme incident or series of incidents before women would mention their perceptions of their subordinate position. Even then, they often obviously felt guilty or excused their complaints away later. To that extent, of course, women volunteers' southern experience inhibited female bonding and a growth of female consciousness, though it provided a shared experience from which some would later be able to begin to articulate a theory of feminist politics.

By far the most common response was to limit severely all social contact, and to practice a form of self-imposed celibacy. Rather like the Victorian women who asserted themselves by denying their sexuality, women volunteers who wanted to assert some control over their sex lives and also to obey the project rules often found themselves living completely (if temporarily) celibate lives. Only by sleeping with no one could women avoid, or lessen the impact of, the charge "racist." In interview after interview, women finally said: "I just cut myself off. I just didn't deal with it."[42] Or "I haven't had any real difficulties, primarily because I just sort of didn't get involved—I just stayed away as far as social life is concerned."[43] Or "I keep it down to a minimum. I don't go out that much."[44]

With these various tactics, women came through the rite of passage. Some ended their summer filled with bitterness, like the volunteer who talked about driving home from a mass meeting with some black men who, "were pretty much under the assumption that we [the volunteers] were all a bunch of bigots . . . and they were taking white girls to bed and started talking about how they were with this bitch or that bitch. You know there was no respect there, no nothing."[45] But most others ended their work pleased with the interracial friendships that they had made, once they had established themselves and passed the "sexual test."

White men volunteers also had a "sexual test" and were discouraged from "playing around" with black women, because of the havoc it wrought in the project.[46] Their experience was different from and less traumatic than white women's, however, because men were supposed, in general, to be the initiators in sexual relationships. They controlled the action and were therefore not as vulnerable to the charge of "racist" as white women were.

Once they passed the "sexual test," women volunteers performed their movement tasks well. Their very competence, as well-educated northerners, often in fact stood in the way of effectively developing indigenous leadership, which was one of the main goals of the Freedom Summers. In the specific case of women volunteers, however, their competence was often doubly resented because of their sex. One 1964 volunteer wrote home, exhibiting both an understanding of the problem and the patronizing attitude which so angered many local staff people:

> Several times I've had to completely re-do press statements or letters written by . . . [local staff]. . . . it's one thing to tell people who have come willingly to Freedom School that they needn't feel ashamed of weakness in these areas, but it's quite another to even acknowledge such weakness in one's fellow workers. Furthermore, I'm a northerner; I'm white; I'm a woman; I'm a college graduate; I've not proven myself yet in jail or in physical danger. . . . Every one of these things is a strike against me as far as they are concerned.[47]

However well deserved the anger directed at the volunteers may have been, white women volunteers found themselves again under double stress, as in the case of sexual relationships. They faced all of the justified suspicion and resentment white men volunteers faced as to their motives and ability, and they also faced hostility because they were women.

Additionally, women volunteers sometimes were scapegoats for black-white hostility in different projects.[48] One woman who worked mainly on the challenge in Washington, D.C., recalled,

> I always dreaded Saturday nights, because we'd all meet in our apartment and drink wine and then when the black guys got a little drunk, they'd pour out all their hatred—racial hatred—at us. But the white guys never got it—sometimes they'd join them—it was always directed at us "white bitches." I couldn't deal with it, not at all. It was just so painful. It tore me up inside.[49]

It was very hard for most women to admit this dilemma and this discrimination. During interviews conducted in the South in 1965 the examples were blurted out in response to unrelated questions, then generally as soon as they were voiced, the accusations were excused away by the interviewees.[50]

Although most women volunteers tried to ignore the sex discrimination, a few strong women dealt with it directly. Generally,
however, they saw the problem in individual terms and tried only
to change their position, not the position of women volunteers as a
whole. Thus, one FDP volunteer, whose high school had been the
Emma Willard Academy, told her story:

One thing I'm finding very difficult in Mississippi is being a northern white
girl, because people, you know, in the north we're used to some sort of
definite organization and people here—first of all, the men are mad
because you're a white girl, because white men have been messing around
with Negro women for so long that they don't really know how to react,
and they feel as if they can run roughshod over you, and this is a very big
hang-up over what to do about a white woman from the north. So one of
the things they do is they put her behind a desk and then get angry at her,
because she's trying to organize, or trying to do something. And they tell
her she's no good, because they can't cope with the black-white problem.
Yeah, and it's very, very strong; they may sort of feel that women are a
little brainless anyway. And I find I have to do twice as much to prove
myself, you know, first, just as a person, to get them to stop thinking about
my being white. It's very difficult. I find a lot of white people coming down
sort of cowered under these Negroes and they get stepped on. Somebody
was stepping on me, and somebody pointed it out to me that I should act
like a person and not like a coward, you know. I did. . . . I just stood up and
said, "cut this out! You can't boss me around just because I'm a woman!"
And I stood up and was a person. I'm me. And people started accepting
me, but it's very difficult.[51]

Black women, staff and volunteers, obviously did not have to
deal with racial resentment from black men, and they were perhaps in a better position to examine sex discrimination than white
women volunteers. Additionally, those long-term white women
staff members, who had years before passed the sexual test, and
were seen as powerful insiders, were also able to begin to question
women's position within the movement, especially since the influx
of white women volunteers made the disparities between men's
and women's experiences clearer than ever.

Within this context, the first analysis of sex discrimination in
SNCC came at the November 1964 staff retreat held to reevaluate
the organization. The major topics of discussion were the future of
SNCC and the role of whites in southern civil rights work, but
additionally an anonymous staff woman, widely assumed at the

time to be Ruby Doris Smith Robinson, wrote a "SNCC Position Paper: Women in the Movement" for the group's consideration in a workshop. The memo began with a list of eleven transgressions by men in SNCC, including several instances of women being excluded from decision-making bodies within the organization and COFO, women being held responsible for office work and minutes taking, experienced women being underutilized in fieldwork, and women being primarily identified as "girls" rather than individuals.

Acknowledging that the "list will seem strange to some, petty to others, laughable to most," the author went on to analyze the problem of women's position and held it was analogous to the position of black people in white society. As the "average white person doesn't realize that *he assumes he is superior,*" and " . . . doesn't understand the problem of paternalism. So too the average SNCC worker finds it difficult to discuss the woman problem because of the assumption of male superiority. Assumptions of male superiority are as widespread and deep rooted and every much as crippling to the woman as the assumptions of white supremacy are to the Negro." She explained that the paper was anonymous, because of the " . . . insinuations, ridicule, and over-exaggerated compensation" which would ensue if her identity were known: "Nothing so final as being fired or outright exclusion, but the kinds of things which are killing to the insides. . . . " After more scrutiny of the problems, she concluded:

Maybe the only thing that can come out of this paper is discussion— amidst the laughter—but still discussion. (Those who laugh the hardest are often those who need the crutch of male supremacy the most.) And maybe some women will begin to recognize day to day discrimination and start the slow process of changing values and ideas so that all of us gradually come to understand that this is no more a man's world than it is a white world.[52]

Her paper did cause a great deal of laughter and some discussion. At the formal meeting to consider it, Stokely Carmichael is supposed to have said, "The position of women in SNCC should be prone," which cut off more debate, though the minutes of the staff retreat reported the workshop seriously.[53] While the movement was not a uniformly hospitable and supportive environment for assessing sex discrimination, black women in SNCC and long-term white staff women were pushed to analyze their position in the civil rights movement precisely because the large numbers of white women volunteers and the increased racial tensions made sex roles, racism, and sexuality stand out in unavoidable stark relief. As one young black woman mused in 1965:

> The Movement is in worse shape now than a year ago. There's conflict between black and white on the staff. Negroes are not prepared for whites coming down. It takes on a sex thing. Most of the Negro men never have been close to a white girl before. . . . [54]

This beginning analysis of institutional sexism came from black women who did not have to wade through charges of racism and from long-term white staff women who had years before dealt with sexual advances and who saw their hard-fought place in the movement slipping away as a result of the Freedom Summers. For a brief time, they tried to deal with the issue head-on, together as a group, unlike the few volunteers who tried to find individual solutions. The sexism that permeated the southern movement was seen and felt so clearly by all women staff, black and white, that no one ever challenged the assumption that the outspoken veteran SNCC organizer Ruby Doris Smith Robinson, a black woman, actually wrote the memo, and she never publicly denied writing it before her tragic and untimely death from cancer in 1967. In fact, however, Casey Hayden and Mary King, long-term white SNCC staff workers, wrote the memo from a discussion group that Robinson organized.[55]

While a few black and white women staff members identified themselves as a group with interests occasionally in conflict with black men, young black women in the movement did not generally join with northern white women in any effort to overcome sexist practices. When there were sexual problems on a project, for the most part young black women remained bitterly divided from white women, whom they saw as stealing their men.[56] As a black SNCC staff woman recounted in 1965:

> Sex is one thing; The Movement is another. And the two shouldn't mix. There's an unhealthy attitude in The Movement toward sex. The Negro girls feel neglected because the white girls get the attention. The white

girls are misused. There are some hot discussions at staff meetings.[57]

The "hot discussions" continued, since in every project black men were pursuing white women volunteers, often with great success, and competent black women felt they were "in some category other than female."[58]

The divisions over sex ultimately meant that all women, black and white, staff and volunteer, could not unite in the civil rights movement to work on problems that were common to them as women. It also meant that the hurt some black women felt as a result of their experiences with white women volunteers would remain long after the Freedom Summers were over.

Exemplifying the kind of long-term effects the summer projects spawned, even among sophisticated movement veterans, Ruby Doris Smith Robinson spoke of her feelings to a white woman interviewer in 1967:

Well, to be honest, I think a lotta white women are screwed up terribly, but . . . that's their problem. I don't worry much about them. I spent three years hatin' white women so much it nearly made me crazy. It came from discovering how the whole world had this white idea of beauty. See, the western world concept of beauty is *your* kind of beauty, not mine. You can't find my African kind of beauty—I mean thick lips and kinky hair—in a picture anywhere except a little bit lately with fashion models. But the ads and all that—they still think in terms of narrow noses and light skin and straight hair. Most Negro women straighten their hair and they're going right on with it. Bleaching cream still sells in the stores. And I mean, I just hated it so much that for three years I wouldn't speak to a white woman.

And then I realized what I was doing to myself. I was losing my self-respect and even losing my looks. I finally had to work myself out of it. I had to find a new sense of my own dignity, and what I really had to do was start *seeing* all over again, in a new way. . . . [59]

Robinson's experience, though certainly sad, was not unusual. What makes her story especially poignant, however, is that she led the first women's sit-in against discrimination by the male SNCC hierarchy and clearly saw the dynamics of male-female power relationships in the organization. One can speculate that if she had to spend years unraveling the psychic damage derived at least in part from working in the integrated southern civil rights movement, it is possible that other women, without her vision, had an even harder time.

In this study of women volunteers in the South, perhaps the most difficult task has been to convey the throbbing pain in many of the interviews. Black women felt invalidated when black men sought white women. White women volunteers often felt used and treated unfairly, but they were too vulnerable to challenge their situation. They also were unable for the most part to see themselves as a group. While the inequality of men and women in most projects played havoc with attempts to gain racial equality, perhaps more importantly in personal terms it placed a tremendous burden on young black and white women, which few were able to overcome easily. And with that, the possibilities for sisterhood and brotherhood on the projects were greatly diminished.

The concept of institutional sexism aids in understanding women's daily life in the movement. Job assignments and responsibilities were clearly sex-role stereotyped. Women volunteers were under double jeopardy for competent performance of their jobs and often caught full-force hostility generated against all whites but vented only on them. In terms of interpersonal dynamics black and white women alike were dehumanized and objectified by black and white men unable to escape their sexism in just the same way that white volunteers unconsciously carried their racism with them to the South. The tensions between black men and women and white women were impossible to overcome without an analysis of sexism in society and the sexism of the projects in particular. Indeed, at the time it was impossible for most of the people who worked in the South to realize what was happening. While both black and white together, in their finer moments, tried to show the nation what true racial equality could be, it did not occur to those involved to strive for sexual equality as well. The Freedom Summers tried to bring black Americans into the mainstream of American society, but they never questioned the unequal status of men and women in that society.

NOTES

1. To understand women volunteers' continuing activities after they left the South, see chap. 8 and Sara Evans, *Personal Politics: The Roots of*

Women's Liberation in the Civil Rights Movement and the New Left (New York: 1979). Evans began with the fact of women's liberation and then traced its roots. In doing so, she interviewed nine women whose papers I have examined because they were volunteers. Additionally, I know from interviews and correspondence that at least twenty more women whose papers I examined or whom I interviewed are or have been active in women's liberation. The major difference between Evans' and my work is where we start our analysis. The most important women from the southern civil rights movement in the early days of women's liberation were women like Mary King and Casey Hayden, white southern women who were powerful SNCC staff members on the inside. Though some women volunteers went on in the North to become seasoned organizers, I have analyzed women volunteers only in the context of their work, experiences, and perceptions of the Freedom Summers.

2. KZSU Interview 0042, p. 6, CORE. In general, citations for this section refer to specific illustrative quotations only.

3. SHSW: Elizabeth Sutherland Prs.: "Uncatalogued and Unused Letters," Copy of article from the *Sunnyvale Standard*, untitled and undated [July 1964].

4. Jan Hillegas Prs.: "SNCC Executive Committee Meeting," April 10, 1964, Atlanta, p. 5.

5. KZSU Interview 0228, p. 6, SCOPE.

6. KZSU Interview 9003, p. 3, FDP.

7. Sellers and Terrell, *The River of No Return*, pp. 79-80.

8. Melish, "Memoir," pp. 83-84.

9. See especially Sutherland, *Letters*, pp. 25-30, and SHSW: Elizabeth Sutherland Prs.: "Uncatalogued and Unused Letters."

10. FDP Compilation, COFO Files, Delta Ministry Collection. See also KZSU Interviews; COFO staff mimeos, Spring 1964 (series).

11. KZSU Interview 9408, p. 13, MCHR.

12. Given the obstacles to their participation, one would expect that fewer women than men would go south and, in absolute numbers, that is true. However, the contention that women were underrepresented might be questioned on the grounds that while 46 percent of the 1964 COFO volunteers, 46 percent of the 1965 SCOPE volunteers, and 44 percent of the 1965 FDP volunteers were women, the proportion of women throughout the United States undergraduate population in 1965 was 40 percent. The real question is, however, "what was the proportion of women in the applicant pool?" And that answer cannot be precisely determined. For example, especially in 1965, northern campus Friends of SNCC groups acted as recruiting organizations and screening agents for volunteers. Women certainly were a large majority of the members of F-SNCC groups

at the Universities of Washington, Wisconsin, California at Berkeley, and Stanford, as well as in Boston. For FDP workers, F–SNCC groups constituted the single most important applicant pool, so women volunteers may well have been underrepresented given an F–SNCC-based pool. Another problem is determining what the 1965 ratio of men to women undergraduates of the upper middle class was. Again, there is some evidence that daughters of upper-middle-class families are educated in more equal numbers than daughters of middle-class and lower-class families. Since the overwhelming majority of volunteers came from the upper middle class, the applicant pool may not be accurately reflected by the lower percentage of women in the total undergraduate population. The problem is a thorny one and not readily solved. Sources for the percentage of COFO volunteers, SCOPE volunteers, FDP volunteers, and 1965 undergraduates are: COFO Address List, COFO Files, Delta Ministry; Aiken et al., *Dynamics of Idealism*, p. 25; FDP Compilation; COFO Files, Delta Ministry; and U.S. Bureau of the Census, *Statistical Abstracts of the United States*, 94th ed. (Washington: 1973), p. 132.

13. KZSU Interviews 1361, p. 2, FDP; p. 6, FDP. Interviews: Donna Goodman, November 30, 1971, Seattle, Wash.; Miriam Feingold Stein, April 1975, San Francisco.

14. KZSU Interview 0242, p. 1, FDP.

15. KZSU Interview 9002, p. 11, FDP.

16. Interview: Donna Goodman.

17. For an example of a black woman's autonomy and power as project director in Bolivar County, Miss., see Cynthia Washington, "We Started at Different Ends of the Spectrum," *Southern Exposure* 4, no. 4 (Winter 1977): 14–15.

18. SHSW: Elizabeth Sutherland Prs.: "Uncatalogued and Unused Letters," Pam |Parker| to Parents, "Dear Mom and Dad," Saturday |July 1964|, pp. 2–3.

19. Sutherland, *Letters*, pp. 182–83.

20. Interviews: Sally Shideler, February 17, 1967, Seattle, Wash., Otis Pease, February 13, 1967, and March 23, 1967, Seattle, Wash.; Melish, *Memoir*; Carter, *So the Heffners Left McComb*, passim.

21. Mississippi Summer Project: Running Summary of Incidents, in possession of the author; Interviews: KZSU Interviews; Miriam Feingold Stein; Gary Good; Sally Shideler.

22. Sellers and Terrell, *River of No Return*, pp. 100–3.

23. Clayborne Carson Papers: Memo 24, "SNCC Position Paper (Women in the Movement)": undated |November 1964|. I am indebted to Clay Carson for sharing this memo with me.

24. KZSU Interviews: Groups 18 and 20. Interviews: Miriam Feingold

Stein; Donna Goodman; Sally Shideler; Liz Fusco Papers, in possession of author.

25. KZSU Interviews 0275, p. 13, SCOPE.

26. Of those SCOPE projects interviewed by KZSU, none had women project directors. The main SCLC staff in Atlanta was primarily male.

27. Interview: Florence Howe and Paul Lauter, June 28, 1972, Seattle, Wash. I am indebted to Howe and Lauter for their frank discussion of sexual tensions on the projects and for their encouragement of this undertaking.

28. Robert C. Sorensen, "Adolescent Sexuality in Contemporary America," *Woman's Day*, March 1973, pp. 73-74, 196-197; Nathaniel Wagner, Department of Obstetrics and Gynecology, University of Washington, unpublished studies; SHSW: Lise Vogel Prs.: Lise Vogel, "Notes at 1964 Orientation for MSP"; KZSU Interviews: FDP Orientation, 0132; SCOPE Orientation, 0099; Sally Belfrage, *Freedom Summer* (New York: 1965), p. 19.

29. Alvin Poussaint, "The Stresses of the White Female Workers in the Civil Rights Movement in the South," *American Journal of Psychiatry* 123, no. 4 (October 1966): 401-7. Dr. Poussaint in this article accurately describes the hostility between black women and men and white women. I think he deals unfairly with white women, however. While black men are excused from aggressive and hostile acts because of their historical experience, white women are not extended the same understanding and compassion. Instead, he sees all of the tensions as the result of white women working in the South. They are the instigators by their very presence, and in his final analysis, he identified "many" as having what he calls the "White African Queen Complex," which is meant to be as derogatory as it sounds. Although I found some women who perhaps fit that "complex," I found none who exhibited those traits in a vacuum. Just as black men had their historical reasons for their hostility—which I think if anything Poussaint downplays—those white women could not escape their historical experience either. More importantly, however, I found most of the white women I studied caught in a horrendous double bind: They could be sex objects or they could be labeled racists. Poussaint seems to have little understanding of the viciousness of that bind.

30. KZSU Interview 0365, p. 36, FDP.

31. KZSU Interview 9006, p. 20, FDP.

32. KZSU Interview 0099, pp. 2-3, SCOPE.

33. Ibid., p. 3, SCOPE; Sellers and Terrell, *The River of No Return*, pp. 95-96; Interviews: Florence Howe; Donna Goodman; Miriam Feingold Stein; Jody Aliesan, Seattle, Wash.

34. Interview: Florence Howe.

35. KZSU Interview 0360, p. 19, FDP.

36. KZSU Interviews: 9009, pp. 9–12, FDP; 9007, pp. 19–20, FDP. Alice Walker, "Advancing Luna—and Ida B. Wells," *Ms.*, July 1977, pp. 75–79, 93–97; Confidential Interviews, 1972–1978.

37. KZSU Interview 9009, p. 1–15.

38. KZSU Interview 0325, pp. 1–2, FDP.

39. KZSU Interview 0365, p. 37, FDP.

40. KZSU Interview 9003, p. 10, FDP.

41. Walker, "Advancing Luna–Ida B. Wells," pp. 78–79; KZSU Interviews 9006, 9009, FDP; Interviews: Donna Goodman, Confidential Interviews.

42. Interview: Donna Goodman.

43. KZSU Interview 9006, p. 19, FDP.

44. KZSU Interview 0364, p. 37, FDP.

45. KZSU Interview 9006, p. 19, FDP.

46. KZSU Interview 0099, p. 3, SCOPE; KZSU Interviews: Group 2.

47. Sutherland, *Letters*, p. 185.

48. Poussaint, "Stresses," pp. 402, 405, KZSU Interviews: 9006, pp. 19–20; 9009, pp. 9–12, FDP.

49. Interview: Donna Goodman. This is one of the few instances where black men and white men bonded together, in this case to attack white women verbally.

50. In none of the KZSU Interviews were sex or sexual relationships specifically asked about. The question "Are there any black-white problems in your project?" however, often unleashed torrents of information that centered on sexual problems and discrimination.

51. KZSU Interview 0138, p. 11, FDP.

52. Clayborne Carson Papers, Stanford, Calif.: Memo 24: "SNCC Position Paper (Women in the Movement)," anonymous, undated [November 1964]. Underlining in original memo.

53. For a description of the meeting and Carmichael, see Julius Lester, *Revolutionary Notes* (New York: 1969), pp. 132–35. See also UCLA, "Special Collection on the Civil Rights Struggle and Black Movement in the United States, 1950 to 1970," XI: Mississippi, folder B, Item 51: "Summary of Staff Retreat Minutes," p. 1. I do not know if the secretary who wrote the minutes was a woman, but it is likely that it was.

54. Jacobs and Landau, *The New Radicals*, p. 145.

55. Evans, *Personal Politics*, pp. 84–85. See also chap. 4, entire, and Washington, "We Started at Different Ends of the Spectrum," pp. 14–15. KZSU Interview 0405, FDP, discusses Dona Richards' well-developed feminism.

56. Poussaint, "Stresses," p. 403; KZSU Interview 0099, p. 3, SCOPE.

57. Jacobs and Landau, *The New Radicals*, p. 145.

58. Washington, "We Started at Different Ends of the Spectrum," p. 14. See Calvin Hernton, *Sex and Racism in America* (New York: 1964), especially pp. 57–85 and 123–68; William H. Grier and Price M. Cobbs, *Black Rage* (New York: 1968), especially pp. 32–62.

59. Josephine Carson, *Silent Voices: The Southern Negro Woman Today* (New York: 1969), pp. 254–55.

6

TO OPEN A NEW COUNTY:
A VOLUNTEER FAILS

Throughout the South, dedicated civil rights workers slowly
opened new communities to movement organization, providing a small community base on which to develop full-scale projects. This phase of civil rights work began in the early 1960s. In
Mississippi, for example, the NAACP had had a statewide organization prior to the student movement, and there were also various
local voter groups, but the direct confrontation associated with the
student civil rights movement did not exist until Robert Moses of
SNCC arrived in 1961.

This slow and dangerous work of extending the movement continued in the South from 1961 at least until 1967. The most successful projects of the Freedom Summers were organized in counties that had been opened sometime before the two summers, but a
small and generally unknown group of volunteers continued this
work well after the first summer project began. At the end of 1964
many counties still had no movement organization at all. Only
twenty-eight of the eighty-two counties in Mississippi, for instance,
had formal community projects.[1] This was the case, in varying
degrees, throughout the South.

Opening a new county was the movement in microcosm. The
assignment was a composite of many jobs and included all of the
individual tasks that the volunteers performed in 1964 and 1965:
voter education, voter registration, and community organization.

Volunteers rarely did this work because it was so hard and discouraging and because people usually needed prior experience in organizing communities. With little guarantee of success, however, in 1965 a few volunteers were delegated to attempt to open new counties.

Jerry Johnson[2] was one of those 1965 volunteers assigned to open a new county. This story is unique, but with minor variations it could in a very real sense be the story of almost any worker assigned the task of gathering a small group of blacks together to build a community base for the movement. The greatest problem that these workers faced was harassment and violence from the white community. When blacks succumbed to fear of white reprisals, workers like Jerry inevitably became discouraged and disheartened. These themes of harassment, fear, and discouragement were constant, but their relative strength varied in each case. In this regard, then, Jerry's story is peculiarly his own.

Jerry Johnson went to Mississippi in September 1965 and stayed there until December. His background was in the mainstream of northern volunteers, and he conformed to the volunteers' group profile remarkably well.

Jerry was born and raised in Washington State and lived in small towns until he went to college. His father was a brakeman for the railroad, and his mother was a first grade teacher. He had one sister older than he. Due to his father's long hours and his parents' joint income, they were in an upper-middle-class income bracket, although they held "workers' ideals" and consistently favored social welfare legislation. They both regularly voted for candidates of the Democratic Party, but neither was active politically.

Jerry's mother was an active member of the Lutheran church, and throughout his childhood Jerry went to church and Sunday school. Jerry himself claimed, "It was mostly a social thing. You know, meet the girls and things."[3]

Jerry had a fairly happy upbringing. He described his family as "very loving." His parents were relatively permissive followers of Dr. Spock. Neither he nor his sister was ever physically punished at home, and he felt this predisposed him to nonviolence and pacifism. He always did well in school both academically and athletically and was always slated to go to college. Both he and his parents thought he would be a dentist, but when he left for Mississippi, he was a junior in sociology.

At age eighteen Jerry enrolled at Seattle University on a basket-ball scholarship. He first became interested in civil rights there because a teammate of his was a Mississippi black. Through his new friend, Jerry became interested in the movement and the lot of the southern black. The next year he transferred to the University of Washington. He joined Friends of SNCC and the Civil Rights Action Group (CRAG), a local organization interested in establishing equal rights in the Seattle area. He began to read everything he could find on blacks and said, " . . . I started identify-ing with the Negro was what happened to me, I became more Negro than most Negroes in the Seattle area. . . . "[4]

In direct proportion to his growing commitment, his relationship with his parents deteriorated. He said he was "in a state of rebel-lion."[5] CRAG protested police brutality, and when Jerry participated in the demonstrations, his father wondered if he was becoming a Communist. Jerry felt he had to change his parents' view of life. Although they believed in the southern blacks' cause, he said, "It evolved to the point that we couldn't talk about Negroes in our house. . . . it always ended in an argument."[6]

After his second year, Jerry finally decided that he had to go south.

It was like a driving force! After awhile, after you've read about it so much and you take part in the North . . . you have to go down. You just feel this is the *biggest* thing in your life; you've committed your life to it.[7]

He worked during the summer of 1965 in order to earn enough money to go.

When Jerry told his parents he was going south, they had ambivalent emotions. While they believed in the southern blacks' cause, they did not understand why Jerry had to try to do some-thing about it. They were afraid for their only son, but they found that they no longer argued with him about his beliefs. They ulti-mately rallied to support him, and their pride and admiration for his actions grew the longer he remained in the South. Indeed Jerry's mother wrote letters to representatives and senators on Jerry's behalf, organized a group letter, and talked about his work to groups.

In September 1965 Jerry Johnson and Anna Sampson left Seattle in Jerry's car for the long drive to Mississippi. Anna was a Filipino woman studying Spanish at the university. She had met Jerry when he joined SNCC, and they had grown to be good friends. They had worked together on SNCC projects for a year and arranged to go south as a couple. In order to be able to work together without offending the black community, Jerry and Anna decided to appear to be husband and wife. In the South, everyone assumed they were married, and they took pains to allow the assumption to go unchallenged. Jerry and Anna knew that as two single people they would never be chosen to work on opening up a new county, because the black community might not tolerate an unmarried couple living together and because the work was too dangerous for a single woman. When they arrived at the SNCC office in Jackson, they were assigned to open Chickasaw County to the movement.

Chickasaw County is in the northeastern part of the state colloquially known as "redneck" country. The population was 16,981 and was 38 percent black. A predominantly rural county, as late as 1950 the census reported no urban population. There are two county seats, Okolona, the county's largest town (population 2,622), and Houston. Black poverty and unemployment are widespread. And the county's blacks suffer deprivation in education and health care. There has, in fact, been a steady decline in the county's black population since 1940.[8]

After a short briefing in Jackson, Jerry and Anna left for Chickasaw. They decided that their best strategy and immediate goal was to find housing in Okolona. They wanted to be in town to establish a base for their work.

When they arrived in Chickasaw, their first impressions were of poverty and fear. That night they stayed in the country with a family of twelve. The house had three rooms, three beds, and no running water or facilities.

The next day Jerry and Anna moved to a shack on the outskirts of Okolona in which a Freedom Rider had previously lived, and they began their search for permanent lodging. Jerry wrote:

No one wants to take us in. Can't blame them really because of the reality of reprisal. Professor from a college in the area was fired because of his attempt to register.... tension [is]... high.... In this community every night for three weeks, a Negro house was fired into.[9]

Jerry and Anna first called on an elderly woman who had said she would take in civil rights workers, but they came too late. Her children had dissuaded her, and she did not know of anyone who would help them.

They then went to see the principal of the black high school. He was sympathetic to the movement but had promised the white school board that "he wouldn't participate in the race issue."[10] He did, however, give them the name of a man who might help them. He said he would keep in touch with them through his friend. Jerry wrote, "[The] fear is fantastic."[11]

In the afternoon Jerry and Anna went to Houston; civil rights workers had never entered the town before. They saw some black women on the courthouse steps and Jerry went over to introduce himself and shake hands; " . . . they cowered back and said, 'No, no don't let the white people see you touch me or I'll get my whole head blown off.' "[12] After visiting the courthouse, which still had "White Only" signs, and facing the white hate stares, Jerry and Anna decided that Houston was too tough to "hit" and returned to Okolona.

They continued to look for housing, because the shack had no cooking facilities or plumbing, and they obviously could not stay there long. Although no one would commit themselves to provide lodging, Jerry and Anna were often given meals, and one woman who lived on the other side of town allowed them to use her bathtub.

Meanwhile in Aberdeen, a town in Monroe County twenty miles from Okolona, the middle-class professional blacks formed a new "Negro Voters League." SNCC had a project in Aberdeen that was trying to organize the poor blacks, and the SNCC workers believed that the league was started to thwart their efforts with the poorer blacks. The formation of the league discouraged both the Aberdeen workers and Jerry and Anna. It seemed to them that the blacks themselves were split and that indigenous black leadership would be harder to attain. Jerry wrote: "I will feel pity for the southern Negro if the Voters League takes over. There is no chance for change for the average Negro without radical revolution."[13]

On the same day in Okolona, blacks formed an armed guard to protect their houses. The park and pool were closed to prevent integration, but a federal injunction demanded school integration, and violence and tension were rising.

Several days went by, and Jerry and Anna still could not find permanent lodging. At this point, the Freedom Rider who had previously used the shack came back and told them to leave. He was very belligerent, and although he had no title to the shack, they both left and spent the night in the car. They now had no lodging of any sort in Chickasaw County.[14]

The next day an older black woman, Mrs. Brown, offered to let them stay with her at her farm in the country. She had never done anything for the movement before, but she thought God had sent Martin Luther King to be a second Moses. As a very religious woman, she thought she should help.[15] Her house had no running water, but there was plenty of room.

Luck seemed to be turning for Jerry and Anna; the same day they met Bobbie McNeal, a nineteen-year-old black, who promised to help them crack the county. Bobbie had done some work with the MFDP and had just returned from Washington, D.C., where an MFDP contingent had been rallying support for the congressional challenge. He lived with his uncle, who was a sharecropper, and helped him with the farm work. Bobbie said he could only help Jerry and Anna when his own work was finished, but as he knew almost everyone in the area, he promised to be a big help once the cotton was harvested. Jerry noted in his diary: "People say he has more nerve than anyone in the county so this will probably come in handy later on. Only hope I can be as brave."[16]

Jerry was soon to find out. The next day whites began harassing his associates. A young black who had been seen with Jerry and Anna was arrested for using obscene language. He claimed he had said, "How do," to a white girl; he was jailed for two and a half hours and fined $100. His life was threatened.[17]

Jerry, Anna, and Bobbie drove to Okolona to find a hall for a voter registration meeting. First they tried the black recreation center, but the black manager said the city did not allow use of the building for political purposes. Then he launched into a speech on black inferiority; he felt blacks were not intelligent enough to vote, and he was, in fact, not registered. The three left and walked to a black cafe. The owner feared arrest and refused the use of her cafe for a meeting. They then approached the minister. He insisted that the church should not be a movement base. They spent the rest of the evening in pouring rain, doorbelling for voter registration.

Frustration began, and Jerry wrote:

What we might have to do is create a disturbance and get . . . arrested.
Then we'll bring in some kids and county folks to hold a demonstration.
This might wake the people up into taking part. Something sure has to be
done.[18]

But Jerry did not try to "get arrested." Instead, he and Anna and
Bobbie held their first mass meeting. It was not in Okolona, as they
had wanted, but in rural Chickasaw near Okolona. About twenty
people came; fifteen were high school students. They sang freedom songs, talked about registering voters, and discussed nonviolence.

The next evening, after a day spent trying to examine voter
registration books, Jerry "got a good taste of southern hospital-
ity. . . . "[19] He, Anna, Bobbie, and two other blacks attempted to
test the Okolona theater. As it was closed, they started home and
on the way decided to test the facilities at a white restaurant. They
entered Moore's Steak House, which was empty of customers, and
sat down at the counter. A cook told them they would be served
shortly. Then Mr. Moore, who weighed an estimated 250 pounds,
came up to Jerry, the only white, and asked him if he were with the
others. Jerry wrote later:

I answered yes and he proceeded to pull me off the stool and threw me on
the floor. He then ran outside and came back with a baseball bat. He
pointed to the other four and said he would serve them but he was going to
beat me . . . and came after me with the bat. I turned to dodge him and he
threw me on the floor. He started beating me with the bat and I was rolling
on the floor in the nonviolent position. . . . I had not had much practice. . . . the first couple blows hit me on the head. But I quickly learned to
protect that and the remainder of the blows landed on my arms and legs.
He hit me about 15 to 25 times before I had a chance to run outside. The
blood was pouring from |my| head as I made it to the car.[20]

Anna called the Jackson office, which contacted a lawyer and
the FBI. The five went to the police station to report the beating
and swear out a warrant for Mr. Moore's arrest. The night officer
would not write out a warrant, but he called the chief of police and
told the group to wait. After ten minutes, Jerry decided he had to

see a doctor. He felt very weak and his head hurt badly. The nearest "friendly" doctor was in Aberdeen and by the time Jerry arrived and began to be treated, the Monroe County sheriff had a warrant for his arrest sworn out by Mr. Moore. The sheriff took Jerry to his jail until the Okolona chief of police could drive over. When the Okolona chief arrived, he charged Jerry with disturbing the peace, handcuffed him, and took him back to Okolona to jail.

In the morning, the lawyer phoned and told Jerry to ask for a continuance of the hearing of his case, which was scheduled for that very day. If it was not granted, he was to plead "not guilty." Two FBI men came to begin the investigation, and Jerry's spirits were revived by the time he was taken to the office of the justice of the peace, who was also the mayor. The continuance was granted, but Jerry found he also was charged with using profane language. He had not said a word during the entire incident. The justice set the bail at $150, and by early afternoon Jerry was free again.

Two days after Jerry was freed, Jerry's lawyer came to get the affidavits charging Jerry of his crimes. The justice of the peace said he would not give them to Jerry or the lawyer until the trial. As it is a violation of a defendant's constitutional rights, to deny him access to the charges against him, Jerry's lawyer petitioned to remove the trial to federal court.[21] He then asked Jerry and Anna to discontinue their activities until the petition was reviewed.

The proscription of their work added to their discouragement. After ten days of virtually no organizing and activity, Anna left to work on the large and established West Point project. As a woman, she had been even more severely fettered than Jerry, since she did not have his social outlet of talking and drinking in the local tavern in the evening.[22]

Completely alone, Jerry awaited his trial. On the appointed day, the federal court removed the case, and Jerry did not have to stand trial. He did, however, have to forfeit his bail, which was $150 and constituted a sizable portion of the money he had saved to go south. To regain it, Jerry began a civil suit against Mr. Moore for damages.

Although in many cases the FBI did not investigate incidents, it did thoroughly examine Jerry's case. The agents took pictures of Jerry's bruises and cuts and questioned all of the people involved. Their investigation was exhaustive, perhaps because the agents thought they could successfully compile a case against Mr. Moore and also perhaps because Senator Henry Jackson wrote at the behest of Jerry's mother requesting a full report of their findings.

There were several thorny problems involved. There was obvious intimidation of witnesses; one of the blacks who was with Jerry later testified he could not remember where he was that night. Although there was some suspicion that a conspiracy may have spurred the beating, there was no substantial evidence. Lastly, although Jerry certainly was beaten, the blacks in the group were theoretically going to be served. Without a proven conspiracy, and without a racially discriminatory act, the FBI and the Justice Department had no jurisdiction to prosecute under federal law. In any event, John Doar himself wrote to Senator Jackson to explain the case. And the senator wrote immediately to Jerry's mother, who had written him initially.[23]

At the end of the month, Jerry and all the other civil rights workers in the South learned of the acquittal of a white man named Coleman accused of murdering Viola Liuzzo outside Selma, Alabama, in February of that year. Along with his anger, he felt a sickening fear and noted:

That decision made it open season on all civil rights workers. As one Negro worker told me yesterday, "It's more like a turkey shoot now." I won't be surprised if some workers get killed in the next month or so. As long as nobody is prosecuted for the slayings of the workers, it's as good as giving every peckerwood a license to kill.[24]

To add to his discouragement, he found that after the Aberdeen newspapers published the names of the nineteen children who had "successfully" integrated the schools earlier in the month, the parents were systematically being fired from their jobs. It was a "very effective warning to any other parents who desire[d] . . . their kids to have a decent education."[25]

October came, and Jerry still could not find a place to live in Okolona. It was the height of the cotton-picking season, and Bobbie McNeal had to work on his uncle's farm. Jerry tried his hand at picking and finally understood the drudgery of the job. After two hours of back-breaking work, he had picked twenty pounds of cotton. At the going rate, he had earned just twenty cents an hour. He wrote tongue-in-cheek, "I decided not to become a sharecropper."[26]

Two days later, Jerry and four others went to Jackson for the state convention of the Freedom Democratic party. There was a call for marchers to reinforce the direct-action protests in Jackson. All the demonstrators were being sent to Parchman Prison. After debating the idea, Jerry decided he was committed to cracking Chickasaw County. He did not think another—and infinitely more dangerous—stay in jail would be his best contribution to the movement. But the call for direct action, coming so soon after his first contact with violence, compelled Jerry to examine his belief in nonviolence. He concluded that he had accepted the concept because of his family background and movement propaganda. With his head still hurting, he wondered if nonviolence really was the answer. He began to read on the subject.

After the convention, Jerry returned to Mrs. Brown's house. Living in her home was one of the most important experiences of his stay in the South. He had never before lived in poverty, nor had he ever really comprehended the dignity a person could have even in poverty. For her part, Mrs. Brown had never contemplated having a white person stay with her. They learned many things from each other.

One evening, after a dinner of collard greens, cornbread, and tomatoes, Mrs. Brown commented on the number of people who wore glasses. Jerry told her he had some and promptly took out his contact lenses. She was astonished, as she had never heard of them before. The next day, Jerry asked her if he could take her picture. She said she would give him one of her and her husband that was taken thirty years ago. Jerry persisted and she finally agreed, if she could change her clothes. "A half hour later she came out all dressed up in earrings, beads, and a brightly colored dress. [It was] really a touching moment."[27]

Several times late at night, Mrs. Brown's friends from neighboring farms came to see a white civil rights worker. Although he was sometimes in bed, she was so proud of Jerry that she would take them into his room to shake his hand. The visitors always left quickly, but they were amazed to meet a young white man who showed them respect. They all called him "Freedom Rider."

After Jerry learned that his case had been removed to federal court, he continued to organize voter registration in Okolona. He and four blacks talked to some local people in a black cafe about registration. The cafe owner called the police, so Jerry and his companions left. Harassment came swift and sure; the five were stopped just out of town for having improper license plates. After his arrival in Mississippi, Jerry had bought local plates for his car, but they were stamped "1966." The patrolman said they could not be used legally until November 1, 1965. He set a hearing for the next day.

Although Jerry thought his plates were legal, he packed his playing cards and books in a sack before he went to see the judge. He pleaded "not guilty" to the charge. The judge seemed reluctant to give a decision; it turned out that neither the judge, the sheriff, nor Jerry actually knew the law on this point. Jerry then phoned the LCDC lawyers in Jackson to have the law clarified. They needed some time to check the question.

While waiting for the return call, Jerry found himself conversing pleasantly with the sheriff and the judge. He wrote:

We discussed football, as they are big sports fans, Seattle, [the] economy in the North . . . just talked in harmony. It makes one realize that these people are human beings after all and have the same interests as myself.[28]

As he had also seen their reactions when he was with blacks, he knew they could be completely different to him. And he noted later in his diary:

It appears to me that this one issue is completely ruining their perspectives on life, because of the large place the Negro holds in southern culture.

A person wouldn't believe these two conflicting attitudes would exist in the same being. Very hard to understand when one sees how damaging this behavior is to our society.[29]

The Jackson lawyers finally called and informed Jerry he was guilty. The judge set the punishment at twenty dollars or a week in jail. Jerry thought he would accept the jail sentence until he was informed he would go to the county prison. He did not feel up to the sure brutality, so he paid his fine and was free again.

Jerry continued voter work, but the next week a friend of Mrs. Brown informed him that Mrs. Brown was too scared to keep him any longer. She had been threatened many times, and all the while Jerry was telling her of the Okolona blacks' fears, she herself had been " . . . shaking in her shoes." Jerry decided one more time to find permanent housing in town. If he failed again, he would leave the county.

The next day, a Monday, Jerry packed everything in his car and drove to Okolona. He was expecting his father to send him another $150 money order, which he now especially needed for rent. He checked at the post office to see if the money had arrived. It had not, and he returned to ask every day that week. Meanwhile he continued to search for a house, even though he was momentarily penniless.

Monday evening, Jerry went to a gambling hall with a black friend. Another black man there, who was just out of the county jail, offered to share his dirt-floored shack. It was filthy and had no plumbing or beds, but Jerry willingly accepted.

On Wednesday, a middle-class black helped Jerry look for a house. As it was very warm, Jerry had the car windows rolled down. Whenever anybody walked near the car, the black talked very loudly about buying insurance from Jerry. He explained later that he could not trust anyone in town; many blacks would report him to the whites if they knew he was sympathetic to the movement. The only house the man could find was one facing the most prominent Okolona Ku Klux Klan member. It had eight easily accessible windows and no black homes nearby. Jerry politely refused " . . . for health reasons."[30]

On Friday Jerry's money order arrived. Jerry asked the postmaster to cash it, but the man demurred. He said he might not be able to finish the day's business if Jerry took $150 and asked if Jerry would return just before closing. It seemed a reasonable request, and, as he needed the money so badly, Jerry went to the library to read until closing. Ten minutes before he was to cash his money order, three young, tough-looking men strode into the library and stood behind Jerry. The three followed him, while the police chief, his deputy, and all the white store owners and clerks stood on the sidewalk staring at him. He went into the post office to cash his money order, but changed his mind abruptly. If they were going to beat him, they were not going to have his money. He kept his money order and ran out a side door to his car.

Jerry started his car immediately and began to drive to Mrs. Brown's house. Nearly halfway to her house, he had to stop; his front tire was slit up the side. He started to panic and remembered: "...what happened...in Philadelphia...I just thought, 'Man! They were caught in their car.' So I'm just going to lock my car and...take off running 'cause they aren't gonna catch me there."[31]

Jerry did lock his car and run; he was scared: "I never felt fear before in my life. I thought, when I was a little kid, you know fear, but you don't. It's terrible! I had to run, you run for your life...."[32] He raced pell mell across a cow pasture to a clump of trees. He stopped for breath and saw a carload of white men pull off the road behind his car. He started running again, always away from the road, until he came to a black home.

In the early evening, the blacks took Jerry out to Bobbie's house. No one in the vicinity had a tire to fix Jerry's car, and the closest phone was three miles away. Bobbie and Jerry walked the distance. They phoned the West Point project, but no one answered. Nobody would let Jerry stay the night; they were all too scared of reprisals. Around ten o'clock, Jerry started walking again and about two hours later he found an empty black church. After prying open a window, Jerry crawled in and spent a cold night on a couch he found in the back.

Jerry awoke early the next morning mainly because of the cold and walked and hitched to Aberdeen for a tire. He cashed his money order and, again unsuccessful in trying to rouse someone at the West Point project, he took his new tire in a taxi to the place he had left his car. It was gone, so Jerry paid the driver and began walking once more. He found a phone and called West Point a third time. Anna answered and said she and another volunteer would come immediately. Jerry waited at the phone and the three of them drove into Okolona.

Jerry's car was at a service station. The state patrol had towed it to Okolona because it was "illegally parked." He could not retrieve it until he answered the charge. The three drove to the state patrol office, but on their way the chief of police stopped them for driving with a faulty muffler. The car had been factory-new only a few weeks before.

The chief of police took Jerry to the justice of the peace for a trial in the justice's garden. He fined Jerry for illegal parking. Upon returning to the police station, Jerry paid the ticket for the "faulty muffler" and the three again visited the service station. The attendants had taken out the transmission for some reason and Jerry had to pay to have that reinstalled. He also had to pay the towing costs. When Jerry added the cost of the new tire, nearly all of his $150 was spent. And he had not accomplished even the most rudimentary of his goals. He wrote:

I left that lousy county and I hope I never see it again. I stayed the night . . . where there are five other workers living in one project. I got to eat also, which was only the third meal I had had in three days.[33]

To violence, fear, and discouragement Jerry and Anna lost the battle to open Chickasaw County to the movement. They could not combat the very real white harassment, nor the well-justified black fear, nor their own discouragement. But in other counties, youths like Jerry and Anna did succeed in organizing black communities. The ultimate outcome of confrontations like Jerry's and Anna's sometimes could not be judged, however, for they often struck fault lines in the wall surrounding the closed society.

NOTES

1. COFO Project Map, Fall 1964, in possession of the author.
2. Jerry Johnson and Anna Sampson are not the real names of the volunteers in this chapter. The names of the Mississippi blacks mentioned are also changed. Jerry's diary, tapes, letters, and affidavits are in my possession and, with the exception of the name changes to preserve anonymity, everything else is a complete recounting, and all quotes are verbatim.
3. Interview: Jerry Johnson, May 19, 1967; hereafter, Jerry Johnson, Tape #2.
4. Ibid.
5. Interview: Jerry Johnson, January 26, 1967; hereafter, Jerry Johnson, Tape #1; Jerry Johnson, Tape #2.
6. Jerry Johnson, Tape #2.
7. Jerry Johnson, Tape #1.

8. U.S. Bureau of the Census, *Census of Population, 1960*; vol. 1: Characteristics of the Population, Part 26: Mississippi (Washington, D.C.: 1963).

9. Author's mss. Jerry Johnson Diary, September 15, 1965, hereafter, Diary.

10. Diary, September 15, 1965.

11. Ibid.

12. Ibid.

13. Ibid., September 16, 1965.

14. Ibid., September 19, 1965. Jerry believed that the Freedom Rider was only in the movement for "excitement." The young man wanted to "raise hell with the police" and was, Jerry thought, the kind of person who had always hurt the movement. Perhaps, instead, he was suffering "battle fatigue." See Robert Coles, "Social Struggle and Weariness," *Psychiatry* 28 (November 1964): 305-15.

15. Diary, September 20, 1965. For feelings on Martin Luther King of those who are religious, see the Rev. Robert Peters' Diary of the Selma March; also interview with the Rev. Mr. Peters. A riddle he heard was, "What's the crookedest thing in the *whole* world? Something Martin Luther King can't straighten out."

16. Diary, September 20, 1965.

17. Ibid., September 21, 1965.

18. Ibid., September 22, 1965.

19. Ibid., September 24, 1965.

20. Ibid.

21. Affidavit of Jerry Johnson, in possession of the author.

22. Jerry Johnson tapes. See also Anne Moody's account of how being a woman civil rights worker compounds the loneliness and frustration of movement work in *Coming of Age in Mississippi*, pp. 335-43, esp. pp. 342-43.

23. Senator H. M. Jackson to Mrs. A. J. Johnson, January 31, 1966; John Doar to Senator H. M. Jackson, January 28, 1966, in possession of the author.

24. Diary, September 30, 1965.

25. Ibid.

26. Ibid., October 2, 1965.

27. Ibid., September 22, 1965.

28. Ibid., October 8, 1965.

29. Ibid.

30. Ibid., October 14, 1965.

31. Jerry Johnson, Tape #2.

32. Jerry Johnson, Tape #1.

33. Jerry Johnson, Tape #2.

7

THE VOLUNTEERS AND THE
SOUTHERN FREEDOM SUMMERS:
SOME CONCLUSIONS

The gamble that the student civil rights movement took in initiating the Freedom Summer Projects paid off in many ways. Fulfilling COFO staff hopes, the volunteers generated enormous media attention and publicity for the movement. Their parents proved, in the main, to be loyal supporters who raised money and lobbied hard for the projects in the North. The volunteers were generally able organizers who gave their prodigious energy and skills to the black community. They made it possible to open projects in communities that the movement had previously never been able to reach, and their sheer numbers kept the projects open, despite white harassment and violence, which covered the spectrum from anonymous threatening calls to bombings, beatings, and murder. Furthermore, because of the disappearance of James Chaney, Michael Schwerner, and Andrew Goodman, the first federal protection for civil rights workers in Mississippi came when droves of FBI agents arrived to find the young men. And, at least partially because of the Freedom Summer Projects, two major civil rights bills became law in 1964 and 1965, desegregating public facilities and banning discrimination in employment and providing federal registrars to ensure voting rights.

In less tangible ways, the volunteers also changed southern black-white relations. Young white adults lived with black families, ate at their tables, and played with black children. For most volunteers and southern blacks alike, those interactions were an important and moving first. Dorothy Smith, who as a thirteen-year-old attended the 1964 McComb Freedom School with Ira Landess and Mario Savio, remembers being "highly impressed with them" partially because "I had not had any dealings with whites prior to that . . . so this was an entirely different experience for me altogether." Fannie Lou Hamer believed that the "bridge" built between white volunteers and black children was one of the greatest achievements of the summers. Never again would southern blacks be so separated from the white community. Likewise, the white community simply could not continue to maintain many of the myths about the "necessity" of separation of the races, which, of course, had never existed anyway when there was work to be done.[1]

The "bridge" that Hamer described was not built by all civil rights workers, however. The dream of what Henry Kirksey, a black Mississippian and the printer for the Summer Projects, called "real integration"—a true melding together of cultures based on openness, honesty, and respect that would transcend all racial, class, and educational differences—was hard to achieve. Kirksey believed "the whole of America is against real integration in those terms," and it was certainly true that some volunteers with the best of intentions were unable to achieve that transcendent integration.[2] Some held rigidly stereotyped views of black people and carried their ethnocentrism with them to the South, where it crippled their ability to work effectively.

But most were good, dedicated workers who believed that their participation in the Freedom Summers was the most important event of their lives. In 1964 more than two hundred volunteers remained in Mississippi, giving up school and their more comfortable northern life, to continue to work for "real integration." As one young woman who stayed wrote back to disapproving friends:

There is a certainty, when you are working in Mississippi, that it is important for you to be alive and doing just what you are doing. And whatever small bit we did for Mississippi this summer, Mississippi did ten times as much for us. Working there has given me clarity about what I want to be learning in college that three years in Widener Library could not give. . . .

I guess the thing that pulls me back most are the people who made us a part of their community. . . . In Mississippi I have felt more love, more sympathy and warmth, more community than I have known in my life. And especially the children pull me back. . . . [3]

Most 1965 volunteers echoed her feelings as well. They were dedicated to the civil rights movement, and they often felt it gave them far more than they gave it.

Evaluations of the success or failure of the programs of the Summer Projects have varied enormously over the ensuing years, depending on the perspective of the evaluator and also the time of the evaluation. Nowhere is that more clear than in the case of assessing the voter registration work and the role of the MFDP. Voter registration, before the Civil Rights Act of 1965, was slogging and dangerous work and seemed during the summers, especially in Mississippi, to be going far too slowly. As early as the winter of 1964–1965, however, it was clear that communities that had had voter registration campaigns during the 1964 summer were much easier than previously untouched communities to organize around various issues. That winter, for instance, civil rights workers found it distinctly easier to organize for the ASCS elections in communities that had housed summer projects; however, in no communities did many blacks succeed in winning ASCS board elections. Several years after the summers, Henry Kirksey made the same assessment the volunteers had about the relative ease of organizing in communities that had had projects. In 1969, Kirksey was an ardent supporter of black separatism, but he still asserted

. . . my view of [the volunteers] . . . coming to Mississippi and the South . . . [is that] . . . without that kind of thing, we'd still be where we were, because places which had no civil rights workers [in 1964] are still essentially the same as they were before the civil rights movement. The *exact* same way as it was before; so to me the Hot Summer Project was *indispensable* to an awakening that had to come. . . . [4]

The case of the MFDP has resulted in differing interpretations as well. After gathering thousands of registrations throughout the state, the MFDP went to the 1964 Democratic convention as a "people's party," optimistic about being seated and convinced of the justice of their cause. The compromise that the national party offered them offended their spirit and denigrated their supporters. The liberals within the national party urged them to accept and increased their disillusion. To outsiders the MFDP appeared to have won a victory with the two seats on the floor, but to local black Mississippians the compromise was humiliating and insulting.

The convention challenge marked a turning point for many in the student civil rights movement. Most volunteers turned away in horror from the compromise, thoroughly disillusioned with the democratic process that they had been brought up to revere and trust. In 1964 with the Humphrey compromise the Democratic Party lost a rare opportunity to affirm its support of the civil rights movement and cement the loyalty of young activist students to the party.

The congressional challenge that followed was also initially judged a failure, although civil rights workers were not shocked or surprised this time that, after months of painstaking research, the challenge to unseat the Mississippi congressional delegation was defeated. Again some argued that the size of the losing vote (143) represented a strong minority and a clear "moral victory." To movement workers weary of moral victories and unkept promises, however, the challenges were perceived and named as failures and betrayals. The ensuing story of politics in Mississippi, as a case for voter registration in the entire South, however, mitigates the initial assessment of failure, though the judgment of liberal betrayal still remains for some.

As a direct result of the Humphrey compromise, an integrated Mississippi delegation was seated at the tumultuous 1968 Democratic convention over a segregationist Mississippi delegation. The origins of the integrated delegation lay in the MFDP, and it was a sweet day for people like Fannie Lou Hamer when they were officially seated in Chicago. Further, other delegations' challenges based on the Humphrey compromise and heard at the 1968 convention resulted in far-reaching changes in Democratic Party rules and a fundamentally changed delegate selection process that later committed the party to proportional representation for ethnic minorities and women.

Politics in Mississippi changed as well due to the addition of blacks to the electorate. By 1971, 307,000 blacks, 68 percent of the eligible black population, were registered to vote. Throughout the decade, more blacks registered, blacks ran for office, often successfully, and by the campaign of 1979, the state had been reapportioned as a result of a legal battle begun in the 1964 summer and conducted by a group of initially volunteer lawyers organized as the Lawyers' Committee for Civil Rights Under the Law. The reapportionment decision, under provisions of the Voting Rights Act of 1965, provided for 461 federal observers to be assigned to polling places around the state and 10 Justice Department lawyers to take complaints of voting irregularities. The election of 1979 resulted in 17 new black state legislators and a total of 343 black elected officials at all levels of city, county, and state government. After the 1979 election, Mississippi had more black elected officials than any state in the Union. Further, many white politicians had also changed their position on civil rights issues. In the 1979 governor's race, for instance, both white candidates were racial moderates for the first time in the state's history. In the most recent special election, in July 1981, the Fourth Congressional District, which includes Jackson, elected Democrat Wayne Dowdy who pledged himself to supporting an extension of the Voting Rights Act, populist economic issues espoused earlier by the MFDP, and complete equity for blacks and poor whites. Seen by political commentators as an "upset," Dowdy credited black voters who are 45 percent of the district population with a "very prominent role" in his victory.[5]

A former volunteer, who joined the movement in the Mississippi Summer Project and who remained through 1965, assessed the voter registration campaign and the success of the MFDP in a letter written in 1977. Responding to what he perceived as criticism of the program, he wrote:

Others can talk of disintegration and co-option. I say with pride that what we volunteers were a part of in Mississippi was a revolutionary experience both for us and for the strong local black leadership it brought out. That effort broke the white stranglehold on the psyche of the rural Mississippi black and created strong resistance which was so successful that Mississippi whites had to knuckle under and were forced to join up with [it] if they were to have delegations to the National Democratic Party. Since this last was the object of the Mississippi Freedom Democratic Party's statewide and nationwide programs, it is no shame that that organization ceased to exist upon accomplishing what it set out to do.

Co-option is a matter of degree. Before 1964, almost all Mississippi black colleges, churches, and black public schools were completely co-opted, and an Uncle Tom leadership picked by the white power structure in the rural communities was in complete control. By 1968, that had significantly changed.[6]

His analysis probably best reflects the state of Mississippi politics today and the view of former volunteers.

Immediately following the large integrated Summer Projects, and as a direct result of them, it was clear to most people involved in the student civil rights movement, staff and volunteer alike, that the movement had evolved to a new stage. Even while acknowledging the ways in which the volunteers had fulfilled the goals the southern movement held for them, southern civil rights staff believed that it was now time for blacks to organize black communities and whites to organize white communities. SNCC staff took the lead in this position, but southern CORE workers followed relatively quickly. Of the activist southern civil rights organizations, only SCLC continued to believe there was an important place for white workers in the South, but SCLC was also not in the forefront of the student movement. Calling the program a move to "self-determination of communities," this next stage in the southern student civil rights movement was not a new ideological stance. All of the ideas and issues of self-determination had been vigorously debated as early as the Greenville meeting in 1963 which birthed the Freedom Summer Projects. Now, however, they seemed a correct and compelling analysis. Partly, of course, this was due to some very real successes in the intervening two years. The passage of the Civil Rights Acts of 1964 and 1965 meant substantially new programs had to be begun if the movement was going to continue. Furthermore, at the moment of some success in legislative terms, it seemed increasingly possible that the attainment of those goals might still not effect fundamental change in the lives of blacks.

The concept of local control, espoused as COFO policy in the winter of 1965, became the vehicle for implementing self-determination. The inherent ability of blacks to organize black communities became canonized as a SNCC credo in the fall of 1965, but before that policy was set, it was clear to both staff and volunteers that the role of whites in the South in the future should be severely limited. Many volunteers realized, for example, that their success at voter registration was often due to their being white. This continuation of the old theme of whites telling blacks what to do made many volunteers extremely uneasy; and even though they believed registration was important, they became convinced that such domination should not be perpetuated. In assessing why it was imperative that blacks organize black communities and whites go to work in the North, one white volunteer explained:

As far as I'm concerned . . . whites are a drawback on any project, whether in the minority or the majority. Because it's a simple fact that, no matter how much I would still like to believe it, a Negro farmer's eyes just don't light up when he sees an integrated team coming toward him. No matter how much he understands the white person's mission and no matter how much he really wants to like him, he just can't talk about the Man, when the Man's sitting in front of him.[7]

While the vast majority of CORE and MFDP volunteers agreed with her, the majority of SCOPE volunteers, like SCLC itself, believed that white workers were still needed in the South. Sometimes their reasons seemed to have little to do with helping southern blacks:

As a white civil rights worker, I encountered hostility from fellow staff workers who feel that white people are generally ineffective civil rights workers. I agree with them that whites are generally ineffective in organizing a Negro community; however, I think the white volunteers gain a great deal from living within the Negro community and take back to their native culture an awareness both of Negro culture and of much of the poverty and Nazi-like oppression that is taking place. . . . I also think that a few people with really creative ability should try and work out some sort of effective program to channel the energies of the many middle- and upper-class white young people, like myself, who are sincerely and seriously interested in eliminating racial discrimination not only so that the Negro has a fair share of our country's riches, but also because we believe that each segment of America's melting pot has something to contribute to the whole, and that the white community is being deprived, spiritually, by setting up artificial barriers.[8]

Even in SCOPE, however, a substantial minority of SCOPE workers disagreed with that position. Representing the minority in SCOPE, one volunteer reflected in the fall of 1965:

> ... the most important thing we did was not voter registration or community organization, but helping make some Negro feel good, to give him a sense of dignity. That's the sort of thing that was most valuable. The summer led me to understand and believe in black power. I realized that most of the things we were doing was not the best way to solve the problem. We didn't have the answers; they can help themselves better, and doing it themselves gives them an important sense.[9]

One volunteer, who worked with COFO in 1964 and the MFDP in 1965, talked about the changes he had seen in the movement:

> ... last year, there was an exuberance, a sort of spirit, which I ... put down to new blood. ... And this spirit is still very much apparent and very much alive among the people of Mississippi, but everyone who's worked in Mississippi, and who's been involved, either constantly or intermittently, there seems to be a whole air of fatigue ... an air of tiredness. ... I was too pushed to feel it last summer, or too much involved in the newness of the work to feel it, but ... I find myself having a genuine longing to be back in the North, where I can be 20 years old again ... and this comes in our feelings about the local people; we talk about the local folks' possibilities, and getting the local folks aware of this, so they can take over. And at first this is just an idea ... because we think it should be done. Because we think it is the right way of going about things—people managing their own affairs. But in addition to this—not replacing it ... there comes the feeling of, "man, I want the local people to take it; I'm tired of having it myself. Please, it's your business. Take it away from me. I've had enough" ... you keep on working ... and maybe you never say this aloud, maybe there's just this little nagging voice. ... I'll be very relieved when the local people can take it and I can do something else.[10]

After the Meredith March in June 1966 when Stokely Carmichael publicly coined the slogan "Black Power," the media, politicians, and civil libertarians across the country expressed absolute horror and outrage at the idea of aggressive black separatism. SNCC and the student movement came under increasing attack as communist-led and inherently racist. Many northerners who decried Black Power charged it was a racist slap-in-the-face to whites who had supported the movement, and many prefaced their criticisms of the new policy by harkening to the devotion and sacrifice of white volunteers in the Freedom Summers. It is hard to remember now what a shock the concept of Black Power was to the liberal establishment in the late 1960s. Of all forty-two separate interviews of former volunteers I have conducted since I began this study in 1966, none of them has ever been critical of the concept of Black Power. Of the thirty-two interviews I conducted from the fall of 1966 until the winter of 1969, during the height of Black Power and the backlash against it, all of the former volunteers saw black nationalism as a positive force in the black community and supported separatism as a necessary community-organizing strategy. To a person, they resented others' charges that their work and ideals were demeaned by black separatism; rather they supported the separatists and believed that their work was properly now in their own white communities. Furthermore, they all saw the development as a logical step in the ongoing movement, one that was partly an outgrowth of their southern work.

For the volunteers themselves, their southern experience proved to be a personal crucible, carrying over to influence the future direction of their lives. The vast majority of the volunteers continued to support the civil rights movement from their home communities in the North. Many also returned home to work on organizing their communities around various issues, particularly opposition to the Vietnam War. Although some volunteers longed to resume a "normal life," for nearly all, work in the South affected their politics and produced a profound skepticism of President Johnson and most government pronouncements. For the first time, the volunteers had lived in poverty and had become aware of the enormous class differences that exist in the country, and this increased their malaise with their upper-middle-class life. Their experience and the dignity of many poor southern blacks left a lasting impression. As one worker wrote:

One of the major results of the summer, for me, was a disgust with the American social system. Clothes, money, and education, and good looks— ugh! I met too many people who lacked all these things, but who were absolutely wonderful, to ever think material things are important again. I will always be willing to fight them and make real values realized.[11]

In both 1964 and 1965 volunteers found it difficult to return to their northern communities. One young woman recounted how hard she found her homecoming to southern California:

[While people are] sympathetic with my stories of problems concerning the South, [they are] terribly, violently against the Negro in the North. Some said they were really beginning to believe in the Negro cause until the Watts riot. Somehow they could not see the problems where they lived and resented any suggestions of mine. They seemed to want me to think that I had been taken in by the communists or (if not that strongly) to a highly emotionalized situation without understanding the whole problem.

I was weary when I returned. I was frustrated, disappointed and hurt to hear the bigoted attitudes of well-liked acquaintances. . . . [12]

This heightened awareness of racism in the North and in their families and friends was particularly difficult for returning volunteers. As one young man noted, "Attitudes and views that white acquaintances have now seem to 'reek of' bias and prejudice. I seem to have developed a more acute ability to sense bigoted individuals."[13] The summer volunteers, then, experienced much the same process of radicalization that the initial civil rights workers had in the early 1960s: The more they witnessed the ubiquitous poverty, the flagrant injustice, the unwillingness of the federal government to use its powers of intervention, and the lack of understanding of the movement in the North, the farther they turned from consensus politics. By no means did the majority leave the two-party system and become political radicals, but most did shift to the left, and a substantial number began to consider themselves radicals.[14]

Although a majority of the volunteers returned to school in the North, many were dissatisfied with the education they were receiving. Often influenced by their Freedom School experiences, they complained that many traditional college courses were not "relevant," that they did not have an experiential base, and that the university system was racist in its admissions and curriculum. In 1964 some two hundred volunteers had dropped out of school to continue working in the South, and the single most dramatic change in attitude of the SCOPE volunteers after their summer work was their belief that the educational system of the country must be changed to become more relevant, particularly to the issue of racism.[15] Many volunteers suffered "culture shock" upon their return to campus:

> To go from ... |Alabama civil rights work| ... to a tree-studded UCLA campus ... is a very hard adjustment to make, especially with all the problems of a multiversity and the questions I have as to just what the hell is going on over there. Is it worth it and the whole value system behind it ... the whole set up? You know, I'm not against education, but what that education is designed to accomplish, which is as Clark Kerr said ... a factory to produce minds for business, the military and government.[16]

Large universities were criticized for their impersonality, their political stance, and their ties to the Defense Department and the "war machine."

The first student eruption at a major university was the Free Speech Movement at Berkeley, catalyzed by Mario Savio shortly after his return from the McComb Freedom School in 1964. Declaring "An End to History," Savio wrote:

> Last summer I went to Mississippi to join the struggle there for civil rights. This fall I am engaged in another phase of the same struggle, this time in Berkeley. The two battlefields may seem quite different to some observers, but this is not the case. The same rights are at stake in both places—the right to participate as citizens in democratic society and the right to due process of law. Further, it is a struggle against the same enemy. In Mississippi an autocratic and powerful minority rules, through organized violence, to suppress the vast, virtually powerless, majority. In California, the privileged minority manipulates the University bureaucracy to suppress the student's political expression. That "respectable" bureaucracy masks the financial plutocrats; that impersonal bureaucracy is the efficient enemy in a "Brave New World."

Following Savio's lead, former southern volunteers took part in demonstrations at Harvard, Yale, Stanford, San Francisco State, Columbia, and the University of Washington over the next four years.[17]

In their personal lives, many volunteers reevaluated their academic plans and career choices.[18] The professions of law, the ministry, medicine, and social work gained new adherents. Women in particular seemed to acquire new career goals at least partially as a result of their movement work. One woman volunteer wrote her sponsor, "Could you ask your husband what he considers should be traits of a lawyer? I'm finding more and more the limited role of white women in the movement and becoming a lawyer has entered my mind as one of the most valuable things one could do for the movement and for the oppressed peoples of this land who don't even know they have any rights."[19] After leaving Mississippi, she became an activist lawyer, specializing in civil liberties and sex discrimination cases.[20] Many other volunteers took up activist, socially relevant careers.

The growing peace movement reaped the major benefit of the volunteers' political apprenticeship in the South. During the summers, especially 1965, many staff and volunteers expressed a link between the civil rights movement and the peace movement. While in the South, several volunteers became committed to the peace movement and filed for conscientious objector (CO) status. For some, it was a logical extension of their belief in nonviolence, but for others, it was more a political decision not tied to pacifism, but expressing a specific objection to the "imperialism" of the Vietnam War. As early as 1965, southern workers were refusing to be drafted. Bruce Maxwell, a volunteer who worked on the "White Folks' Project," burned his induction papers and told his draft board, "I would rather go to jail." He applied for CO status, but did not use a traditional religious argument:

The freedom movement in the South, of which I am a part, is trying to destroy what is destroying humanity in the South. I also realize that the U.S. military is destroying humanity all over the world, for instance, it is trying to prevent a free election in Vietnam. . . . Now the U.S. government is saying to me: "Join the world's largest force of destruction or go to jail and sacrifice your future effectiveness in the freedom struggle in the South." Now I have never wanted to fight a CO battle because that is not the most effective way I can function in humanity's struggle for freedom. But since fate sees fit to have me drafted, I cannot stand before God willing to destroy humanity for two years or six months and still claim that I am a valid part of the people's struggle for freedom when I return to the South.[21]

When the volunteers returned north to organize their own communities, the war in Vietnam was the strongest issue of concern. Former volunteers were involved in organizing the first "Anti-

Vietnam Teach-Ins" at universities across the country. SDS, many of whose members were former volunteers, grew enormously and came to represent the New Left on more than a hundred campuses by early 1966. SDS and the student mobilization continued to organize anti-Vietnam demonstrations for several years.

In the summer and fall of 1966 David Harris, Dennis Sweeney, Mary King Sweeney, and a few others started talking about the draft. All of them had worked in Mississippi, and Harris and Sweeney were students at Stanford University. They lived in "the commune" in East Palo Alto, worked in the community and experimented with drugs, especially acid (LSD). The considered themselves conscientious objectors, but after talking about the draft, Sweeney recalled later, " . . . it became obvious that it was pointless to say you 'won't go' if you weren't being asked to."[22] Late in the summer, Mendy Samstein, another white SNCC veteran, came through the Bay Area and called for draft resistance. Both Samstein and Sweeney wanted to create "a white SNCC," which would require the kind of daring that civil rights workers had displayed in the South. Early in the next year, the commune formed The Resistance, which spread dramatically across the country and called on young men to turn in their draft cards and actively resist the draft. As David Harris said later, the commune and then The Resistance represented "a synthesis of the style developed in the South, and what may have been my generation's contribution to the synthesis, centering around a vision of self." Many former volunteers joined The Resistance.[23]

Also in 1967 several New Left groups sponsored the Vietnam Summer Project. The project was the largest organizing effort the New Left ever attempted. In an endeavor to organize white communities around the issue of the war, the Vietnam Summer Project modelled itself on the Freedom Summer Projects. The antiwar organizing was based on "self-determination" and was aimed at different "constituencies," like labor unions, professional groups, teachers, and so on. Over twenty thousand volunteers were involved at least part time on the project. About two hundred worked full time at the national office and another five hundred worked full time in local communities. Every major city had a project, and the goal of the Vietnam Summer was to build local, "multi-issue" groups, which would develop indigenous leadership and continue after the summer. All of the major national office organizers were veterans of the southern civil rights movement. Many of the local community organizers were also former volunteers. Although it is impossible to measure the degree of "success" of the summer project, it certainly added to the growing public opposition to the war. The organizing of local groups with indigenous leaders proved difficult, however, especially since the vast majority of volunteers were students who went back to school in September. Ironically, the Vietnam Summer Project staff, many of them former civil rights volunteers, saw their local groups dissolve when the Vietnam summer volunteers left for school.[24]

Particularly through the antiwar movement and a new activist approach to the professions, the majority of the former volunteers continued the work they began in the South. A minority, however, reacted to their experience by going inward and dropping out of activist work altogether. For some their dissatisfaction and frustration from the South served to crystallize their desire to work for goals they had held prior to their southern work and which had previously conflicted with their movement orientation. As one SCOPE worker explained:

I'm afraid the summer sort of contributed *negatively* toward my interest in civil rights. I am less enthused, less hopeful. Sometimes I feel that the summer's experience contributed to my increasing interest in *violin playing*, by making me feel less convinced of any possible personal effectiveness in civil rights. This is an exaggeration—but I have always felt that music and civil rights conflict in that each demands full-time work if you really "believe" in them. Now I lean toward music as something obviously more achievable.[25]

More commonly, however, the people who dropped out had no cohesive plans for their lives. They drifted, delved into mystical philosophies, and experimented with drugs. A former SCOPE worker, who considered herself a "hippie," rejected her former involvement:

I think now there should be no movements. Things should be on a more personal basis. With love we will help without causes. The trouble with causes is that the people involved forget about love.[26]

A nonrandom follow-up of forty SCOPE volunteers conducted in

1969 indicated that about 25 percent worked full time in radical causes; about 40 percent were active "reformists"; another 25 percent were "disengaged"; and the remaining 10 percent were dropouts. Since 1965 all had come to oppose the Vietnam War. Roughly 65 percent of the former SCOPE volunteers were actively working for social change in 1969. Before they went south in 1965, however, only 18 percent were active in the civil rights movement. Also in 1965 only 5 percent considered themselves "radicals," as opposed to 25 percent in 1969. The effect of the summer was clear even on former SCOPE workers, who were widely recognized as the most conservative volunteers in 1965.[27]

Of course, the volunteers' lives were not static, and many went through several phases after their civil rights work. An example is the continuation of the story of Jerry Johnson, the volunteer who tried to open Chickasaw County in 1965.

In the winter of 1966, Jerry Johnson returned to Seattle and renewed his ties with CRAG, CORE, and Friends of SNCC. He reentered the University of Washington and began to read voraciously on nonviolence and pacifism. With a clear philosophical base for his "instinctive belief," he filed for CO status and began lecturing locally against the war in Vietnam.

Jerry started experimenting with drugs, especially marijuana and "mind-expanding" drugs like LSD and peyote. By 1967 he was beginning to become "genuinely confused" about his allegiance to the movement. His civil rights and peace work could take all of his time, but he also wanted "to explore his mind" and read in the Eastern religions. He debated this quandary for nearly a year, juggling his movement work to make time for his "selfish" needs. He completed all the coursework for his B.A. degree, except for the language requirement, but he did not attempt to find a full-time job.

Jerry actively demonstrated against the war and went to San Francisco for the big Student Mobilization March in 1969. His draft board had meanwhile denied his CO request, because he did not base it on traditional religious reasons. Undaunted, Jerry took his case to court and was one of the first persons in the area to win CO status over a draft board denial.

Resigning himself to the language requirement, Jerry returned to school to learn Swahili and acquire a teaching credential. He wanted to go to Mississippi and teach in a black school, if he could get hired. While in school, Jerry was drafted into alternative service. He worked nights in the psychiatric ward at Harborview Hospital in Seattle and continued work on his credential during the days. The open drug use by hospital authorities, juxtaposed with his student teaching while,

> patients gloriously
> struggled with their
>   sanity
>   • • •
>   made for catalyst to reach
>   the point
>   where
>   i abandoned
> "the creeping
>   meatball"
> so i stopped all activities
>   of previous patterned
>   life style and began tuning
>   in to life process.[28]

As soon as his alternative service was over, Jerry set off with a pack and haiku books to "find his soul." He went into the Canadian wilderness, meditated, and "found himself." He cast off his old name and became "Shalimar." For the past several years, he has lived with a woman, worked in the apple and pear harvests, gardened in the wilderness, and practiced yoga and meditation. He and his friend had a child in 1971. Jerry is obviously happy, though he has "very little contact with people or their events."[29]

Women volunteers added another dimension to the evolving movement of the late 1960s. Like the men volunteers, they continued movement work in the North. Primarily involved in the peace movement and SDS, they began to analyze their position in the movement. The first serious paper on the subject of sex discrimination within the movement publicly claimed by white women was dated November 18, 1965, and was published in *Liberation* in 1966. Mary King and Casey Hayden, both of whom had worked in the Jackson COFO office, co-authored "Sex and Caste: A Kind of Memo." They drew the analogy between women's status in society and the movement and the black's status in society. In a very tentative way, they discussed "inequities" in the movement between men and women, and they asked for responses from other movement people; the concept of "self-determination" was enlarged again. Predictably, women by and large reacted favorably and men treated the ideas as a joke.[30]

In late 1966 SDS held its yearly convention and set itself the task of formulating a "student-power strategy," organizing antidraft unions. When a caucus of women demanded a plank on "women's liberation," male SDS members harassed the women and told them to leave. After several scenes like the SDS convention, the first independent women's groups began in Chicago and New York in 1967. Like The Resistance, women's groups proliferated across the country. Generally they began first as women's caucuses within radical groups, and then they graduated to independent women's organizations. The first national women's liberation conference took place in Chicago in 1968, and many participants brought position papers on theoretical points about women's liberation.

The early women's movement owed a great deal to the civil rights movement. Many of the founding women had been volunteers in the South and their initial, unmistakable dose of sexism came from the movement. While the intertwining of racism and sexism had inhibited the volunteers from making a collective feminist analysis during their southern work, the strength they gained in the South profoundly influenced their later analysis and organizing. One 1965 volunteer commented at the end of the summer, "I've always had the feeling that women can be sort of helpless nonentities, and I'm learning that women can be real and have to be strong."[31] That realization, reinforced by sexism in the northern movement now separated from the southern complexities of intertwined race and sex, made it possible for former volunteers in the North to develop a feminist ideology and political analysis. One of the first organizing techniques of the women's movement evolved from a combination of Maoist theory and the southern freedom school teaching method. The experiential basis for identifying and analyzing oppression came directly from the freedom school tradition and was called "consciousness raising." The movement slogan "The Personal is Political" was precisely the point of view behind a great deal of southern organizing, especially in 1965.[32]

By the turn of the decade, the Freedom Summers already seemed light-years away. The student branch of the civil rights movement had dissolved into small, scattered projects, mostly outside the South and committed to black power and black separatism. Throughout the South, the political status of blacks had changed profoundly and continued to develop during the 1970s, but the economic status of blacks has not changed much since Freedom Summer days. The concept of self-determination, or "liberation politics," is a political standard now, with women, nonblack minorities, and gay and lesbian activists, as well as blacks, expressing their need to organize around their own identities. Slogans like "La Raza," "Gay Pride," and "Women's Liberation" are acceptable and expected political rhetoric. The "summer project concept" has also become a staple of Left politics, from the 1967 Vietnam Summer Project to the 1981 Summer ERA Project, which had sex-integrated teams doorbelling in Utah to register people in support of the ERA.

Out of the summers, northern students developed a radical critique of American society that was experientially based in their southern work and a profound disillusionment with the federal government's willingness or ability to practice its ideals. That critique, coupled with the new policy of self-determination, led former volunteers to organize their own movement in the North. Their main political issues were demanding educational change, combatting northern racism, opposing the Vietnam War, and beginning women's liberation. Former volunteers were active in organizing all of these movements, which received a great deal of their initial impetus and strength from the Freedom Summer veterans.

The concept of "self-determination" ushered in Black Power and the northern student movement. A natural evolution of the southern student civil rights movement, it closed the chapter of purposeful integration, of "black and white together." The programmatic success of the projects, in addition to the difficulty of realizing "true integration," assured the acceptance in the movement of the philosophy of self-determination, first strongly articulated in 1963. The northern volunteers, tempered by their southern work, became active participants in their own movement in the North. For the next decade, their experience profoundly changed their lives, their politics, and their communities.

NOTES

1. Interviews: Dorothy Smith, January 24, 1979, Lawrence, Kans.; Fannie Lou Hamer, November 2, 1969, Ruleville, Miss.

2. Interview: Henry Kirksey, November 11, 1969, Jackson, Miss.

3. Sutherland, *Letters*, pp. 225–26.

4. Interview: Henry Kirksey.

5. "You Gotta Love Me," *Newsweek*, August 2, 1971, pp. 22 and 24; "Winter Wins Mississippi Governor's Race," *The New York Times*, November 7, 1979, p. 15; "Mississippi Governor-Elect Plans to Guide State to Turning Point," *New York Times*, November 8, 1979, p. A17; "Natchez Pilgrimage," *The Today Show*, April 2, 1980; "Howdy, Dowdy," *Newsweek*, July 20, 1981, p. 22; "Black Voters Credited in Democrat's Victory," *The Phoenix Gazette*, July 8, 1981, p. A9.

6. Bruce Maxwell to Grace Maxwell Brooks, January 20, 1977, p. 2, in possession of the author.

7. KZSU Interview 0211, p. 11.

8. SHSW: Gerald Marwell Prs: SCOPE Questionnaire Comment.

9. Ibid.

10. KZSU Interview 0218, pp. 3 and 11.

11. SHSW: Gerald Marwell Prs: SCOPE Questionnaire Comment.

12. Ibid.

13. Ibid.

14. Kenniston, *Young Radicals*, p. 120; Aiken et al., *Dynamics of Idealism*, p. 149, 171–77.

15. Aiken et al., *Dynamics of Idealism*, p. 163.

16. SHSW: Gerald Marwell Prs: SCOPE Questionnaire Comment.

17. Michael Miller and Susan Gilmore, eds., *Revolution at Berkeley* (New York: 1965), p. 239. For information on these student demonstrations, see Joanne Grant, *Confrontation on Campus: The Columbia Pattern for the New Protest* (New York: 1969); Cox Commission, *Crisis at Columbia* (New York: 1968); Mitchell Cohen and Dennis Hall, *The New Student Left, An Anthology* (Boston: 1967), pp. 215–90; Jacobs and Landau, *The New Radicals*, pp. 59–64, 206–48; Paul Lauter and Florence Howe, *The Conspiracy of the Young* (New York: 1971), pp. 3–147; Mitchell Goodman, *The Movement Toward a New America: The Beginning of a Long Revolution* (New York: 1970); Jerry Farber, *The Student as Nigger* (New York: 1970). Also see, James O'Brien, "A History of the New Left, 1960–1968," *Radical America* 2 (May–June, September–October, November–December 1968, reprint ed., Boston: n.d.).

18. Aiken et al., *Dynamics of Idealism*, pp. 161–65.

19. SHSW: Linda Seese Prs: Linda Seese, "Dear Mrs. Rice," January 23, 1965, Indianola, Miss.

20. Interview: Linda Davis, October 1973, Washington, D.C. (by telephone).

21. SHSW: Bruce Maxwell Prs.: Bruce Maxwell, "Dear Unitarians," May 8, 1965, Mayersville, Miss., and enclosure "Series II" (draft statement), mss., Bruce Maxwell to Grace Maxwell Brooks, January 20, 1977.

22. Michael Ferber and Staughton Lynd, *The Resistance* (Boston: 1971), p. 81. In the years of intense political change that have swirled by and witnessed mindless assassinations and terrible violence in and out of the South of this country and in Southeast Asia, some individuals have fallen victims of that intensity. The movement has had its darker side. Dennis Sweeney, for instance, was one of the few whites allowed in McComb in 1964. Dedicated to nonviolence, he helped found The Resistance in 1966. In the ensuing years, after several mental breakdowns in which he became obsessed with the idea that Allard Lowenstein was inhabiting his mind and killing him, as he believed that Lowenstein and others like him had killed the movement, Dennis Sweeney in 1980 calmly murdered his former Mississippi mentor Allard Lowenstein in cold blood in his New York office. Although Lowenstein was once Sweeney's best and most trusted professor and friend, he and Sweeney had fallen out late in 1964 over the challenge, the direction of SNCC, and Lowenstein's belief that Communists were taking over the movement.

23. Ferber and Lynd, *The Resistance*, pp. 81-82. See also Willard Gaylin, *In the Service of Their Country: War Resisters in Prison* (New York: 1970); Roger Neville Williams, *The New Exiles: American War Resisters in Canada* (New York: 1971).

24. Kenniston, *Young Radicals*, pp. 3-19. The entire book is devoted to a study of the fourteen people who directed the project. All had served in the South.

25. Aiken et al., *Dynamics of Idealism*, p. 153.

26. Ibid.

27. Ibid, pp. 168-85. Aiken et al. do not make any connection between the changes in the volunteers' previous lack of political activity and their sustained active work in the movement since the summer. Indeed, because only 25 percent are full-time radicals, they indicate movement activity is at least partially a phase, whereas it is as logical to argue that civil rights work profoundly changed their lives when they returned to the North.

28. Jerry Johnson (Shalimar), Letter (in poem form), September 8, 1973, in possession of the author.

29. Jerry Johnson (Shalimar), Letter, September 8, 1973, in possession of the author. This entire story is constructed from a series of conversations with Jerry from 1967 to 1969 and from his extraordinary letter.

30. Casey Hayden and Mary King, "Sex and Caste: A Kind of Memo," *Liberation* 10 (April 1966): 35–36; George Owen, Betty Rozak, Gene Hoffman, Jeanne Bagby, "Sex and Caste: II," *Liberation* 10 (December 1966): pp. 26–33.

31. KZSU Interview, 0138, p. 13.

32. See Judith Hole and Ellen Levine, *Rebirth of Feminism* (New York: 1971); Maren Lockwood Carden, *The New Feminist Movement* (New York: 1974); Shulamith Firestone and Anne Koedt, *Notes From the Second Year* (New York: 1970); Robin Morgan, ed., *Sisterhood Is Powerful* (New York: 1970); Florence Howe, *Female Studies II* (Pittsburgh, Pa.: 1970); and Jo Freeman, *The Politics of Women's Liberation* (New York: 1975). The best historical analysis is Sara Evans, *Personal Politics: The Roots of Women's Liberation in the Civil Rights Movement and the New Left* (New York: 1979).

BIBLIOGRAPHY

PRIMARY SOURCES

This work is based mainly on traditional historical primary sources: organization records and files; participants' letters, diaries and memorabilia, and tape recorded interviews. In addition, I have read three newspapers for 1964 and 1965, popular journals, liberal political journals, and radical student movement journals. Perhaps the only unusual feature is the abundance of data, which brings with it the painful process of winnowing and paring down.

The Contemporary Social Action Collection at the State Historical Society of Wisconsin is the single most varied and important collection. It has all of the national and southern CORE papers and a massive collection of volunteers' letters, diaries, and memorabilia, spanning all of the southern civil rights groups, and it will continue to grow, since the archivists are committed to continuing an active acquisitions policy. The "showy" collections for the volunteers are the Rev. Harry Bowie Papers, the R. Hunter Morey Papers, and the Elizabeth Sutherland Papers; yet, I found that the "ordinary" individual volunteers' collections—often a folder—were studded with gems and were well worth painstaking examination. The next most important collection is the KZSU Transcripts now housed in the Stanford University Library. With over four hundred hours of interviews completely transcribed, the KZSU tapes have just begun to be tapped as a source of information on the entire student movement. Likewise, UCLA's Special Collection on the Civil Rights Struggle and Black Movement in the United States, 1950 to 1970, is very useful and extensive. What I have loosely called "The Delta Ministry Collection" is of tremendous importance to anyone interested in the COFO or FDP projects. In the fall of 1969, at the Delta Ministry "office" in the old plantation at Mount Beulah, Mississippi, Charlie Horwitz said casually, "Oh, you might be interested in some FDP stuff upstairs," and he opened a closet door onto every single COFO and FDP volunteer's file. For seven days I slept on an old broken couch and the moths, mice, and I typed what I call the "COFO Compilation" and the "FDP Compilation." There was a great deal more material there, especially the files of the Delta Ministry project and the languishing FDP. Unfortunately, I do not know what has happened to the "Delta Ministry Collection." In 1969 I immediately contacted both the State Historical Society of Wisconsin and the Center for the Study of the Black World in Atlanta and urged them to give a permanent home to the material. I have never heard what actually happened, but I believe the material is still in the South. The Southern Regional Council's files on the Voter Education Project were very useful background material; their scope is extensive and they are well organized. The files of the Freedom Information Service were also well organized and incredibly extensive, especially for Mississippi work. Jan Hillegas planned to leave them in Mississippi, if she left the state, but I do not know where they are now. The same is true of the Medical Committee for Human Rights (MCHR) Files. In 1969, two *full* four-drawer filing cabinets were in Dr. Justin Simon's garage in Brooklyn. The records not only delineate the birth of the MCHR as a support group for the Freedom Summers, but they also contain reams of information, particularly in the form of staff reports, about the movement throughout the South and about health conditions of blacks. The MCHR still exists and represents a constant liberal challenge to the American Medical Association; their slogan is still "Health Care Is a Human Right." Again, unfortunately, I do not know what has happened to the papers, since I tried to contact the Simons and they have moved. Otis Pease, as a professional historian, has an excellent and organized personal collection and, obviously, the diary of Jerry Johnson is a true jewel.

COLLECTIONS OF UNPUBLISHED DOCUMENTS

Public Collections

Boston University: Martin Luther King, Jr. Papers
Southern Regional Council: Voter Education Project Files
Stanford University: KZSU Radio Interview Transcripts; Quote Cards; Commitment Sheets
  Lorna Smith Papers
UCLA: Special Collection on the Civil Rights Struggle and Black Movement in the United States, 1950–1970
University of Washington: John and Ellen Fawcett Papers
  Mary Gibson Papers
  Francis Hoague Papers
  Timothy Lynch Papers
  Seattle Friends of SNCC Papers
  James Wilson Papers
State Historical Society of Wisconsin: (Because of the size of this collection, I will simply list in two columns the names of the collections I examined)

Meldon Acheson
Sandy Adickes
Mary R. Aickin
Pam Allen
Russell Allen
James Amory
Douglas Baer
Robert Bailey
Ella Baker
Michael Bambiger
Lee Bankhead
Rabbi Arie Becker
Jacqueline Bernard
Steven Bingham
Jacob Bloom
Bogalusa, La., Freedom School
Julian Bond
The Rev. Harry Bowie
Bambi Brown
Candy Brown
Carroll Co. Freedom Democratic Party

Chicago Area Draft Resisters (CADRE)
Bradley Clark
John and Pat Coatsworth
Robert Cook
CORE
CORE East and West Feliciana Parrish
CORE-Monroe, La.
CORE Southern Regional Office
Harriet Danyman
JoAnn Darken
Michael Davis
Ruby Davis
Delta Ministry of the National Council of Churches
Jerry DeMuth
Dion Diamond
Stuart Ewen
Ellice Fatoullah
Robert Feinglass
Mimi Feingold

Ferriday, La., Freedom House
The Rev. W. W. Finlator
Nicholas Fischer
Laura Foner
Freedom Democratic Party,
    Lauderdale and Sunflower
    Counties
Freedom Information Service
Erskine Fuller
Aviva Futorian
Vickie and Robert Gabriner
Alan Gartner
Jack Geiger
Tod Gitlin and Nanci Hollander
Sue Gladstone
Carolyn Goodman
Richard Gould
Raymond Gozzi, Jr.
Kenneth P. Griswold
Dale Gronemeir
Florence Halpern
Lillian Hamwee
Jan L. Handke
William Hansen
Sandra Dungan Hard
David Haspel
Charles Haynie
Rita Headrick
Frederick Heinze
Marjorie Henderson
Christopher Hexter
Jan Hillegas
Jane Hodes
Harold Ickes
Dilla Irwin
Gayle Jenkins
Florence Jones
Kathleen Kahn
Alicia Kaplow
Jean Kates
Walter Kaufman
Harry Koger

Louis Kreinberg
Ellen Lake
Martin Lanfield
Phillip Lapansky
Lee Bankhead Larson
Robert S. Lehman
Marilyn Lowen
Timothy Lynch
Staughton Lynd
Jan Maedke
Fred Mangrum
Gerald Marwell
Bruce Maxwell
James Mays
Joseph Martin
Charles Miller
Collin Minert
James Moore
R. Hunter Morey
Ahmed Abboud Najha
NAACP Legal Defense and
    Educational Fund
Mr. and Mrs. Martin Nicolaus
Alvin Oderman
Robert W. Park
Brian Peterson
Jane Polsey
Sally Belfrage Pomerance
Poor People's Cooperative of
    Mississippi
Peter Praetz
Presbyterian Church, Board of
    Christian Education
Quitman Co., Mississippi
JoAnn Ooiman Robinson
Susan Ruff
Linda Seese
Sam Shirah
Mary Short
E. W. Steptoe
Charles Stewart
Elizabeth Sutherland

Harriet Tanzman
Jerry Tecklin
Thomas Patrick
Ottar Tinglum
Silas Townsend
Mary Varela
Lise Vogel
Judy Walborn

Sam Walker
Herb Warner
Christopher Wilson
William Winfield
Rabbi Richard W. Winograd
Mitchell Zimmerman
Howard Zinn
Matthew Zwerling

Private Collections

Norman Ackley Papers, Seattle, Washington
COFO Papers; Delta Ministry, Mount Beulah, Mississippi
Gerald Marwell Papers, Madison, Wisconsin
Roger Dankert Papers, Stanford, California
Delta Ministry Papers, Mount Beulah, Mississippi
FDP Papers, Delta Ministry, Mount Beulah, Mississippi
Mary Gibson Papers, Seattle, Washington
Richard Gillam Papers, Stanford, California
Jerry Johnson Papers, Seattle, Washington
Jan Hillegas Papers, Tougaloo, Mississippi
David Hood Papers, Seattle, Washington
Margaret Kalberg Papers, Seattle, Washington
Carol Koppel Papers, Seattle, Washington
Medical Committee for Human Rights Papers, Dr. Justin Simon, Brooklyn,
    New York
Otis Pease Papers, Seattle, Washington
Justin Simon Papers, Brooklyn, New York

INTERVIEWS

Uptaped Interviews

Jody Aliesan, December 1972, Seattle, Washington
Roger Dankert, January 1967, Stanford, California
Linda Davis, September 1973, San Francisco, California
Nancy Davis, October 1973, Washington, D.C.
Richard Gillam, January 1967 and November 1969, Stanford, California
Fannie Lou Hamer, November 2, 1967, Ruleville, Mississippi
Jan Hillegas, November 11, 1969, Tougaloo, Mississippi
Carel Horwitz, November 12, 1969, Jackson, Mississippi
Charles Horwitz, November 6-12, 1969, Jackson, Mississippi
Florence Howe, June 28, 1972, October 6, 1973, July 1974, Seattle,
    Washington

Jerry Johnson, Series 1967–1976, Seattle, Washington
Henry Kirksey, November 11, 1969, Jackson, Mississippi
Paul Lauter, June 28, 1972, July 18, 1974, Seattle, Washington
Timothy Lynch, November 1966, Seattle, Washington
Frayda Simon, November 19, 1969, Brooklyn, New York
Justin Simon, November 20, 1969, Brooklyn, New York
The Rev. Roger Smith, November 6–8, 1969, Mount Beulah, Mississippi
Pat Watters, November 16, 1969, Atlanta, Georgia

Taped Interviews

Norman Ackley, February 1, 1967, Seattle, Washington
John Darrah, February 21, 1967, Seattle, Washington
Ellen and John Fawcett, January 25, 1967, Seattle, Washington
Mary Gibson, February 9, 1967, Seattle, Washington
Donna Goodman, November 20, 1971, Seattle, Washington
Francis Hoague, January 24, 1967, Seattle, Washington
David Hood, January 24, 1967, Seattle, Washington
Charles Horwitz, November 5, 1969, Mount Beulah, Mississippi
Billy Jackson, February 14, 1967, Seattle, Washington
Jerry Johnson, January 26, 1967, and May 15 and 17, 1967, Seattle,
    Washington
Carol Koppel, January 30, 1967, Seattle, Washington
KZSU Tapes, June-August 1965, Stanford, California
Thomas Lynch, November 7, 1967, Spokane, Washington
Otis Pease, February 13, 1967, and March 23, 1967, Seattle, Washington
The Rev. Robert Peters, March 16, 1967, Seattle, Washington
Jean Phillips, November 5, 1969, Mount Beulah, Mississippi
Barbara Rosen, January 26, 1967, Seattle, Washington
Michael Rosen, February 7, 1967, Seattle, Washington
Miriam Feingold Stein, May 1975, San Francisco; May 1976, Los Angeles,
    California
Sally Shideler, February 15, 1967, Seattle, Washington
Dorothy Smith, January 29, 1979, Lawrence, Kansas
The Rev. Roger Smith, November 1969, Mount Beulah, Mississippi
James Wilson, February 1, 1967, Seattle, Washington

NEWSPAPERS AND SOURCE JOURNALS

Atlanta Constitution, April 1964–January 1966
Clarion-Ledger (Jackson, Miss.), April 1964–September 1965
Freedomways, 1963–1968
New York Times, June 1964–September 1965
Southern Education News, 1955–1965

BOOKS AND ARTICLES

Belfrage, Sally. *Freedom Summer*. New York: Viking Press, 1965.

Buckley, William; Bond, Julian; and Lewis, John. "Politics and Black Progress," *Firing Line Transcript*, January 23, 1974.

Custer, Dick. *They Should Have Served That Cup of Coffee: 7 Radicals Remember the 60's*. Boston: South End Press, 1979.

Forman, James. *The Making of Black Revolutionaries: A Personal Account*. New York: Macmillan, 1972.

Franklin, John Hope, and Starr, Isidore. *The Negro in Twentieth Century America: A Reader on the Struggle for Civil Rights*. New York: Vintage Books, 1967.

Grant, Joanne. *Black Protest: History, Documents, and Analyses, 1619 to the Present*. Greenwich, Conn.: Fawcett Publications, 1968.

Holt, Len. *The Summer That Didn't End*. New York: Wm. Morrow, 1965.

Howe, Florence. "Mississippi's Freedom Schools; The Politics of Education," *The Harvard Educational Review* 34 (Spring 1965): 144-60.

Jacobs, Paul, and Landau, Saul. *The New Radicals: A Report with Documents*. New York: Vintage Books, 1966.

Louis, Debbie. *And We Are Not Saved: A History of the Movement As People*. New York: Doubleday, 1970.

McCord, William. *Mississippi: The Long, Hot Summer*. New York: W. W. Norton, 1965.

Moody, Anne. *Coming of Age in Mississippi: An Autobiography*. New York: Dell, 1968.

Sellers, Cleveland, and Terrell, Robert. *The River of No Return: The Autobiography of a Black Militant and the Life and Death of SNCC*. New York: Wm. Morrow, 1973.

Silver, James W. *Mississippi: The Closed Society*. New York: Harcourt, Brace and World, 1966.

Sugarman, Tracy. *Stranger at the Gates: A Summer in Mississippi*. New York: Hill and Wang, 1966.

Sutherland, Elizabeth. *Letters from Mississippi*. New York: McGraw-Hill, 1965.

Tucker, Shirley. *Mississippi from Within*. New York: Arco Publishing, 1965.

U.S. Civil Rights Commission. *Voting in Mississippi: A Report*. Washington, D.C.: U.S. Government Printing Office, 1965.

Van Hoffman, Nicholas. *Mississippi Notebook*. New York: David White Co., 1964.

SECONDARY SOURCES

PERIODICALS

Liberation, 1963–1967
Life, April 1964–September 1965
Look, April 1964–September 1965
The Nation, September 1963–December 1965
New Republic, September 1963–December 1965
Newsweek, April 1964–September 1965
The Progressive, April 1964–December 1965
Studies on the Left, 1963–1967
Time, April 1964–September 1965

UNPUBLISHED STUDIES

Carson, Clayborne, Jr. "Toward Freedom and Community: The Evolution of Ideas in the Student Nonviolent Coordinating Committee, 1960–1966." Ph.D. diss., UCLA, 1975.

Derber, Charles, and Flacks, Richard. "An Exploration of the Value System of Radical Student Activists and Their Parents." Paper delivered at the American Sociological Association Meeting, San Francisco, 1967.

McLemore, Leslie Burl. "The Mississippi Freedom Democratic Party: A Case Study of Grass Roots Politics," Ph.D. diss., University of Massachusetts, 1971.

Stoper, Emily. "Student Nonviolent Coordinating Committee: The Growth of Radicalism in a Civil Rights Organization," Ph.D. diss., Harvard University, 1968.

PUBLISHED STUDIES

Aiken, Michael; Demareth, N. J. III, and Marwell, Gerald. "Conscience and Confrontation," *New South* 21 (Spring 1966): 19–28.

_____. *The Dynamics of Idealism: White Activists in a Black Movement*. San Francisco: Jossey-Bass, 1971.

Allen, Pam. *Free Space*. New York: Times Change Press, 1971.

Alther, Lisa. *Original Sins*. New York: Knopf, 1981.

Bass, Jack, and DeVries, Walter. *The Transformation of Southern Politics: Social Change and Political Consequence Since 1945*. New York: New American Library, 1977.

Bolton, Charles D. "Alienation and Action: A Study of Peace Group Members," *American Journal of Sociology* 78, no. 3 (November 1972): 537–61.

Brink, William, and Harris, Louis. *Black and White*. New York: Simon and Schuster, 1967.

Carden, Maren Lockwood. *The New Feminist Movement*. New York: Russell Sage Foundation, 1974.

Carmichael, Stokely. *Stokely Speaks: Black Power to Pan Africanism*. New York: Vintage Books, 1971.

_____, and Hamilton, Charles V. *Black Power: The Politics of Liberation in America*. New York: Vintage Books, 1967.

Carson, Clayborne, Jr. *In Struggle: SNCC and the Black Awakening of the 1960's*. Cambridge, Mass.: Harvard University Press, 1981.

Carter, Hodding. *So the Heffners Left McComb*. New York: Doubleday, 1965.

Carson, Josephine. *Silent Voices: The Southern Negro Woman Today*. New York: Delacorte Press, 1969.

Cohen, Mitchell, and Hale, Dennis. *The New Student Left: An Anthology*. Boston: Beacon Press, 1967.

Coles, Robert. *Children of Crisis: A Study of Courage and Fear*. Boston: Little Brown, 1967.

_____. "Public Evils and Private Problems: Segregation and Psychiatry," *Yale Review* 44 (Summer 1965): 513-31.

_____. "Social Struggle and Weariness," *Psychiatry* 27, no. 4 (November 1964): 301-15.

Cox Commission. *Crisis at Columbia, Report of the Fact-Finding Commission on the Columbia Disturbances*. New York: Vintage Books, 1968.

Deming, Barbara. *Prison Notes*. Boston: Beacon Press, 1966.

_____. *Revolution and Equilibrium*. New York: Grossman Publishers, 1971.

Dienst, Evelyn. "On Alienation and Activism," *The Research Reporter* 7, no. 1 (1972): 1-4.

Duberman, Martin. *In White America: A Documentary Play*. New York: The New American Library, 1964.

Dunson, Josh. *Freedom in the Air: Song Movements of the Sixties*. New York: International Publishers, 1965.

Erikson, Erik H. *Youth: Change and Challenge*. New York: Basic Books, 1963.

Evans, Sara. *Personal Politics: The Roots of Women's Liberation in the Civil Rights Movement and the New Left*. New York: Knopf, 1979.

Farber, Jerry. *The Student as Nigger, Essays and Stories*. New York: Pocket Books, 1970.

Ferber, Michael, and Lynd, Staughton. *The Resistance*. Boston: Beacon Press, 1971.

Firestone, Shulamith. *The Dialectic of Sex*. New York: Wm. Morrow, 1970.

————, and Koedt, Anne. *Notes From the Second Year*. New York: n. p., 1970.

Flacks, Richard W. "The Liberated Generation: An Exploration of the Roots of Social Protest," *Journal of Social Issues* 23, no. 3 (1967): 52-75.

Freeman, Jo. *The Politics of Women's Liberation*. New York: David McKay Co., 1975.

Friedman, Leon. *Southern Justice*. Cleveland, Ohio: World Publishing Co., 1965.

Gaylin, Willard. *In the Service of Their Country: War Resisters in Prison*. New York: Grosset and Dunlop, 1970.

Gettleman, Marvin E., and Mermelstein, David. *The Great Society Reader: The Failure of American Liberalism*. New York: Vintage Books, 1967.

Goodman, Mitchell. *The Movement Toward a New America: The Beginnings of a Long Revolution*. Philadelphia: Pilgrim Press, 1971.

Grant, Joanne. *Confrontation on Campus: The Columbia Pattern for the New Protest*. New York: Signet Books, 1969.

Harris, Louis. "The Backlash Issue," *Newsweek*, July 13, 1964, pp. 24-27.

Hayden, Casey, and King, Mary. "Sex and Caste: A Kind of Memo," *Liberation* 10 (April 1966): 35-36.

Hilton, Bruce. *The Delta Ministry*. New York: Macmillan, 1969.

Hole, Judith, and Levine, Ellen. *The Rebirth of Feminism*. New York: Quadrangle Books, 1971.

Holloway, Harry. *The Politics of the Southern Negro: From Exclusion to Big City Organization*. New York: Random House, 1969.

Holt, Len. *An Act of Conscience*. Boston: Beacon Press, 1965.

Horn, John L., and Knott, Paul. "Activist Youth of the 1960's: Summary and Prognosis," *Science* 171, no. 3975 (March 12, 1971): 977-85.

Huie, William Bradford. *Three Lives for Mississippi*. New York: WCC Books, 1965.

"Integrate or Get Nothing—How Big Is the Crackdown?" *U.S. News and World Report*, May 3, 1965, pp. 41-44.

Kampf, Louis, and Lauter, Paul. *The Politics of Literature: Dissenting Essays on the Teaching of English*. New York: Vintage Books, 1973.

Keniston, Kenneth. *Young Radicals: Notes on Committed Youth*. New York: Harcourt, Brace and World, 1968.

————. *Youth and Dissent: The Rise of a New Opposition*. New York: Harcourt, Brace and World, 1971.

Killian, Lewis, and Grigg, Charles. *Racial Crisis in America: Leadership in Conflict.* Englewood Cliffs, N.J.: Prentice-Hall, 1964.

King, Martin Luther, Jr. *Strength to Love.* New York: Pocket Books, 1964.

_____. *Stride Toward Freedom: The Montgomery Story.* New York: Ballantine Books, 1961.

_____. *Where Do We Go From Here: Chaos or Community?* New York: Bantam Books, 1968.

_____. *Why We Can't Wait.* New York: Harper and Row, 1963.

Lasch, Christopher. *The New Radicalism in America, 1889-1963: The Intellectual as a Social Type.* New York: Knopf, 1965.

Lauter, Paul, and Howe, Florence. *The Conspiracy of the Young.* New York: Meridian Books, 1971.

Lester, Julius. *Look Out, Whitey! Black Power's Gon' Get Your Mama!* New York: Dial Press, 1969.

_____. *Revolutionary Notes.* New York: Grove Press, 1969.

Levy, Charles J. *Voluntary Servitude: Whites in the Negro Movement.* New York: Appleton-Century-Crofts, 1968.

Lewis, Anthony. *Portrait of a Decade: The Second American Revolution.* New York: Random House, 1965.

Lewis, David L. *King: A Critical Biography.* New York: Praeger Publishers, 1970.

Lynd, Staughton. *Nonviolence in America: A Documentary History.* Indianapolis, Ind.: Bobbs-Merrill Co., 1966.

Matthews, Donald R., and Prothro, James W. *The Negro and the New Southern Politics.* New York: Harcourt, Brace and World, 1966.

Matusow, Allen J. "From Civil Rights to Black Power: The Case of SNCC, 1960-1966." In *Twentieth Century America: Recent Interpretations,* edited by Barton J. Bernstein and Allen J. Matusow. New York: Harcourt, Brace and World, 1969.

Meier, August. "The Dilemmas of Negro Protest Strategy," *New South* 21 (Spring 1966): 1-18.

_____, and Rudwick, Elliott. *CORE: A Study in the Civil Rights Movement.* New York: Oxford University Press, 1973.

Miller, Michael, and Gilmore, Susan. *Revolution at Berkeley.* New York: Dell Publishing Co., 1965.

Misseduc Foundation, Inc. *Mississippi Black Paper.* New York: Random House, 1965.

"Mississippi: 'You Gotta Love Me,'" *Newsweek,* August 2, 1971, pp. 22 and 24.

Morgan, Robin. *Sisterhood Is Powerful.* New York: Vintage, 1970.

Moses, Robert. "Questions Raised by Moses," *The Movement* 1 (April 1965): 1 and 8.

Muse, Benjamin. *The American Negro Revolution From Nonviolence to Black Power, 1963 to 1967.* Bloomington, Ind.: Indiana University Press, 1968.

Namorato, Michael V. *Have We Overcome? Race Relations Since Brown.* Jackson, Miss.: University Press of Mississippi, 1979.

National Advisory Commission on Civil Disorders. *Report of the National Advisory Commission on Civil Disorders.* New York: New York Times Co., 1968.

National Commission on the Causes and Prevention of Violence. *Rights in Conflict.* New York: Signet Books, 1968.

Navasky, Victor S. *Kennedy Justice.* New York: Atheneum, 1971.

Newfield, Jack. *A Prophetic Minority.* New York: Signet Books, 1966.

_____. *Bread and Roses Too: Reporting About America.* New York: E. P. Dutton, 1971.

O'Brien, James. "A History of the New Left, 1960–1968," *Radical America* 2 (May–December 1968), reprint ed., Boston: New England Free Press, n.d.

Owen, George; Roszak, Betty; Hoffman, Gene; and Bagby, Jeanne. "Of Sex and Caste: II," *Liberation* 10 (December 1966): 26 and 33.

Peck, James. *Freedom Ride.* New York: Simon and Schuster, 1962.

Pettigrew, Thomas F. *A Profile of the Negro American.* Princeton, N.J.: D. Van Nostrand, 1964.

Piercy, Marge. "The Grand Coolie Damn," *Leviathon*, November 1969; reprint ed., Boston: New England Free Press, n.d.

Poussaint, Alvin. "The Stresses of the White Female Workers in the Civil Rights Movement in the South," *American Journal of Psychiatry* 123, no. 4 (October 1966): 401–7.

Rustin, Bayard. *Down the Line: The Collected Writings of Bayard Rustin.* Chicago: Quadrangle Books, 1971.

Sale, Kirkpatrick. *SDS.* New York: Vintage Books, 1973.

Smith, Lillian. *Our Faces, Our Words.* New York: W. W. Norton, 1964.

_____. *Killers of the Dream.* New York: W. W. Norton, 1969.

Sobel, Lester A. *Civil Rights, 1960–1963.* New York: Facts on File, 1964.

Solomon, Fredric, and Fishman, Jacob R. "The Psychosocial Meaning of Nonviolence in the Student Civil Rights Activities," *Psychiatry* 27 (May 1964): 91–99.

The Venceremos Brigade. *The Venceremos Brigade.* New York: Simon and Schuster, 1971.

Walker, Alice. *Meridian.* New York: Pocket Books, 1977.

_____. "Advancing Luna—And Ida B. Wells," *Ms.*, July 1977, pp. 75–79, 93–97.

Wallace, Michele. *Black Macho and the Myth of the Superwoman.* New York: Warner Books, 1980.

Washington, Cynthia. "We Started At Different Ends of the Spectrum," *Southern Exposure* 4, no. 4 (Winter 1977): 14–15.

Waskow, Arthur I. *From Race Riot to Sit-In, 1919 and the 1960's: A Study in the Connections Between Conflict and Violence.* New York: Doubleday, 1966.

Watters, Pat. *Down to Now: Reflections on the Southern Civil Rights Movement.* New York: Pantheon Books, 1971.

————. *Encounter With the Future.* Atlanta, Ga.: Southern Regional Council, 1965.

————, and Cleghorn, Reese. *Climbing Jacob's Ladder, The Arrival of Negroes in Southern Politics.* New York: Harcourt, Brace and World, 1967.

Weltner, Charles. *Southerners.* Philadelphia, Pa.: Lippincott Press, 1966.

Williams, Roger Neville. *The New Exiles: American War Resisters in Canada.* New York: Liveright Publishers, 1971.

Woodward, C. Vann. "What Happened to the Civil Rights Movement?" *Harper's Magazine* 234 (January 1967): 29–37.

Zinn, Howard. *SNCC: The New Abolitionists.* Boston: Beacon Press, 1964.

INDEX

About the Author

MARY AICKIN ROTHSCHILD is Director of Women's Studies and Assistant Professor of History at Arizona State University in Tempe. She has published numerous works on women in history and currently is working on a history of the Girl Scouts in the United States and a booklength collection of oral histories of Arizona women.